WARRIOR OF THE HEART

DAN A. BARKER

FOR DUKE, FOR MY
FOR MY FRI

This Burning Cities Press edition is published by arrangement with Viet Nam Generation, Inc., 2921 Terrace Drive, Chevy Chase, MD 20815.

We used a Macintosh IIcx computer and a Radius 19" monitor to typeset the manuscript. Software employed for word processing and page layout includes Microsoft Word 5.0 and PageMaker 4.2. Title font is Collage 24pt, and body text is Palatino 11 pt. Camera-ready copy was printed on an Apple Laserwriter IINTX. The book was printed by BookMasters, Inc. of Mansfield, OH.

Book design by Dan Barker and Kali Tal.

Contents

OAKLAND, DECIDING

There was no love to be found in Oakland. Serving my corpsman apprenticeship on the neurosurgery ward at Oak Knoll Naval Hospital I'd go into San Francisco on my nights off looking for some willing woman to make love with, to make a future with, to gain loving acceptance from, to embrace and hold, but would mostly wander the streets broke and wanting, too young to buy a drink, too poor to offer a future, too confused to make or know love, the serene face of an enraptured young woman seen in my imagination as through a gauzed lens, my eyes begging with profound need. There had been a highschool virgin lovemate. Brown hair and dark eyes, slender, the soul of her in desperate tears. Our union was based on deep need neither of us could fulfill. Seeing her fat father sitting drunk on the curb in front of her basement apartment so deeply shamed her that I promised that if I could, when I could, we'd marry, I'd take her to live with me in some apartment complex in San Leandro on my enlisted sailor's pay. But there was really little I could offer her but unending need.

On the pretext of engagement she and I would sneak into the Senator Hotel in Sacramento, rent a room with two weeks' pay, and have furtive, guilty, forbidden sex. Oh, the first time, in her childhood bed, I could feel the singularity of self split and slide away like the skin of a salamander, hymenal blood an anointment. And at church on Sunday afternoons we'd hide in a closet where I'd suckle at her tender breasts, selfish and in ecstasy.

But the ardor faded and the ecstasy became the work of cajoling her from eighty miles away, by jealousy and manipulation, to own the very core of her love and thereby ensure a constant source of loving sustenance; I consumed her until her innate wisdom of self-possession ended my illness for possessing her. It didn't matter that was how I'd learned to love, nor that it was not my nature. She strained hard to become what would please me. She was kind. She'd learned to be a chameleon to survive with her boozer wife-beating father and her screeching supplicating mother. She yielded to our mutual desperation for being loved, but desperation was not ground enough on which two children could found a life together. My possessive jealousy had once more robbed her of actual love, and she had had her fill. Just because my dependency felt like home was sufficient reason for her to run for her life.

On a walk through downtown in November, as I expounded on my new medical knowledge and arrogantly claimed mastery of the world, she became bored, and told me that her new friend, a woman experienced at men, was leading her away from her alcoholic parents, was teaching her to be a whole woman, and that I'd changed. I didn't seem to care about her except as someone to fuck. "That's all you want to do when you come up from the hospital." And, "You're not a doctor, you don't have licence to be an asshole." As a subject of the Playboy Philosophy, and the time being before the Pill, coupled with the fact that she was right, I accepted the marquis cut diamond ring back and caught the bus for Oakland, alone and without connection to a woman for the first time in life. War was a distant succubus.

◆◆◆◆

The girls attending Mills College had been well schooled to reject come-ons from sailors, buffeted constantly at the shared bus-stop on the freeway into the City. No luck there; our destinies were divergent. The superior heart of social good found no resonance in the thrum and beat of war pulsing in our naval blood. And though a nurse from the ward next to mine did me a kindness once by donating a picnic at Stinson Beach where it was cold and we were miserable ("The music on the car radio was good," she said to her friend) there was a social level of women reserved for servicemen, and there was no breach in the walls above them. Somehow two of them found me.

They were half-sisters who lived with their cocktail-waitress mother in some huge public housing facility in Alameda near the Air-station. One was thin and blond, the evident product of fetal alcohol syndrome, the other fat and brunette, smelling of neglect and taco grease. Both sported pachuco tattoos, victims of gang-boy cruelty, their ankles claimed and pierced by needles wrapped with India ink soaked thread while drunk and stoned and laughing at the boy taking pictures of their twats. The cross, the rays of murder, rape and armed robbery permanent, leaking its meaning and claim into their centers. When my friend and I showed up in his Corvette for a night of Thunderbird and downers, the fat one glanced knowingly at her sister like they'd fallen into something good, boys with regular paychecks and money from home, boys with access to cheap cigarettes and pharmaceutical quality drugs. They took us home, and promised to come downstairs after their mother was asleep, to give us what we came for. But after waiting anxiously, chastising myself for even allowing myself to fall into such conniving company, even in the name of manly conquest, I passed out. In the morning they said they'd decided they needed to know us better before they fucked us, come again, when you do bring us some....

And because we never paid for it, we drifted apart, and my friend drifted away from me. So once again I was roaming the gaudy streets of the City, counting the days until I would be released from the self-imposed poverty of pocket and spirit, manufacturing a mental future filled with comfort and ease in some Tahitian paradise where the work was done freely, the food grew on trees, the children belonged to everyone, and no enemies clamored at the gates or impelled the glands to massacre, ever so lonely.

On the ward we'd tend the sick and injured; the Filipino steward who lay comatose after a car crash that swept away half of his brain, the fifteen year old athlete with a brain abscess (terminal), the nine year old boy named Skipper with cerebral lesions (no cause known, no cure known, God's retribution upon the boy's father for serving nuclear catastrophe, we theorized), and Kenny who had jumped from a cab over a bridge rail and fell 150 feet to the rocks below—and lived—as a contorted spasmodic capable only of smoking and an occasional burst of keenly rational thought. And all the others with spinal lesions, gunshot wounds, fused vertebrae, broken backs and broken necks, smashed skulls and subdural hematomas, the colossal egotism of the resident surgeon, the fine and dedicated caring of the nursing staff, the long slow narrow burn of the healing process from our hands to their bodies. And the dead.

On the ward, working alone at night, I found myself looking forward to placing the huge penis of a back-injured man into the stainless steel urinal, and stroking it. I was so unselfconscious that when the head nurse told me I wasn't to do any more than take that patient's vital signs, it didn't dawn on me until several days later that the wishful dreams of a thirteen year old's want of a manly cock was leaking into my tough guy persona, adopted for the fear of men.

Fearing for my station among men I had a dragon tattooed on my leg, showing it still scabbed to my dorm mates. And, I ran back to the City looking for a girl or a woman, any female who would so much as talk to me, my urgency for contact and manly affirmation so utter that when I saw a fifteen year old girl whose hair was disheveled and smelled of cum and man-sweat riding the bus back to the hospital I approached her. Her neck was splotched with monkey-bites, her eyes glazed from drugging, her worn and tattered sweater opened and exposing whisker reddened breasts. She looked like the mouths of many boys had taken succor from her tortured flesh.

It's hard to say what she saw in me, perhaps just another hungry boy who talked of befriending her, but she agreed to come with me to the apartment of some friends where we would fuck and then she could finally get some sleep, there was nowhere else in America left for her to go. We walked through the October mercury vapor street

10

lights, she lagging behind, not knowing me from Adam, not knowing what horror awaited her in another cheesy apartment full of sexhungry young men. She was so tired, perhaps sleep, perhaps strangulation, what difference did it make, maybe this is the last nice guy in the world and all he wants is some pussy, maybe he'll protect me, yeah, sure.

The apartment complex was a squalor of noise, television, crying babies, yelling parents, the smells of hamburger and onions. The door of my friends apartment opened, releasing tobacco and marijuana smoke, fraternal sweat, cheap beer and hi-fi Dion and the Belmonts. The group leader came to the center of the ragged room, saying, "What can we do for you and your, uh, girlfriend, Doc?" His posture was challenging, chest inflated, shoulders hunched, eyes menacing, a killer waiting for his moment. The other four pair of eyes in the room were licking the girl. Her eyes darted between the boys, looking for a way out. She'd already been in the same place that night. "We just want to use one of the bedrooms for tonight, Gene." He looked the girl over like a broker and said, "No way, man. No way in the world. Shit, you fucking idiot, she ain't any older than fifteen She's statutory, man. I don't even want her in the same room with us!"

Having gone as far as to beg a favor, I added, "Hey, man, she's a runaway, she don't give a shit. She ain't gonna bring down the heat."

"Maybe not tonight, but what's going to happen when her momma and poppa beat the truth out of her? She'll be right back here and we'll get busted by the cops, court-martialled, General Discharge, fucked forever."

One of the onlooking boys said, "General discharge is what we had in mind, Gene." and the other boys laughed. The girl stiffened, touched my elbow, and said, "You guys work it out, I'll wait for you outside." She tugged her sweater closed and went out the door.

And that may have been the moment that death in war loomed a brighter promise than living through life in an interminable argument. I can still feel the swarm of thought demons tearing at my conscience. The steamy leers of the other boys were the same as mine, pussy was pussy, a further claim in the realm of manhood. I could feel their desires reaching into me, persuading me. I could become known as someone who could find women, and knew what to do with them, and thus become larger than them. My own desire to gain access to the central cleft of a woman from which all mankind flowed, to have the rapture of mutual joy coiling through my body despite teenage mental chaff, to feel the silky lubric barrel grasping and accepting was beyond pleasure or measure. It would be absolution of my faggot-fear. I could reclaim the ennobled image of a man interested only in women, cunt-conquistador, maker of children. And to escape that fear was worth any cost required in the realm of duplicitous men.

It was then that I was self-impelled to act on thoughts seemingly not my own. I felt my mouth and tongue form the words, but the sphere of my brain felt attacked as if possessed by an inchoate personality made from the scraps of life lived until then. Punchy and nauseated, I offered Gene and the boys, "Tell you what, let us stay the night, and you all can have her when I'm done." Psychotic pimp. I was instantly ashamed, fervently wishing that Gene's fear of being arrested for statutory rape would prevail. At the center of the offer was the notion of being a tough son of a bitch, like a motorcycle gang member who offers his mamma to his assembled clutch of sociopaths, disdaining women as mere pleasure holes, my attempt to appear a big man in their eyes turning to deep self loathing, the kernel of suicide speaking. As a boy my mother taught there was no lower form of man on earth than the pimp, a man who gained his livelihood from the flesh of beaten and subjugated women, and such a man deserves no place in civilization or stance in the face of God. To make such an offer was to abandon one's soul to Hell, to seek annihilation in the sleazy alleys of desperate monsters, to be drawn and quartered by your own hand, fishbait even the Styx's sharks would spit out. Anything horrible that happened to you after that was chosen fate, and the women of the world would cheer, righteously.

12

I could see Gene considering the offer. To say yes would admit me into their group, he'd have another boychick to control, he'd get sloppy seconds, there was the real risk of being found out by the law, each and every one of them would know something dishonorable about each other, opening a destiny of continued degradation and bonding blackmail. But Gene was boss; there could be no sloppy seconds.

"Get outahere, man, you're too much trouble. What a bumfucker idea to bring that little girl here. And don't come back. Ever. Ain't no place for you here," Gene said, fists balled, contempt aimed at my heart, pushing me backward through the open door with his chest. The other boys looked at each other like Christmas had been cancelled. My relief was immense. It was easy to agree to his demand, to absent myself from the company of the boys who would know me as a pimp; all I had to do was avoid them for the rest of my life. Resolutions of pure circumspection, clean and honorable living, of never again injuring anyone, rose up in me as the door slammed.

Turning to the girl waiting in the fog, seeing her face twisted by perhaps having to work through another mob of grasping hands, sucking mouths and jabbing pricks, their disease poisons spurting into her womb in clots of jism, I couched a neutral disarming sentence and told her, "They don't want to let us use the bedroom," egotistically hoping for a look of disappointment. Her anxiety turned to fury.

"Don't hand me that bullshit, you son-of-a-bitch. I know what happened in there. You think I'm stupid? I know about your kind! Come on like the white knight, then sell me out. You offered to let them have me, to use me, you cocksucker. Fuck you man, fuck you and fuck them, and fuck everyone you ever knew! You think I'm some kinda trash, human garbage! Your mother was a woman! Use me and throw me away. I hope you die!" she screeched.

Swallowing her ominate, assuming the regrettable truth, I forced a handful of Darvons and my last two dollars for bus-fare on her, and drifted into the chilling haze.

◆◆◆◆

When we were kids we'd go shoplifting to get the bright and shiny gewgaws that we thought would move us from being kids to being powerful. We'd go to Merchant's Hardware and steal knives and fishing tackle, and my favorite, the Jonie Handwarmer that needed lighter fluid and came in a keen red velvet bag. Carrying it in my pocket was like toting an eternal flame. But we weren't fooling anyone. After our first two or three forays into the stores the clerks would watch us so closely we could feel their eyes inside our heads and we'd have to leave. We'd take the knives we stole and sell them to the other kids, effectively arming the Junior High School like William Casey passing out a million handguns in the Philippines.

All roads in our neighborhood led to war. John Wayne wetdreams and the Boy Scouts, Frank Sinatra and Steve McQueen playing jungle fighters were just fuel added to the lives stretched behind the men who lived on our block. There was Mr. Snow who lived in a dark house in his wheelchair—a Chinese bayonet had sliced through his spine. And Mr. Frank down the street—quiet, moving as if he still felt the weight of the ambush that killed his squad, and the burden of his survival—knocked out by a bullet creasing his skull. He said he could still hear the Germans jeering as they sauntered away. And Mr. Johnson, the fireman, who'd served on Okinawa, and sadly told the story of the Japanese throwing themselves into the sea, intimating that the cowardly horde fleeing Christian righteousness could only redeem themselves in the eyes of man by suicide. And Mr. Chatworth who drank a fifth a day to balm the wound in his soul, self-inflicted by slipping over the Communist lines in freezing Korea to kill them in their sleep with his commando knife, their every ghost ripping at his center like the beaks of metallic crows.

Also implicit in my family was the acceptance of lamed and maimed men. The women would care for men of valor, and would send their sons to serve the Country, granting themselves a kind of guarantee. Three sisters had married veterans who hailed from the

South, two of them wife beaters and child abusers, and one a gentle, childless, teary man whose right leg had been blown off in the Battle of the Bulge. And Uncle Sly who spent four years on Guadalcanal, and suffered from sergeant's fury, often beating his son, and whose eyes were twisted into white stars of barely controlled insanity, pouring out incessant rage and perplexity. At first light and at dusk he'd step out onto the porch to smoke five or six Camel straights, and gaze back into island warfare, his eyes fixed on the dark treeline from which the Japs would rise up to slaughter him and his friends. We children would long to touch the medals and rifles enshrined in a glass case upstairs, to absorb the power of the tools used to cleanse the world of monstrous tyrants. We couldn't hear the voices of our dead; the images of the bulldozers pushing the bodies of the millions of Jews, the millions of Chinese, into huge pits, collective knowledge generated ample cause to extinguish tyranny in any form. They had fought to save the world, and they had won. For me, to have joined the Navy and become a corpsman only half fulfilled my family's ambition for me. My father had stayed stateside with the women, hence to not be a Marine was subject for shame.

Working on the ward at night I'd listen to the men shipped in from Vietnam or northern Thailand moan from their wounds. Kidney failure, severed spinal cords, shell fragments lodged in their brains. Some of them would rise up from their exhaustion screaming in incomprehensible terror, their sheets soaked with urine and sweat, their panic still shaking through their nerves. Mystery surrounded their failing bodies, currents of combat action like ghosts of our futures. But even wounded or dying they were beyond any claim any one of us could make in our present realm. We'd gather around them to drink in the glory, as if to be pierced by steel would release the years of fantasy in a furious hour and gain us absolute realization as men to be reckoned with. And I'd callous myself against the struggle of a man trapped in a Stryker-bed grieving his loss of half of the world by charging him with not being good enough, not hacking it. His not a fate that would befall me or anyone I loved, immortal at eighteen.

Lying in bed, whole, the world new and relatively safe, moving stately through the universe, I'd work up hero-mayhem fantasies to push me further toward dying in war. Vietnam's dark current floated in the blood, stretching past cavalry hunting Indians, the Japs, the millions of already dead Chinese surging into machine-gunfire in the flat timeless black and white of newsreels, unreal, the dead and maimed not actually our own flesh but members of races inherently inferior, their maxim of no regard for human life threat enough to bring an end to their existence. The war-blood current would open into aneurysms of fetid rice land swarmed with dark little men sacrificing their living bodies on pikes of exploding steel, me or someone like me at the center, boydream manufactury at once future seeing and shielding a fearful heart. I'd force myself to see me standing outside the ward at the Saigon Military Hospital protecting the wounded men inside the tent-ward, the eerie flare-light showing me crouched over a mound of dead Viet Cong, .45 smoking in my right hand, gunshot in the left shoulder.

There was something horribly sick and horribly wrong with wishing for such expectations, even if they were imbued by the heart of the country. The two sets of teachings, the Christian good, and the political good, were churned and twisted like the snakes entwined on my caduceus. In such schizophrenia preparational fantasy was inevitable. After all, the magnificent machinery of war, the aircraft carriers and jets, the troop transports, tanks, missiles and small-arms, the two million men sworn to annihilate any named enemy, were waiting for me to join them and were just a signature away.

So what if you got killed? Killed like the millions upon millions who died before you and would die beyond you. The concrete agonies of hopeful immortality would slough away beneath a black curtain of blood, reducing you to pure atomed ease, starlight breathed through with God. What if you were wounded in your body, scarred in your soul? The world offered provision. Veteran's hospitals to cure you until you died, women to bring you lunch on a tray, the crump of the grenade that blew off your leg or your arms or your hands, or your eyes, or your balls, still resonant in your strobe-eyed recollection, never again to be expected to act as a complete and whole man, and therein lay a kind of freedom. War was a way to run from my despicable deed of pimping.

But there was no Naval Hospital in Saigon. There was only one way to free oneself from bedpan duty and the lovelessness of Oakland. It was also the way to escape the low opinion of my friends, family and self and the requirement of life to make a future: ship F.M.F. Fleet Marine Force, Seventh Fleet, bound for Vietnam. As I signed the papers I could feel myself abandoning the World.

OKINAWA

Okinawa was a low dark green volcanic hummock rising out of the December Pacific. Our A.P.A. approached it with grand slow bulk, the deck rails lined with a battalion of young Marines whose dreams were about to come true. Bye-bye California, Quantico and the land of the big PX; hello jungle tangles, cane swamps, habu and kraits, scent of rotted canvas and laterite dust, and women that smelled of sandalwood and fish. Vietnam was due south. We were going, it was certain, it bloomed in our collective mind like a chain of DNA plugged into itself, generating metastic violence. All we had to do was wait, train and wait. The Mickey Mouse would pay off.

Tugs broached the hull as we passed the concrete breakwater, and pushed the great grey hulk of ship into a long pier. Barnacles and purple seastars coated the pilings. In the sunlight, the water was clear tropical turquoise slicked with oily rainbows.

Our fathers' legacy greeted us from the pier. Forty Okinawan women wearing splendid traditional costumes swayed to an ancient military drum and twang, their bird pitch voices echoing off the corrugated-tin warehouse behind them. Then, without the courtesy of waiting for the Oriental women to stop their song and welcoming dance, a band of Air Force men began their brass blare, drowning the women's delicate tribute. The two musics collided until the diesel roar of seventy-five olive drab 6x6s overwhelmed them both.

My first glimpse of Asia was from the back of a canvas-covered truck. The road leading to the farthest military installation on the island, our future place of training and waiting, ran through Naha. Naha was the principle port of the island and was adjacent to

Kadena Air Force Base. Its main street was lined with tiny shops filled to brimming with bright futons, tinware, kerosene lamps, cookware, silk shirts and kimonos, and crowded with the shopkeepers and their families, the noise and chatter of their foreign talk at once exotic and disconcerting.

That all those people were somehow inferior, beaten, therefore subjects to the American Way and hence servants, seemed to be the concurrent opinion. But it wasn't working for me. I was amazed at their industry, their persistent conduct of business with primitive resources, their lives going on in spite of massive military presence and the sacrifice of their daughters to the sexual demands of their conquerors. As we neared the Air Base the bars and honky-tonks made a neon ghetto being swept out and readied for payday night. Kadena Air Force Base was the largest military complex north of the Philippines, hosting thousands of airmen and hundreds of planes, including B-52s that carried nuclear bombs. You could see world annihilation in the way the men moved around the planes, like they were holding a horrible secret in their hearts, one that made them crazy and ultimately powerful, a tireless arrogant swagger that allowed bargaining with a woman for access to her sex and made men fight with each other over tiny slights. The machines demanded all the caring and polish, the work. And the women in the bars fed the needs of the men so the men could feed the needs of the machines so the machines could kill us all.

But we Marines were different. We were down on the ground grunts. Fundamental infantry who looked upon the Air Force boys as something less than ourselves, almost girls without the guts to stand up and die like a man. As we passed them we hooted and jeered at their conspiratorial mechanical safety.

Then we broke into the countryside; rice paddies and ditches clogged with weeds, small tile-roofed stucco houses grey with dilapidation, people working their fields with walk-behind tractors and water buffalo. The open ocean lay to the north and hills covered in jungle scrub lay to our south. Japanese taxis flashed by our convoy. We passed the tank farm at Camp Butler, the huge tracked beasts facing the road, their turrets aimed into the town below the camp, relentless warning. Then further and further up the island's spine until we could hardly wait to shake off the twenty-five days at sea and the ponderous travel up that narrow ridge of road, finally reaching Camp Schwab, home for a year unless Vietnam happened, as it surely would, it was Uncle Sugar's gift to us, and finally, the beginning of real life.

◆◆◆◆

We corpsmen weren't quite full fledged men. The Marines let us know about that one right away. There were four of us assigned to each company in the battalion, one to each platoon and a senior corpsman. The medical team was given a special room at the back of one of the concrete squad-bays and instructed to conduct its duties from there, nevermind going out on the training exercises unless the brass assigns you.

Separate and unequal, our duties consisted of setting-up shot lines for inoculations, holding sick-call for the respiratory ailments and malingerers, the hangovers and crabs, passing out daily medications and daily injections for colds, gastritis, headache, gonorrhea, in general maintaining the health of a healthy group of young men. We would stand inspection, do PT, pick up the trash, and go on some of the training marches.

But there was some training we peckercheckers weren't privileged to. Like the lecture where the sergeant tells the boys that "Ambush is killing and killing is fun." They came back from that one snarly and absolute, and there was no liberty granted that night. It was part of their necessary information, imprint for well-armed killer-kids who could easily die without it, cynical initiative couched in classroom parlance, nevermind those who died beneath the fire, the dead were dead and couldn't hurt you anymore. Being the healers, the ones who would staunch the wound and hold you while you died, the onus of the good savers of life was upon us so there were secrets our souls should not be stained by. Keeping the roles separated, healer from killer, kept us as simply defensive

personnel, marking us as lesser men allowed only a .45, versus their
M-14s, M-79s, M-60s, mortars and grenades. It devolved to us to
keep the peace and keep the flame of life and compassion alive. And
to fulfill even that noble purpose in secret. The communion of our
Esprit de Corps was Pray for War, and every thought, word and
action was dedicated to that end. If you were among Marines and
not willing to fight and die, to kill, and to incessantly talk of killing,
they had no use for you. Tits on boar, they'd say.

We four corpsmen would frequently find ourselves excluded,
and would occupy the time discussing strategies of how to get
along with our hosts. We played a lot of back-alley, telling ourselves
we had it knocked, let the poor dumb grunt mutherfuckers slough
through the mud, take that hill while simulating fire, we'd be ready
when the time came. We'd seen all the right movies. Especially the
one starring one of our training sergeants, where his platoon was
pinned down by raking machine-gun fire and he was dashing to the
wounded, more athletic than Burt Lancaster, applying battle
dressings, injecting morphine, checking for exit wounds, using the
bodies of the dead and wounded as cover. The Marines knew about
that one, too, and resented our presumption that we should stay
alive to keep them alive and not die equally with them, or instead
of them, or first.

We all had notions of how it was going to be once we got there,
got in the thick of it, got the war going. There seemed no sense of
time, just action that took three or four minutes, the winners heroes
of the world, us. Then, as our reward, we'd be spirited back to the
World to live out our lives in easy, glorious honor. Waiting for the
order for our battalion to go on "float," surely headed south, was
like a prison sentence. How were we to know that working for a
year to make our dreams come true could corrupt a lifetime?

The question wasn't if we were conducting right lives, but how
well could we do what we were supposed to do. Could we hack it?
We were where we were supposed to be. We'd each and every one
followed the bold psychic drumming down to the warrior's garden
to eat the crimson poppy and drink deep the bloody mead. Despite
the threat of being drafted, no true warrior child would join the

Army. Every man in the battalion had volunteered, and taken the abuse of bootcamp, and allowed themselves, even worked and abetted, to transform themselves into ideal men of action, members of the green machine whose mission was clear—kill the enemy. And the enemy was supposed to get killed. He was not supposed to kill you back. He was supposed to lay down and die as if blown asunder by God for life-malfeasance.

There was no question that we were being trained for fighting in Vietnam. We were sneaking through jungles, hiding in rice muck, learning the dangerous insects and reptiles of Asia, practicing camouflage and night movements with grease painted faces, learning to spot booby-traps and punji pits, setting up mock ambushes, "L" and "X," practicing retrograde movements (Marines never retreat, they kill the enemy even as they run), doing the slide for life and trying to talk the sergeant into letting us breathe through reeds underwater. Fun with a deathly edge of danger. Training, so the body moves despite the mind screaming in holy terror. Readying the body so at the first crack from an enemy rifle the reaction is immediate and on target, the medulla kicks in, squeezing every drop of adrenalin from the kidneys. Keep your canteens full; you might need the juice. We walked behind tanks over open ground, climbed trees as snipers, crossed tumbling streams on fallen logs, and learned each other inside and out. Who could read the terrain, who could read a compass, who was accurate with a rifle, who had the most daring, the most physical strength, who could carry a mortar base-plate, full field pack and still hack it, and who'd help you when you couldn't. Though the Okinawans would run or watch the entertainment from hiding when they happened across our maneuvers, the enemy remained imaginary.

After all, the enemy was he who was out to kill you. He could expect no quarter. He was dedicated down to the last molecule of his sinew to obliterate you, as you were to obliterate him, we'd be dead fools to entertain any other truth, and the Okinawans were never really our enemy, merely collaborators with the Japanese who were no longer our enemy, either. Besides, when we'd come in out of the field it was the island daughters with whom we'd dally.

◆◆◆◆

On the knoll overlooking the whore-town of Hinnoko, Sgt. Hurlock, ten year veteran of the Corps, was explaining the Okinawan viewpoint to me. "We're fish, Doc. These people have been fisherfolk and farmers for centuries. Then we show upon their shores like Columbus and crew, just as dangerous, and they gotta do something to keep their shit together. You got a lot of sex-crazy killer boys running around hoping for rape and pillage, like it's their right because they're bigger and better armed and have the whole fucking Armed Forces behind their every move, you gotta give up the booty. You see this part of town? The part closest to the Camp? That's our part. That's where we get to hoot and holler and get our dicks wet. Every building down there is a combo bar and whorehouse. Quaint, ain't it? You got the Blue Moon, The American Bar, The California Bar, The Cave, The Galaxy Club, hell, they even got The Apollo for the Splib Bros. It's like they got us figured out down to the last stitch in our skivvies. Speaking of which, there's even a couple of Hong Kong tailors in case you got a James Bond number going. But see down the hill, beyond that treeline? That's where the real folk live. There's Commies down there, agitating to kick our ass off this stinking Rock. Think if you had a wife or a daughter or a sister, and you had to give her ass up to get fucked by a couple of thousand hairy shitheads, how'd you feel?"

"The word I got was that whoring was strictly business with these people, an honorable profession."

"That's where the fish part comes in. They know we're gonna leave someday, we gotta, we have a treaty or some such shit, not that that's ever made a difference in U.S. policy, and even at three bucks a throw, compared to what you can make mucking rice, a woman can get rich on her back. They got the wisdom, baby, money talks, shit walks and dies broke and alone. Ain't nothing inscrutable about these folks, they got it all worked out. We're the ones running around without a rudder, ready to die in a combat zone, box me up and ship me home."

"So that part of town is off-limits?"

"Slip onto that side of the tracks and some patriot will stick a shiv between your ribs. Nothing nobody can do about it, either. You sure ain't gonna talk, and neither will they. Besides, they got an agreement with the brass. Over there, you're just wrong. They don't want you to meet your snake's mamma. Anyhow, you ain't got time or permission to fall in love, Doc."

Looking down into the far end of Hinnoko I could see the fifty or so houses were well whitewashed, their roofs in good repair, the courtyards fenced with bamboo, the gardens tended, the dirt streets swept, and children dressed in blue school uniforms coming home. I could imagine their fathers oiling their weapons, keeping the past alive by planning a future pure and free of the hairy ones and their African half-brothers.

"I thought fucking Marines was just a way of life for women here, I mean after twenty years of occupation I figured a fuck was casual as a handshake." I said.

"Well, it is and it ain't. These people always had the geishas, trained concubines, but, man, we're meat. A starving people will turn any trick to put rice in their bowl. Might as well sell what they fear we'd take anyway. I got a feeling like our fucks don't count, it's like copulating with a demon in a dream, next time around on the wheel they won't have to. Sacrifice to the good of the family, and all that karma shit. It ain't like every girl down there is Mary. You gotta remember, these people have been having their asses kicked for centuries. First the Japs, then us, and we weren't none too kind. Hell, it's the ambition of every Top-kick in the Corps to retire here, open up a skivvy house and drink himself to death. Long as there's a profit to be turned, you think good ol' Christian morality gonna come out on top? Besides, it's how they keep us in our place. We're customers. There ain't a boy in our platoon that ain't said he'd never pay for it, then got himself sent here the first chance he saw."

In the gathering dusk neon was beckoning. We put on our pisscutters and sauntered down the hill. Several taxis full of Marines sped past us, getting the jump on the evening. Hurlock remained calm. He'd been there before. He knew how fast the boys were. He knew there was plenty to go around. For a moment Hinnoko was like the negro section of Santa Cruz where my Uncle Sly warned against ever entering for fear of disease or stabbing.

We walked past the Hong Kong tailor, then past The Crystal Club, The Movie Bar, past the restaurant where you could get a hamburger and fried rice, where Roy Orbison's "Pretty Woman" played constantly, loudly, and on down the street to Hurlock's hang-out, The Texas Club.

Inside the greying clapboard building was a dimly lit barroom, and behind the bar was a Confederate flag surrounded by Marine Corps memorabilia, chevrons, swagger sticks, embroidered dragons from sailor suits, a DI's hat, the comforting signals of occupation.

We ordered a typhoon fifth so we'd be sure to be good and drunk by the time we decided to get laid. Remembering the ritual of pouring the "fusil oil" off the top, refuse for the gods, we began burning our throats from tiny porcelain cups. We were soon joined by six women wearing Chinese silk dresses slit up the thigh. They would partake of no wine, but insisted on iced-tea-whiskey purchased in their name from the mamasan controlling the bar.

Their time purchased for the time it took to drink their tea, they began the work of the courtesan. While they started the conversation, Hurlock and I knocked back the rice wine with purposeful abandon. The desired state to be achieved was that of loss of inhibition, loss of recognition that these were Oriental women bent only on taking our money, loss of our cultural injunctions against using prostitutes, loss of the knowledge that any one of the women had just fucked five or ten of your friends, that night, and hundreds before then, while the constant virgins at home waited patient in our holding. The wine was to make her come around in mind as a fresh being dedicated solely to you, and to desensitize your genitals so the usual thirty seconds of thrusting could be stretched into a respectable two minutes. Any man coming back out of the door leading to the cribs in less than fifteen minutes didn't have a hair on his ass. Many a young Marine lingered long over his socks.

On the other hand, the profit mechanism of the bar was constructed just like a used-car lot. Every woman had an up. Her

26

turn came after her trick came and she had no choice in whether or not to service a customer. It was first come first serve. The system had evolved to encourage competition and prevent fighting between the women over quick and easy pickings. Efficiency, standardization, sober control and production were the mamasan's watchwords. We could see her dark shining eyes darting between the women, the back door, the drinks and the abacus.

Showered with affection, freely groped, and after they had determined our hometowns, our length in service, our arrival date, our departure date, the number and amount of our allotments, our names and the names of our girl friends back home, the amount of cash on hand, my willingness to go to one of their homes to treat a son's abscessed tooth, accomplished with little girl innocence and well-schooled pidgin, four of the women left us as four more Marines banged through the door. They already knew it was payday. "Eagle shit today, na?" one of them asked coquettishly, as if Mamasan didn't have the pay schedule tattooed on her eyelids.

It didn't matter that she was being paid. To be in the presence of a willing woman after such a long string of disasters with women, and months and months of only the company of men, was intoxicating beyond the wine. Even after twenty years she is still distinct in my mind. Her name was Michiko and she was somewhere past thirty-five. Through the furze of my battered nineteen year old personality I could feel the central spring of her, a deep of opiated drifting, as if her soul opened into space itself. And as I absorbed her dark well of energy I could feel the thousands of bright flames of young men she'd lain with flickering through her like a course of mirrored starlight. Her hair was long and held in a bun by a pearl-inlaid comb. Her eyes looked backward in time, not seeing me, or even, perhaps, herself. Her musculature had grown supple in the yoga of short-time.

Passing my five dollar bill to the mamasan, we went out the back, down a narrow alley and through a sliding door into her workroom. She lit a kerosene lamp with my borrowed Zippo. In the soft orange light I could see a swaybacked futon resting on unraveling tatami. Beside the mattress stood a stack of hand towels,

27

a metal basin and a galvanized bucket full of water. The walls were bare.

Had I been calmer and less impelled to be manly among men I could have been satisfied to simply live time with her, not speaking, simply being in the same place at the same moment in the history of the world together. But business was business and she slipped out of her Suzi Wong dress, then helped me with my shirt buttons. "You big boy," she flattered, reaching into my trousers, a gesture which spoiled my delirious mood by its commonality. I was thankful to merely be there with her. I sensed kindness.

Suppressing my timidity, instinct took over. As she knelt facing me I could see her breasts had swollen with milk for several children but had since flattened and sagged long. Lamplight shadowed in the skin crevices left from boyhands pulling them into their mouths. Her expert hand guided me into her; smooth, hollow, lubric; her cervix like small hard lips, her labia like doe skin, yielding, empty.

Finished too soon, she let me lay on top of her, feeling her swim through me like a dark undulant current, her skin a memory of musky tired scent. Pushing me away with a giggle, she said, "You go now. Get stinko. Comeback later. Not too stinko."

There must've been some other look on my face than shy embarrassment when I followed her back into the bar. Sgt. Hurlock took one look at me, guffawed and said, "Ha Ha, Doc's been snake-bit."

And snake-bit I was. During our six weeks on the Rock we'd prowl the bars at night, often finding our friends huddled into the comforting arms of the Hinnoko women like they were back in the World with their girlfriends, talking pidgin, drinking local or blackmarket beer, getting stinko, pretending there was no difference between the women on Okinawa and their girlfriends back home, pretending that there was no difference between females anywhere, cunt was all they were really interested in after all. They'd spend their pay laying claim to the women by occupying their time, dollar a drink, and when drunk enough, would defend their right to them with fists, teeth and feet, until midnight rolled around and it was time to go back to the Camp. And I confess I took many a sample from those women, but kept going back to Michiko.

She was working, so there was no resentment when I'd gone to the Texas Club and found her milking some other poor homesick boy. We'd simply acknowledge each other and I'd go on to spend my money with some other woman. Her job was comfort and illusion, ours was will and violence. Both risked life, limb, and soul.

Access to the vital socket quickly became like plugging into a battery on half charge, the envelope of woman flesh fueling the separation from the World and the transformation into agents of destruction. Neither woman nor man could give completely, or realize beyond role. Girlish placidity combined with strutting arrogance, precipitating half lives in small towns, the illusion of sexual conquest and competence feeding the illusion of warrior invulnerability. In what pretended to be intimate moments, the woman's soft and yielding light would close and she'd just be body, so you felt like you were a complicitor in a life-long slow serial rape, the numbers of the same young you stretching back twenty years, enough bodies to march across the Pacific. So, enraptured with orgasmic immediacy, we could not feel the bones of the 48,000 American dead buried beneath the towns calling for us to live, find love, make peace, become men who embraced all the world and life.

Entering into life as it had always been on Okinawa (in our lifetimes, anyway) it was plain that official resignation to the call of Marine and Air Force genitalia wasn't the only force driving the women onto their backs—any woman willing to accept the price. If you didn't go to town on payday and get laid you were suspected of being either homo or, worse, Mormon. Promises to the girls back home were dismissed with a condom and a snigger. Recognition that the whole of Asia was predicated on garnering the American dollar, that Asian life was predicated on feudalism or slavery, made using prostitutes like contributing to the free-market system. The damage done to their souls was deemed the cost of doing business. Life was cheap, the dinks throw away or drown girl babies; do 'em a huss, fuck their brains out. To use them was to be a man because a man was all dick and weapon and his stay might be short.

But nobody ever dies in a war. Just the enemy, and they aren't people anyway. Rape was the right of the conqueror, went the warrior lore. So what if the process had been going on for twenty years, and it had become institutional instead of violent.

As hard as I tried to adopt the prevailing attitudes, that first lovely moment with Michiko had woken in me the knowledge that she was a soul, distinct and whole, a woman with her life radiating from the Asian past and into the Asian future. The pearl-inlaid comb had been made by skilled hands dedicated to beauty. Her little boy would become a man required to hold up his part of the world. What kind of man would he become in the midst of such example as us? Taxi driver pimp? Guerrilla taking a bead on my son? Opium smoking wastrel begging in a Hong Kong alley? Commissar of Social Purity armed with dictums and a pistol?

And no matter how frequently I visited the town, measuring my money to gain the most pleasure for the nickel, there was never any moment of real satisfaction. No relaxation or sleep after bedding with a woman, no giggles of mutual pleasure or recognition. Just a kind of widening emptiness like Asia was a great swallowing cave of shadows sucking me down into its sultry maw. The dragon may have held the pearl, but we were inside the dragon. Whore talk said the words we wanted to hear, two decades of demands had educated them, but there remained a persistent nostalgia for some girl back home. I wrote a plaintive letter to a Navy girl back at the Oakland hospital, but received no reply. My need must've been oozing off the pages like a swarm of serpents.

Beyond my own sad perceptions were the exultant faces of a battalion of young Marines who claimed to have died and gone to heaven. Between paydays the E.M. club would be filled to capacity with Marines drinking as hard as they could, clamoring in fraternal glee and telling each other just how bad the war was going to be and how bad they were going to be fighting it. They were getting drunk, they were getting laid, they were destined for glory! a Silver Star at least, Purple Hearts by the basket full, jungle fighters par-excellence. Life was supposed to be short; drunk and feisty was the way they were supposed to be, every sign permitted it.

In the competition for who could get the drunkest, drunk past smashing a beer can flat on your forehead, Ortiz came up the winner. Ortiz was a Private in Hurlock's squad, a short reedy boy none too bright, but earnest in his efforts to please. Demonstrating his camaraderie one night, he drank the entire contents of a typhoon fifth—a half gallon of 40 proof rice wine. His friends, nearly as drunk themselves, had to dump him into his rack. Even though he'd vomited in the taxi on the way back to Camp, there was enough alcohol remaining in his system to cause respiratory failure. His bunk mate had heard his breathing go into rales, then stop. In a panic he woke the rest of the squad-bay, but no one knew how to get Ortiz back to the land of the living and breathing. A rifle team was organized and dispatched to wake me, over a minute away across the camp street.

By the time I got there Ortiz was only a few seconds away from being dead. His skin was sallow and clammy, his fingernails cyanotic blue, his pupils dilated. I had to press hard into his jugular to find his sporadic pulse. I could still see the spark of life deep in his eyes.

I began giving him mouth-to-mouth, between breaths ordering his squad to make a stretcher out of a blanket. After a few minutes he was breathing raggedly on his own, so we loaded him onto the blanket and ran with him down to the Regimental Sick Bay. The doctor there had seen many such cases, and casually injected Ortiz with paraldehyde. His life functions working, we left him there and went back to sleep.

Up to that moment my reputation among the Marines had been based on bravado and acting like them, whoring in the town, drinking until I puked, hacking it in the field. After saving Ortiz's life, I gained status. I knew what to do in an emergency and wasn't afraid to do it. For all the professed confidence of Marines, the boys left it to the corpsman to do the mouth-to-mouth. But what I saw in their eyes the next morning when they congratulated me was the taint of homosexuality. The taboo against homosexuality was so powerfully ingrained that to touch lips with a man in any form made you suspect.

Two days later we packed to go on float. The last night in Okinawa, my last night there perhaps forever, I went to see Michiko.

I babbled on about going to sea, probably going to Vietnam, "No good, no good. Many boys die," she said. She'd seen many an outfit pull out. All it meant was a change of indistinguishable faces. But instead of leading me back to her crib, she took me out of the Texas Club and down the street to her own house on the edge of the town. Inside her tiny apartment I could see oriental scrolls depicting serene landscapes, a calendar featuring a Japanese movie star and her unmade bed. We made a long slow compassionate love. It was free.

◆◆◆◆

While the women in Hinnoko were lighting their braziers to heat their work rooms, the U.S. 7th Fleet was deploying its long arc of destruction from Hokkaido to Indonesia. As Marines on float we were to be ready to fight any Asian enemy at any time. The possibilities ran from suppressing rioting in Japan, repelling invasion in Korea, quelling Communist uprising in the Philippines, shelling Quemoy and Matsu and stopping the Chinese in their tracks, showing the Commies in Thailand we meant to honor the SEATO pact, and to supporting our advisors already occupying South Vietnam. We were sent to Mt. Fuji for winter training in response to North Korea's threats to steal South Korea's industry.

All during that miserable freezing February our urgency to get to Vietnam compounded, our time overseas restricted to thirteen months, and that month of winter training was cutting into our war time. It was with great relief that we heard the news that North Korea had decided against a winter invasion, and that we'd be moving south, into the South China Sea, down into the tropical sun to be on call while we waited for an invitation to come to the aid of the South Vietnamese—many of whom were Catholic refugees from the oppressive Ho Chi Min regime. Catholic: almost Filipino, almost Irish, almost us.

The whole battalion, plus headquarters company including Regimental headquarters, plus field kitchens, medical equipment, jeeps, Ontos, weapons, every item necessary to keep a battalion supplied in the field for ninety days, was stuffed onto a six hundred foot long APA named the *Galveston*.

The upper decks were reserved for the officers. We men occupied the holds, sleeping stacked five high with eighteen inches of breathing space between our racks. There was no privacy whatsoever, and we lived playing cards on deck and standing lines for our three meals a day.

As we cruised south the weather warmed, and I was awed by the vast spaces between the areas of our protection. There was never the question of our right to be there. We were dedicated and sworn to carry out national policy, trained to absolute obedience, simple instruments of our country's will.

The long grey water heaving with storms off Japan gave way to deep quiet blue, then to calm azure as we crossed onto the shallows of the South China Sea. Great ribbons of sulphur colored brit wound endlessly through the sunbright water. Sea snakes hunted through the brit. We expected to see whales and other ships, but found ourselves singular, unwatched by Chinese or Russian trawlers. A dreamy serenity pervaded the ship, and at night the stars were bright enough to read by. I'd often find myself staring into the diamond water nearly vanished in revery. The abundant miracle was evident and at hand, and I was enraptured. But there was also the boredom that comes with listening to the hundreds of stories from the hundreds of men, told between card hands, brave exploits committed by prisoners. And being merely attached to the Marine Corps, I found I had to seek true friendship only with other corpsmen, one of whom was a dental technician named Duke. It was from him I learned that I wasn't the only one driven by shame to volunteer for war.

It was a condition of his friendship that I secrete myself with him in the tiny stateroom that served as the dental office, and drink the medicinal alcohol only he and the dentist had access to. We'd spend our dimes on cups of orange flavored soda and mix in the 190 proof to get giddy, sick and lugubrious. I'd tell lies about racing motorcycles and he'd tell lies about racing sports cars. We'd remember body surfing at Del Mar and physically challenging the older men in our training class. But there was always a welling of violence in him, and when he'd get to a releasing state of drunkenness, his eyes would squint and his mouth would tighten into a drooling maniacal snarl, and it became my job in the friendship to keep him under control. He told me his story about having to search the bars of Kansas City and San Mateo for his mother while his father was conducting executive conferences with the secretarial staff. A habit of life that went on until his mother became such a notorious embarrassment to her wealthy family that she was committed to a sanitarium, diagnosed with dementia praecox, divorced and left to cure herself.

And like too many of the others aboard that ship, Duke had been forced to make the choice of either jail or service. As a dental student at Whitman College in Spokane he and his frat brothers had spent all of a Saturday night drinking until the sun came up, and they had all come to a similar conclusion. Student poverty had denied them Michelins for their hoopies, the liberation of capital goods was politically correct action, and Duke knew exactly where the tire store was located. Driving there as a rolling party, Duke took a trash can from the alley and threw it through the plate glass storefront. Inside, he and the boys began rolling tires out, figuring to mount them later in the day, a pit crew in beanies. The police responded to the Sunday morning alarm and arrested the working half of Sigma Chi. His friends gave him up, they were poor lost sheep sobbing for their mothers whose fathers would make bail, pay damages and any fines the city cared to impose. Duke was certainly the ring leader. His father was far south in San Francisco, and wrote the judge a letter saying Duke's fate was in his own hands. The judge said a long sea voyage would do him and the community some good. At the urging of his father, Duke agreed.

But that wasn't what was really driving him. He and I would argue about what we'd do after we got out of the war, and he'd tell me that his family expected him to be a good businessman, and the only way to be a good businessman was to acquire property. The more property you had, the more power you had. You could say to a thousand men, go, you could command a thousand women, come. "You got no future, Doc," he'd say. "All your good-heartedness don't mean shit in the real world. You gotta be hard, man, ruthless, slash and burn, get your rocks off doing the other guy dirty. Guys like you just make it hard for guys like me, with all your liberal bullshit. You can run the world if you want to, shit, get elected. I just want to own it."

And even when that argument once erupted into a wrestling match, the heft of his shoulder smashing into my solar plexus, knocking me against the office bulkhead, me finally having to choke him into quietude, living up to his family's expectations didn't explain his volatility.

After our fight, and after drinking quite a bit more, I extracted his confession with a solemn promise of unending care. He'd never told anyone. The incident had happened three years before. The tire store invasion was just a way to leave home. It seems that he took great pride in his Ford LTD, had installed a blower on the engine, put in a new rear-end, beefed-up the suspension—bored and stroked and the rest of the mechanical adjustments necessary to make a passenger sedan into a hurtling menace. Challenged by some other boys in a similar car to a race down the coast highway, for pink slips, as was the macho fashion at the time, he took the bet. The road was slick with evening fog. The other boys were beating him. He couldn't stand the thought of losing his car. What would he say to his father who'd bought it for him and forbade him to race? His honor among his friends would be stained. To lose property as valuable as a new car was utterly unthinkable. In a desperate lurch of speed to win he smashed into the back end of the other car and sent it flying through the guard rail and two hundred feet down onto the rocks below. The other boys were killed.

After hearing him out, and still as hungry for love as he, he sealed my burden by promising to cut me in on his grandmother's will. She was very rich, matriarch of an old Kansas City medical family. She was living in Boca Raton. She was eighty-six and sick.

"It'll be soon, man, we'll buy some businesses, hire some managers, we'll be sitting pretty, get drunk all the time. Suck on the fat of the land." Terriers nipped at sybarery sugar plums. It was the first time anyone had bid my acceptance with so rich a bribe, besides the Marine Corps. But it held no real promise. It was only a new kind of game we could play between seeking violence and abandon, a fantasy we could spin to extract ourselves from our shame. I didn't tell him why I was there, but I knew I'd have a friend when I needed one.

There was a distinction between befriending a murderer and being amongst a troop of killers. Back in the World Duke would be a pariah, and deservedly. His secret would infect every relationship, standing between souls until the furious whirl of consequence drove him into a dark room with a shotgun plugged into his mouth or he smashed his car into a locomotive, which he did twenty years later. But the point and purpose of Marines was to hunt and kill other men who were as just as dedicated to hunting and killing them. With God on the side of the righteous forgiveness could wipe a slate clean.

◆◆◆◆

It was only a few days after I'd knelt beside Duke's rack and heard his story that we got the scoop that the battalion was being sent to suppress Communist activity on the peninsula dividing Thailand and Malaysia. We'd get to practice an amphibious landing. We'd be issued live ammunition. We'd be well armed and dangerous and the sergeants would have to cut us some slack. The operation was to be conducted as "joint maneuvers" with the Thai Navy, a training exercise. No, we wouldn't be getting combat pay, there was only the suspicion of Commies in the area, but just in case we're fired upon take these magazines.

Grumbles registered the Marine's disappointment that we wouldn't be rushing the beach and firing from the hip at pillboxes. It was chickenshit to require that they place a piece of tape over the bullets in each magazine and the sergeants would be checking them every four hours. How will we be able to identify the enemy? Don't sweat the small shit, do as you're told, if they're shooting at you they're the enemy. What if they just fucking gun us down? We'll be busy peeling tape off our bullets while they shoot the shit out of us. Better'n you gettin' pissed off at your buddy and shooting the shit out of him. Hey, man, I thought we was going to Vietnam. What's this practice shit? I'm ready.

From the ship rail we could see the jungle, palms and thick green, spreading on, maybe forever. The sea had changed from azure to dirty grey. We were in the wash of a river. Three rusty destroyer escorts, bearing both U.S. and Thai insignia, wallowed beside our APA. We climbed down the cargo nets into the landing boats, then formed up on the beach. And there we were, the full battalion including weapons, standing in ranks dressed in fatigues, rifles, web-gear, machine guns and bandoliers, helmets and boots, mortar tubes and .81 mm rounds, M-79s, an indomitable show of mastered force and will. We were infantry back on land, flags flying over tropical Asia, jaws tight and ready to fight, and about to step into Paradise.

The maneuvers went on for a week, but the impression remains for a lifetime. The whole body of us, the entire battalion of uniformed armed fierce Marines could have been mere apparitions to the people living on the peninsula. We marched through the little town that bordered the river and its beautiful people stood in their courtyards watching us pass in review, not threats and not liberators, just curiosities. Their bright smiling eyes and grinning mouths chattered at us, then they went on about their daily business. Gardens grew pineapples and vegetables. Small orchards grew guava and papaya. Pigs and chickens roamed under houses built on stilts. Rice straw thatched the roofs. The houses were built in the shade of mahogany and ironwood, and down beside the quiet streams leading to the river. The road led to open parks where children dressed in sarongs played and fished for loaches. Men with trained gibbons harvested coconuts from palms lining the road. They seemed uniquely happy, and disregarded our desire to be seen as fearsome warriors and their protective saviors.

It wasn't long before we started talking among ourselves about how to disappear into the jungle for a few days just as the troop ship was pulling out. Many a young man fashioned a mental letter home asking for a steady supply of money. The girls were very beautiful. Some walked about with their luscious breasts exposed. The living was easy, the sun comfortable and warm, there was a Shell station for the boat traffic, a European medical clinic to rid you of worms and malaria, there'd be no more hurry up and wait, no more sergeants and officers, no more threats of K.P. and the brig, no miserable future back in the World to battle to win. A man with a piece of ground and a boat could trade up and down the coast, dive for pearls, be a pirate, live one adventure after another, more than one wife with long black hair and yielding hips was possible to a man rich enough. What more could a man want? The food grew on trees or fattened on garbage. No wonder the Commies wanted it. A man with a couple of rifles or an M-60 could do all right for himself and get these people to adopt him, a hero, Lord Jim, the armed missionary.

But no one would talk to us, and the girls weren't for sale, and the land was all owned and passed from generation to generation, and we were barbarians ultimately unwelcome. What else could the men of the town do but ignore us? We were temporary apparitions who they'd have to kill if we decided to stay. What seemed abundance to our city trained eyes was simply stasis achieved over several thousand years. The line of children stretched back into unrecorded time and the ghosts of ancestors guarded the people's well-being. To include these great brawling monsters into life would soil harmony. Soon they'd be hungry for more, like the angry taxcollectors from the next village who came in the night taking the money and the young men, and defiling the women. To be so large and so healthy, so well armed and rich with canned meat to eat, bespoke huge appetite as well as cavernous wealth, and there was only ever enough to feed themselves rain by rain, and crop by crop.

The battalion was deployed to surround the town and be on the lookout for invaders. We traipsed into the jungle and established a loose perimeter, listening for enemy footfalls, and hearing the insects mate in the succulent moonlight. Tranquility laced with fear, yearning to be rid of the World and be alive in serenity, rocked us to sleep. There were no invaders, at least none we could distinguish from the people who lived there.

On the last day of the operation my platoon was humping down a thickly overgrown trail beside one of the many streams, heaving our packs through the muggy heat, grimacing at our loads and our purposeless effort. We heard a man's voice call to us from across the stream. An American's voice, high pitched and mocking. Definitely not the authoritative growl of a Marine. We spotted him standing taller than the twelve or so Thais he was walking with. They were all dressed in sarongs, but he was distinct. His hair was long and red and his beard wild and flowing. The only other Americans we'd expected to see in that neck of the woods were CIA. spooks, but he was certainly not the soldier type. He wore a tape recorder on a sash around his chest. Anthropologist, someone guessed. When he had our attention he pointed at us and burst into a long howling laugh, an orangutang's ridicule. No matter how tough and gung-ho we pretended to be, we knew the sound of being called dufus jerks. And even if Cpls. Rameriz and Orrick did point their rifles at him while he was laughing, saying,"Get that Zeke mutherfucker," he knew as well as we knew where we were headed, and the joke was on us.

Going In

Going in, the landing craft beat against the seas above Da Nang. Disobeying the order to stay knelt down on the bottom of the boat I stood up to find out where we were and how far we had to go. The APA was a mile behind us, and the beach a mile ahead of us. I don't know how scared I looked, but I remember how scared everyone around me looked. Full field packs, helmets strapped on, rifles loaded with live ammunition, brass-cartridged bandoliers framed frightened boy-faces I would never see again.

The bravado of the night before was gone. Then we were invincible jungle fighters backed up by the finest military mechanism developed in the history of mankind. The Viet Cong were grungy riceballs infected with evil who deserved to die. We'd go into this quaint little country with their backward ways, almost China, on the Russian tit, and kick some ass, wipe the wily little fuckers out, and rise victorious over evil. God-damn, this is what we been waiting for all our lives, Uncle Sugar's promise is going to come true. The boys who acted toughest claimed they were there to collect some ears, they were ready to shove the bastards into the ovens, burn the villages down, Hell, burn the whole fucking country down. In a moment of detached clarity I remembered the golden rule and feared that every injury we delivered would be returned to us ten fold, and our blood of mind would carry it into ten generations. We'd been waiting weeks for the announcement that we were going in, and when it came, the Marines cheered. In jaw clenching panic I resolved to never again wish for anything but peace and benevolence, but by necessity kept it to myself.

This time wishes and prayers and magic would hold no sway. This time it was for real. No more simulated fire. Real war with real men who were out to kill us. Booby traps that could blow off your foot or your leg or your balls. Punji traps made of sharpened knives of bamboo dipped in diseased filth. Ambushes where all you'd see was the flash of the rifles as blackness swallowed your soul. Entering into a land whose people were so crazy for violence their priests burned themselves down in a blaze of gasoline scream. Embracing an enemy who'd suddenly become at once real and as elusive as a ghost. He wasn't going to just stand up and let us shoot him down. He was going to sneak through the moonless night and wait for his moment and then kill us for trespassing. And we wouldn't know him in daylight, because what made him the enemy was his mind and that didn't show when he came to cut our hair or pick up the laundry. And not only was it the men who drove the jeepneys who were the enemy; it was the farmers and their wives and their children and the most insidious cadre down from the North absolutely resolved to expel the lumbering imperialist giants, and to do it as close up as a knife in the eye while we slept. We were each and all inhabited by a boundless paranoia, homemade and hot.

Each of us knew what awaited us in the Vietnam dark. You could see particular fates working behind the eyes of the boys huddled in the bottom of the landing craft. Some feared being blown in half by a mortar round and having to live out life a breathing stump in a wheelchair, their suicide already decided. Some feared a bullet in the brain from an unseen unknowable sniper, no chance to fight back. For some it was to lay wounded and paralyzed in a filthy benjo ditch and be eaten by rats. Or to be shot out of the sky, look mom—no chute!, the last sound heard a sickening crump, if you didn't die first from screaming. Or to wake up with your own hands choking yourself to death while you tried to stop your jugular from feeding your life into the leached out soil of Asia, your killer grinning his ancient triumph. Or maybe they'd come en masse, marching the peasants we were sworn to protect in front of their troops in numbers so vast they could absorb every ounce of death stored in our magazines and Claymores until it was hand-to-hand and they cut you apart with their bayonets, as merciless as we'd be. Or maybe it'd be something quick and lethal as the bite of a cobra or habu or krait when you were turning over a rock to sit on and eat your ham and limas. Or even something smaller, like microbes infecting your bloodstream, picked up from some mamasan's rice pot or some village well or from quenching your thirst from a jungle stream or from a mosquito biting you while you waited on ambush and could not slap.

We'd watched the jungled coast for weeks while we waited, expecting, even hoping, to see fire fights erupt in the dark. We'd see helicopters and jets taking off from the air base at Da Nang and feel jealousy that our brother battalion, 1/3, had already landed and taken up defensive positions. Already the jungle smell and paddy water steam was mixing in our blood. But during those weeks we'd seen only one fire fight, a brief exchange of bright orange tracers and white hot rifle flashes—between a squad of Viet Cong and some ARVN soldiers, no kills, no wounded, we were told. The officers monitored the military net with relish and expectation. In mind movie there were no long stretches of boredom blowing up into fierce moments of wrenching terror, or hunts for the enemy that went on for weeks, even months, culminating in some horrible bloodletting catastrophe that lasted only a few minutes and would haunt our nights for centuries.

Although each one of us carried the whole of America like a mantle around our person, we were about to invade another sovereign nation, even if it was in disarray, disintegrating before our very eyes. It mattered little to us that the Gulf of Tonkin incident had been provoked. As warriors of the just and the mighty we had the right to be anywhere in the world we wished to be, and if the North Vietnamese were foolish enough to pluck at the eagle's feathers, then all hell could be unleashed upon them. And if they were angered enough to compose their armies into phalanx upon phalanx to be fed into our killing machine, then so be it. We'd serve the best interests of the world and eliminate their Communist effrontery from the sight of God. Our mechanism soared high and struck with precision. Our weapons were the most awesome ever devised. We could sear a village from the face of the earth with a flight of napalm laden jets. We could put a round in every square foot of a football field in thirty seconds, killing every thing that metabolized. Our tactics were tested and questioned and redesigned at universities dedicated to the execution of war. And if deeply enough wounded, in men or in pride, there was always The Big One, twice used. The whole Seventh Fleet, including a thousand jet fighters and bombers, the Air Force bombers on Guam and in Saigon and in Thailand, could be called upon to flatten any enemy stronghold or blast down whole cities. Napalm, willy peter, fragmentation, massive destruction designed to kill and terrorize by mere mention, if we could get it to work in the split seconds when we would need it.

When the landing craft ramp lowered and we rushed into the gentle waves lapping the beach north of Da Nang there was no enemy to greet us with machine-gun fire. Secretly thankful for the insult, we failed to surmise how deeply ran their impacted rage or how deeply coursed their ancient fury. Movie children, what did we know of the patience of the perverted Wheel?

Our outrage at Communism's tyranny was real enough. The Viet Cong were a formidable enemy, one led and inspired by their brethren Chinese and capable of hideous acts of mass murder. Before we were shipped overseas we were shown documentary evidence, film taken by State Department representatives, of Communist solutions to social problems. The swarm constituting Mao's liberation army had swept into Nanking, a million strong, hungry and vengeful. To insure their place in society, Mao's army rounded up all the city's notables. They took over the communications facilities, the government infrastructure, the banks, the major industrial and commodity outlets, installing their own managers, and took the Capitalist Roaders to the city square. With a gesture designed to eliminate any further resistance from any entity, free man or free government or incensed world, they buried ten thousand people up to their necks, setting them out in a neat grid like planting onions. Then the murderous henchmen went down the rows harvesting heads.

They were the enemy. They were utterly contemptible. The tenet claimed that Asians found life so miserable that it held no value for them.They enforced their will for order and profit under the guise of providing health and well being for their citizen charges and thus allowed their leaders to sacrifice the lives of less valued people—who would die of disease or starvation or feudal struggle anyway, so why not line them up in front of the trained armies to become soil for the next and future generations?—and this made them anathema to life. Seeing that horror convinced that it was forgivable to shower them with bombs, to wipe out their gene-pool, to burn their mothers down, to protect yourself from even breathing the same atoms of air they'd breathed. Ho Chi Minh was one of them, as was any vile dink who followed him. It could be you or any man who aspired to freedom they planted like an onion.

It was that collective history, that fearsome knowledge held by both us and the Viet Cong, that made them seem so dangerous. While our tradition threatened to shoot deserters, only one had ever been court-martialled and killed. We were held together, no matter the strength of the opposition or the horror invoked, by pride, honor and mutual love. That the Viet Cong were willing to subject themselves to leaders who led with the barrel of a gun made them more suicidal than any of us could truly comprehend, more insanely dangerous because they were so willing to die, and dishonorable as human beings. Bound by fear of each other, infected by singular economic structure, fired by the cause of expelling us enemies of the people, inspired to rid the culture of corruption and claim once more a unified Vietnam purified of foreign exploitation, they gave us ample reason to fear them. Their zeal for sacrifice and death was evidenced by the million death-seeking corpses reddening the Yalu River. Kali scattering lost souls like mouldy grain, her flame burning black in the masters of eternal China. To squelch their heinous power was a significant burden to be assumed by nineteen-year olds potent with American righteousness.

Certain the enemy surrounded us, the men in the battalion were skittish when the officers formed us into ranks. The jungle just beyond the beach was dark and brimmed with menace. If they feared a fight on the open beach they could easily snipe at us from spider holes, taking us out one by one until we fell into chaos. Suddenly all the yelling and anger of sergeants thrashing us into obedience made sense. Still our eyes watched the jungle and only half heard the captain as he told us, "Listen up. We are part of the Twentysixth Marine Expeditionary Brigade. We are in the Republic of South Vietnam at the invitation of the Government of South Vietnam. We are here to demonstrate the United States alliance with South Vietnam. Presently we will meet with units of the South Vietnamese Rangers. We will remain at attention. There has been no enemy activity reported in this sector, and none is expected. Relax. That is all." But we knew he was lying to us. We could feel Charlie in the bushes. Arrows of hate were singing in our brains.

We spent the next few hours marching toward the air base. Heading inland and away from the water the heat was stifling. To cover my anxiety I passed up and down the ranks distributing salt tablets, and reaffirming that we were all in this together. Despite the sure and certain knowledge that the whole of the American military machine was behind us, our isolation and distance from any mechanism that could help us if the Viet Cong decided upon a mass attack was equally certain. My red salt tablet dispenser made a great target. The lore went that killing corpsmen earned a larger bounty. For a troop to lose its corpsman was to lose its connection to rescue, hence its morale. Dumb grunts were worth ten dollars. Corpsmen, thirty-five, a day's pay back in the World, six months' pay for them.

Twenty H-34 helicopters were waiting for us just outside the air base, their rotors spraying out bright orange dust and pebbles that stung our anxious faces. In the distance we could see men wearing conical hats and black pajamas working the paddies with water buffalo. Farmers by day, Viet Cong by night. So we'd be, were we them. Better to regard them as someone who could and would kill you than to trust to good will and luck.

No one in charge bothered to tell us what to expect. We didn't know if getting on the helicopters meant transport to a safe haven or dropping into a nest of Viet Cong. The door gunner's face was different than ours. Alert, strained from months without sleep, his eyes looking out and down and within like he was an animal living on pulsed instinct. How can you kill women and children, the joke went, easy, just don't lead 'em as much. Har Har. But he was a worried young man, contemptuous at our greenness, yet on the verge of tears. Bringing down a helicopter and crew, plus nine dumb grunts and a corpsman, you could feed a family for a couple of years.

Until our arrival the helicopters had been used to ferry the ARVN soldiers into combat. But adding another battalion of Americans to the mix changed the odds. Certainly the Marines would start aggressive operations against the Viet Cong: more chopper rides, more exposure, angrier Charlies. And while he worried about getting home and having more war, many of us worried that there wouldn't be enough war to go around. In a few months our faces would look like his.

I took the door seat. More exposure, and last man on is first man off, but I wanted to see. The thought of travelling so fast toward the unknown, maybe even getting killed, closed up inside the greasy metal shell of the chopper, was easier to bear the more I knew by seeing. I hadn't volunteered to be killed or maimed or to assume the burden of this country and not get to know.

From two thousand feet we looked out upon a land of splendid beauty. Sharp lush green hills rolled into darker green mountains on our left, and the South China Sea lay serene and blue on our right. Below us spread a long broad flat plain divided by paddy dikes and silvered into expanses of shining water. Round fish nets hanging from bamboo tripods stood at canal junctures. Thatch villages shaded by palms and teak interspersed with banana trees passed quietly beneath us. In the hottest part of the day the people had retired from their work, leaving the paddies bright and tranquil. The villages were islands floating on a sky silver sea.

The plains then gave way to densely green hills. Narrow waterfalls poured down from rock shelves in the clefts of the hills, and we could see the thin columns of woodcutter charcoal fires rising in the still air. It seemed impossible that so much hate and menace could be lurking down in that jungle waiting to find and exterminate us. We crossed the spur of hills, sliding along the strip of white beach sand beside the sea, imagining skin diving and surfing, beer and girls.

◆◆◆◆

Catching sight of the red beacon from the yellow flight control tower at the Phu Bai airport we began our descent. We landed, unloaded, and were formed into ranks, then left to stand at attention for several hours while we awaited the arrival of a company of ARVN Rangers, pro forma military ritual none us any longer believed in. After two men fainted from heat prostration the captain relented in his demand for a demonstration of physical stamina and let us sit in formation, the heat rising off the tarmac in bellowing waves, sweat soaking our garrison fatigues.

Well into darkness, we heard the prop noise of several C-47s approach the field. The pilots used the sharp angular descent of military landings into short and contested air-strips, the three planes touching down within minutes of each other. It was time for our meeting with our allies.

The two companies of men stood facing each other at attention. Draped in the notion that the war couldn't start without us, our minds alert for an as yet unseen enemy just beyond our reach, it didn't dawn on me until years later that the war was standing right in front of us.

There we were, a fully equipped Marine Corps company; M-14s, M-79s, M-60s, .81 mm mortars, .45s, K-bars, M-2 carbines, ammo and rounds, disciplined to a fierce readiness, a hundred and sixty young men ready to fight and die, and we were made fools by a scraggly band of fewer than a hundred Vietnamese.

We could see their last fifty years of active war in their faces. They were taut with measured violence. The sheen of dirt and oil that collects on men in combat coated their cheeks and brows. And though they smiled shyly at first, feeling our curiosity and the distinct possibility that at some juncture in history we'd become their enemy, their lips tightened into impenetrable passivity. We could feel their eyes taking our measure just as we measured them. We were large and well armed, but only three of our hundred and sixty had ever seen combat, and that was long ago in Korea. Each one of them had crossed the savage line, we could tell. There was no uniformity in their weapons. They had greaseguns, SKSs, AK-47s, carbines and M-1s, U.S. issue M-60s and old BARs, weapons won by killing the enemy. Their thin musculature let them slip easily through jungle tangles and live on stream snails and rice. If you closed your eyes you could see in each of them the hollow dark flame of instinct orbited by the ghosts of the brothers and fellow countrymen they'd killed. They seemed capable of disappearing into the night, blending with the fetid atmosphere, of counting themselves already dead and thus conscienceless. Ideology implied future, but there seemed no connection to land or family about them, just the honed energy of the hunt, the snarling joy of momentary triumph. We had home to go to, but home for them was Avici Hell. The rules were clear—find the enemy and kill him before he knew he was found. Ambush is killing and killing is fun. War was what they did at night and after the rice was planted, instead of TV. After the French, the Japs, the French again, then so confused and embroiled in corruption, the families sold into slavery to the landlords, war had become the national way of life. These were the finest savages, and as we stiffened into daring arrogance we must have seemed like sensitive children easily provoked and dangerously equipped.

The meeting was over. The Rangers' officers, CIA mysterymen, marched them into the waiting Air America C-47s, to fly them over to Pleiku to hunt down the Cong infiltrating down the Ho Chi Minh Trail. After they left we congratulated ourselves for being superior soldiers by claiming the Rangers' allegiance because we trained and paid them. But inside, we knew.

SEARCH AND DESTROY, FIRST DEAD

Marching out to the ruins of the French fort that commanded the hamlet of Le Mai and the Song De River basin, our company passed through ten miles of country that made Okinawa look like a highly civilized nation. The shattered stucco walls of shelled houses and rusting hulks of blown open armored personnel carriers stood in weed clotted paddies. The walls surrounding the courtyards of the colonial masters were studded with concrete embedded broken glass and rusted barbed wire. Off from the main dirt road thatch villages huddled behind thorn hedges. At the juncture between the road that led to the river and to the Dai Lai Pass stood a thatch covered barracks consisting of bamboo sleeping platforms that served the ARVNs as a semi-permanent rest area. Across from the barracks a warren of corrugated tin and ammo crate refugee dwellings had erupted. The concept of heaven was nowhere to be found.

Along the road women and children stopped to rest and watch us swing our broad shoulders past, staring from under their sun hats at yet another massively armed troop of raw young men injecting themselves into the balance of their lives. Although they carried baskets bearing piglets and rice, and even babies, rumor had it that even they were dangerous. The story went that a man from 1/3 had approached a ten year old boy to buy a Coke and was handed a grenade which killed them both, and wounded several other men. Betel spittle and blackened teeth bespoke a depth of

51

misery that would allow any member of their society to thank death for release as they embraced your young body to the grenade strapped to their chest.

And though we each carried in our heads the comforting future of the American Way, and the magnanimity inherent in surplus, to the people we were passing we must have appeared as plain compounded danger. America was vast and wealthy, so rich she could spend even her sons. Looking into their eyes, past the impassivity, the fear and hatred, there was bewilderment that even so noble a gesture as fighting to save them from whatever tyranny was at hand was at once frivolous and destructive. That so great a people would recklessly add their formidable weight to the Wheel could only hurry the spin into chaos.

A current of excited adventure ran through our double column. We'd finally been turned from our clumsy waiting, stuck in some dry rice paddies while the brass figured out what to do next. While we waited we'd continually bitched about getting this stinking little war off the launching pad, earning our combat pay, getting into the action instead of doing side-straddle hops in front of our canvas tent-city, the sergeants still calling us girls. Now we were marching down the Asian road carrying the weapons of occupation, entering enemy territory. Charlie was about, we knew he knew every step we took, that he was watching, that every woman we saw along the road was plugged into his information network. Instead of driving out to the French ruins in trucks, we were marching the ten miles to show our stamina and determination, our strength and bravery, to a people who'd suffered centuries of war and toil. The air was alive with the fragments of souls shattered by bullets and bombs.

When we reached the spur of hills that ran beside the Song De River we found that word of our arrival had preceded us. People from the hamlet were busy working on the lower southern slopes with hoes and digging sticks, removing tea bushes and urns that contained the ashes of their ancestors. The sacred tea and sacred bones would not be defiled by these demon driven people.

It had only been eleven years since the French had lost their slave-hold on the fort we occupied, but it was a shamble of brick and leached mortar. The low outside wall still stood, but the interior buildings had been knocked into a rubble of brick and cracked concrete floors by furious men out to erase any sign of their oppression. Our first detail upon reaching the hilltop was to clear away the rubble, and toss it down the hillsides, furthering the villager's work while becoming the phantoms of the past. If there were this many of us showing our strength, there would be more and more, until no other response than expulsion by violence was possible.

For another two weeks we cleaned up the ruins, set up listening posts, strung concertina and hung C-ration cans with pebbles in them to the wire, made sand bags and dug latrines. Two Ontos were assigned to our position, to fire into the expected hordes of doped up swarming Viet Cong rushing up the hill. A mortar pit was dug, and a comm-line laid to Battalion Headquarters. Each man was given a position behind the wall to defend and sleep on, just like the Alamo. And every day and night for that two weeks the sergeants would attempt to keep our fighting spirit fired by spreading the word that the VC would be coming that night, hundreds of them, G-2 had the skinny that they were massing for a human wave attack and weren't taking any prisoners. And we'd stare into the dank night imagining the shadows assuming flesh and arms, the sounds of already dead men's footfalls and breath rising to warn us they were coming. Staring until our eyes hurt, no one ever sleeping on watch, a round in the chamber and fear like a steady drip of pain hollowing a channel down your spine.

But the VC never came. They were patient, letting our anxiety etch into our confidence, and our sleeplessness erode our caution. After a while we stopped listening to the sergeants, but not to the dark. The urgency to engage the enemy was building, though, and the officers began talking about patrols and ambush. The best defense is a good offense, went the motto.

◆◆◆◆

"Doc, I mean, would you tell them. If you were captured, would you tell them?" they would ask, and I'd say, "What is there to tell them that they can't already see for themselves? They know where the company is at all times. If they catch us out there some night, they're just going to blow us away. A grunt ain't worth nothing." But their real question was did I think they could withstand the torture. No one ever really does.

Of course there are demons. Monster and demon are the same word, the toothed beast that eats you, released in the man-brain, the blood-brain, by life jeopardized. Memory is older than algae. But demons have no more power than you give them. If they vex you, gift them with a piece of your soul, discovered or made. They'll leave you alone forever, I'd tell them.

◆◆◆◆

We could tell something momentous was afoot when the platoon sergeants started passing out metal toy crickets as an adjunct to our hand grenades and ammo. Some major had seen a movie and figured we could identify each other in the dark by clicking our little crickets; we'd be the only ones possessing them, the villagers were too poor to buy them and there wasn't anywhere to buy them anyway. So we took them and played with them like halloween kids, then threw them in the latrines. The dark was much too full of dread for such imbecility.

Those weeks also gave us a chance to survey the surrounds. Looking west the Le Mai hamlet spread under a half square mile of palm, teak and camphor trees. Beyond the hamlet lay miles of diked paddies and canals, then the beach of the South China Sea. South lay the road to Da Nang and more paddies, Iron Bridge Ridge and the road to Dai Lai Pass protected by another French ruin. Behind our fort ran a steep ridge that led into a tangle of jungled mountains where the Viet Cong hid and lived. And north, across the dirt road that ran beside our hill and across the river was another smaller village holding to a bend in the river. It was completely Viet Cong, we heard, and everything north of it, a sea of elephant grass and jungled hills, was Indian Country.

◆◆◆◆

We loaded into the 6-bys that had been dispatched to take us to where the the Viet Cong had been seen, grumbling our reluctance, ponchos over our helmets making us look like penitents. The trucks took us to some hills that ran beside the Tourane River, let us out, and sped away like something was chasing them.

We were standing around on the road in fire teams and squads, hoping some miracle would countermand our orders. No such luck. The lieutenant caught our attention, and said, "I don't know what we're getting into here. G-2 says there are VC out behind us here. We're supposed to go in and find them and kill them if we have to. They're supposed to be getting ready to mount an attack on the Airbase. Now you know as much about this as I do. First squad, take the point, head due west."

Forming into a column we began the trudge into the hills, following a small stream toward the low ground in the distance. Bamboo sagged from the weight of the recent monsoons. The sky was roiling grey. Within an hour we reached the low ground, and before us spread a seeming endless expanse of swamp water, still and thickly grown with clutches of bamboo. It gave off the sense of being the most desolate place on earth. The potential for life was there, but some hideous pocket of entropy prevented it from taking a foothold.

Entering the swamp was spooky, dangerous. It emanated dread. We slid down a bank of slick red mud and splashed into water up to our chests. Instinctively we split into two columns, silent and slow moving, the mud sucking at our boots, our ponchos snagging in the vegetation. Venomous snakes glided on our wakes. Dead leaves and sinuous leeches floated up through the brown water. It took every erg of energy just to keep moving, to keep our weapons held over our heads, to pull our feet loose for one more step, to keep our noses open for the scent of Charlie.

We pushed further and further into the swamp, our fear growing with each step. We were completely exposed. There was no way for a helicopter to reach us in the event we needed a medevac. There was no way jets could rocket or strafe the VC if we were attacked. The enemy was already there, had the hiding places, had the advantage. Even as quiet as we were trying to be they would have known we were coming by the way the animals were broadcasting our fear. They could wait until we were bunched up and cursing, then open up on us. My own fear felt like a silk thread being pulled by bulldozers, and I'm sure it was akin to that felt by every other man in the platoon.

Our collective dread became a kind of psychic magnet eroding the will of the lieutenant. We pushed on further, peering into the bamboo thickets, expecting men using breathing tubes to rise up before us and kill us by surprise, expecting to wander into some impenetrable clump of bamboo and be attacked from behind, death by bullets and drowning. It became abundantly clear to our frightened minds that we were only out there in that horrible swamp as bait, to be killed in a skirmish, to slow up the VC. The Viet Cong could no sooner attack the Airbase from that swamp than we could defeat Hanoi with our teeth.

We kept pushing in though, until the lieutenant could no longer ignore our recalcitrance or his own fear. Our faces were each registering the intensely murderous eyes drawing beads on us, waiting for the exact moment of foolhardy weariness when we would be the most vulnerable, when death was blooming black in our souls, welcome, called for. Finally, and not a second too soon, to our great relief, the lieutenant relinquished the Captain's hold on our fate, saying, "This is fucked. Let's get out of here." Tail-end Charlie led us out by dead reckoning.

◆◆◆◆

Le Mai had been searched many times by ARVN troops, but hadn't been entered by foreigners for at least twelve years. In the categorical imperatives of MACV it was considered a hamlet aligned with the Saigon government, though we knew better. There were at least five hundred people living there, mostly women, children and old men, and how could you tell if any one of them had embraced a new version of tyranny? We got the honor of being the first American outfit to sweep the village.

Nobody had to wake me up the morning of the operation. I had lain tucked in a little cubbyhole in the French ruins, smoking a pack an hour all night, thinking about what it was going to be like to kick through the hedges and get a bullet though my lungs or step on a punji stake and die slow of septicemia, or get killed outright, a bullet in the head like a long nurtured notion of suicide grasped by some other mind and delivered, free, and with malice. Or worse, that I would freeze in the middle of a fire fight, in the midst of a kind of violence I had never even seen much less been part of, and that I wouldn't be able to perform my function as life saver, wound stauncher, and thus be thought of as the lowest form of military man, a coward. My medical kit was well stocked with morphine, dexedrine, battle dressings, minor surgery kit, tourniquets, an air-way. I'd even saved the cellophane of my cigarette packs to place over sucking chest wounds. I chambered a round in my pistol, certain I'd end up using it on some maddened squad of Viet Cong before the day was over, and looked around me for some mislaid rifle to better insure my survival and to better fit with the men around me.

The men around me looked frightened and grim. For all the bravado of even the night before, there was no grab-ass and skylarking this morning. They were a thoughtful, apprehensive group about to get what they came for, and no doubt each man harbored similar thoughts to mine. They were cleaning their weapons, checking each other's backpacks (change of socks, two meals, extra ammo), adjusting their pack straps so they would ride over the hard shells of their flack jackets—hot, heavy, new, and no one was convinced they worked against bullets. Some men were writing letters home, others spooning up the last of their peaches, the acts of self comforting on perhaps the last day of life.

No one knew what awaited us when we entered the village. Maybe the Viet Cong were there, maybe they'd come in the night and had strung new trip wires, maybe they were waiting just inside the hedges with their rifles trained on our hearts, maybe they weren't there at all, maybe there were hundreds of them set to slaughter us in mid stride.

A thought that possessed me the whole of the night before was remembering a junior high school bully, huge, sixteen, who challenged me to a fist fight kick you in the balls cream your ass after school. He claimed that I had dared to talk to his fourteen year old girlfriend, the one with the big knockers. And I yawned all day through classes, and tried to enlist help from my friends, who were as afraid of the bruiser as I was and refused. Out of honor I showed up for the fight, and lied, and said, no I didn't talk to her, I know she's your girl. Which satisfied him and disappointed the audience. I didn't tell him that it was she who had talked to me, and from kindness I had listened to her tale of brutal ownership. And as the years flew, it wasn't long before I and my buddies went looking for a gang fight to be in—it was the manly fashion amongst fourteen-year-olds—and had failed to find one.

And that morning I had the same feelings, except this morning I could be permanently maimed or dead. But believing in the great power of the gun, somehow it would be easier to walk into the arena, especially with everyone else on my side. Just as it was my job to save their lives, it was the Marine's job to protect mine.

Our lieutenant, a fairhaired running-back from Annapolis and recent graduate of OTS, Quantico, called us into a huddle. We gathered around him to hear the rules. He said, with remarkable calm. "The purpose of our mission here is to conduct a sweep of the hamlet out in front of us. We will enter the ville, search the hootches, and flush out any military aged men. Any men in this area not already conscripted to the ARVN forces are presumed to be Viet

Cong or VC sympathizers. We will place them under military arrest, and send them to Da Nang for processing." Someone asked, "Does that mean execution? Shit, Lieutenant, let's just kill 'em here and save the paperwork." The lieutenant then added, "No good. We don't know who is what. Better to let their own people deal with them. We are not to fire unless fired upon. We will not take the chance of injuring innocent bystanders." Another grunt spoke, expressing our general mood, "Innocent bystanders, my ass. These people are all VC," seeing us at home rather than them in theirs. Another man spoke, saying, "You expect us to die behind some dufus police action bullshit? Them fuckers show their faces once to me and I'm gonna blow them away."

The lieutenant had heard hardchargers talk before, and though this was as new to him as it was to any one of us, he was still in command and had to quiet our fear and zeal.

"There are five hundred people down there, and if we start shooting up the place a lot of people are going to die needlessly. We aren't here for you to do your John Wayne number. We're here to win these people's hearts and minds. Better to have them on our side than on Charlie's. Never know when we're going to need them. We'll go in and take any weapons we find, disarm any booby traps, and you, Doc, tend to any kind of sickness you find. You get those people mad and they will be up here cutting off our heads. I don't want you people fucking up this war 'cause you got an itchy trigger finger. Has everybody got the word?"

We all nodded our obedient assent, though the message profoundly disagreed with our expectations. We were prepared for what the Marines do best, a frontal assault. We would be foolish to expect anything less than total defense by the enemy. If we were in their place and a troop of big hairy gun toting foreigners came attacking us, we'd take them out, damn betcha.

Reading our faces, the lieutenant added, "Don't get your balls in an uproar, people. Nothing is going to happen. We'll go in, do the sweep, spread a little fear of God, and be back for evening chow. No sweat. Now, saddle up."

The whole company, save a reserve rifle squad, collected on the helicopter landing pad below the French ruins. The sergeants passed among the men, making last minute checks, seeing that everyone was accounted for, armed, ready. They were grinning, still teasing us about having balls and cocks and nowhere to put them but five finger Rosy. Ours was the lead platoon, and when the Captain passed the word from his hilltop lookout, a commander who planned to be around to command, our lieutenant led us, in formation, down the hill.

We were grumbling among ourselves, saying, "This shit is fucked. Up to me we'd sneak in there just before dawn, burn the hootches and shoot anyone who runs out," as if the Vietnamese were Salem witches subject to testing by fire.

Through the wire, beyond the bell of sanctuary afforded by our hill positions, crossing into enemy territory like entering a swarm of disembodied insects. We spread out down the length of the dirt road facing the hamlet. In front of us we could see the twelve foot tall thorny hedges surrounding the thatch houses comprising the hamlet. The walls and shattered roofs of the few outlying stucco houses had long ago been blown out by grenades and rockets. Paths that led from the drying weed-choked paddies widened as they approached the breaks in the hedges. Camphor smoke rose in thin straight columns from inside the village. Barely an hour after dawn and the heat was already staggering. Salty sweat blurred our vision, making the village waver in the heat, making it appear to be made of entropy, of particles of the physical world held together by gravity and perception alone, peopled by ghosts. A thought could extinguish two thousand years.

When we were on line I was standing behind the lieutenant and heard the radio crackle for us to begin. It felt like a huge invisible blade swept out of the insubstantial sky and had severed me from my past. There was only this upcoming moment, only the next steps, and the next until our time in-country was up or I or we were killed or maimed and finally released from this dream that was out to kill us and owned us body and soul.

60

A gloomy silence came from the village, as if even the house gekkos had stopped breathing. The villagers had been through this before, and were about their daily business silently praying no horror would befall them, no crazy Marine would toss a grenade and laugh when it blew up the women and old men and sick little children hiding in the dugout bunker under the house. We knew they knew we were coming. We were sure the Viet Cong were waiting for us in pillboxes or behind paddy dikes or in underground spiderholes or tied to tree limbs to snipe at us, hiding invisible instant death, the bullet that would kill you silent and unknowable (if you heard it, it was already gone, went the lore). But even scared and not knowing how truly destructive our own guns and minds were, we stepped toward the village. Incredible courage.

To the villagers it was inevitable that we would enter their homes and search for weapons and men. A hundred years of occupation was fated by the Wheel. The specters would rise and fall away, dying deservedly. The seed of a life's end is in its beginning. The rice told them that. Violent men sought violent death. Viet Cong, ARVN, Marines; it didn't matter much which killed you; you were just as dead.

The ground approaching the hedges was rough with clods of weedy sod. As we advanced, the NCO's attempted to keep our courage up by shouting, stay on line, keep your interval. Everyone was walking forward with their rifles held waist high, aimed toward the village. A fusillade could burst from the hedges at any second.

Several men had nervously stumbled, so when we saw Gonzales go down we kept moving. It hardly registered to the most of us that Gonzales hadn't merely stumbled, but had flown backward ten feet, as if slammed by a huge invisible fist, then dropped like the heaviest stone in the world. Four men on either side of him instinctively knelt into firing positions, their eyes searching forward, but the sound of the single shot that had killed him had been muffled by the clump his body made hitting the ground. His corporal went over to his prone body, and kicked him in the thigh, telling him to get up. But there was something funny about his face.

It was grimacing in a state of profound shock, rictus baring his dust coated teeth. His eyes were wide open and blank, as if the flame of his life had been snatched by an unseen god. It was unbelievable. No one in his squad or his platoon had ever really seen a dead person before, especially not a person who was as much a part of your own life and your own body as was a fellow Marine. The reality of his death had no place to register. It wasn't a dream anymore. The platoon corpsman rushed to the clot of men forming around Gonzales, and the radio instructed the squad leader to keep the line moving, to break up that clusterfuck. The corpsman knelt down and checked for a pulse. Gonzales was still warm, but there was no heartbeat. He was as still as a rock. The corpsman opened Gonzales's flack jacket and without looking leaned down to listen for a heart beat. Hearing nothing but black hollow soundlessness, and feeling the thick sticky blood coagulating on his ear he looked down and saw the neat silver dollar sized hole that is made by a .50 caliber bullet as it rips you into death. "Fuck, corporal, this fucker is dead," the corpsman said, as surprised at his proclamation as the men around him. It wasn't until then that the squad leader ordered his men to take cover, and asked if anyone had seen anything.

"Maybe from that house, there, at two o'clock," the man who'd been walking next to Gonzales said. "Maybe I saw a rifle flash, I don't know. Is he really dead?" he said, and the look of a scared little boy came over his face. The Prick-6 asked the corporal, "What's the hold up, Bates?" "Got a man down here. He's shot lieutenant, no shit." "Shot? Are you sure?" "Fucking-A, sir. Shot right through the heart. He's deader than a mutherfucker, sir." The copper-jacketed bullet the size of a man's thumb, travelling at ten times the speed of sound, had torn a hole in Gonzales's young chest, gathered up a massive clot of bone and muscle, torn into his lungs and heart, ripped away every shred of sinew, vein and artery, obliterated his heart, and exited through a jagged hole in the back of his flack jacket, so shocking his brain that it shut down mercifully unthinking.

"We can't hold up this operation because one man is down." the Captain on the hill radioed. "Leave two men with him, and get that line moving. I'll call in a medevac." So two men from Gonzales' squad were detailed to sit with his body until a helicopter could pick him up, and the line of men continued to move toward the village. Only one shot had been fired, a direct hit that kinked and confused our minds. Charlie had fired first, but no one had presence of mind to even name what had happened, much less fire back. Word of Gonzales' death spread quickly up and down the line, and by the time we kicked through the hedges our fear and shame had twisted into a sharp desire for violent engagement. The enemy was there, and every eye sought him out.

Mindful for trip wires and debris disguised punji pits we filed through the hedges down lanes bordered with thatch and bamboo houses. Many were empty. Some were occupied by betel-chewing old women tending their cookfires. Some held four generations of women, the fourteen-year old with her baby held to her hip, her mother protecting eight and ten year old boys who tended the water buffalo and the ducks, her mother who swept the courtyard, and her mother who leaned into the thatch wall, smoking and chewing, waiting for the tuberculosis to consume her. The lanes split and divided, winding around a tree trunk, bordering the small stream that ran toward the sandy graveyard just outside the hamlet, heading toward the hamlet's central square.

We entered the houses unbidden, poking our bayonets into the roof thatch looking for weapons and ammunition. We roughly forced the women and children and the few bearded old men out of the homes and escorted them at gun point to the square. Not one of the Vietnamese offered protest or resistance. They'd been through this before, with the ARVNs, with the Viet Cong, the French, the Japanese, and now with these Americans. What we saw as passivity was actually stoic wisdom; armed frightened boys were dangerous.

At one of the houses three Marines had rousted the people huddled in a corner, then swept through their cookpots and their makeshift altar looking for Viet Cong tracts, when one of them noticed a woven mat under a rope-frame bed. He wrenched the bed aside, and pulled up the mat. Under the mat was the opening to an underground bunker. It was the first one we'd seen and he was only a second away from firing into it when his corporal stopped him.

"Use a grenade," the corporal said. When the Marine produced the grenade and was about to pull the pin, the woman of the house reached out to stop him, calling shrilly into the hole. Brown calloused hands fluttered into the opening, followed by two older women and several children. The woman who'd called the warning was sobbing, impossibly explaining that they were frightened, they didn't know what to expect, how would you feel, they hid from us. The corporal seemed to understand, and made a motion with his hand, first pointing to each of the women and children, then drawing a circle, and pointing outside. The woman nodded assent. The corporal shooed them out of the house, and when they were twenty yards away, called over his shoulder, "Blow it." and the Marine tossed the grenade down into the hole, then ran to catch up. No one knew if there was anyone else down in the bunker, if they were VC or too old to walk or too scared to trust us. The grenade exploded with a muffled crump. If they were in there, they were dead.

Word passed among the squads to check for bunkers, and through the next three hours of searching we heard the muffled crumps of many more grenades exploding. The hamlet people had no other course of self protection but to burrow underground, and most of the houses had bomb shelter bunkers.

Dappled sunlight filtered into the village square, and most of the population was standing around its edge, women with lank black hair tied at the back of their heads, dressed in serf black, children in singlets and no bottoms, many with protruding bellies and oozing patches of ringworm, flies nursing at their eyelids. Old men with wispy white hair and dirty breechcloths sat on their haunches watching the mad parade. No military aged men had been found. The Viet Cong who had shot Gonzales through the heart had not been found. No weapons had been found. The punji pits had already been located and backfilled by an earlier ARVN sweep.

The Marines took up standing positions behind the crowd, and the company's executive officer strutted to the middle of the square. No one in the company spoke the least word of Vietnamese and there was no one able or willing to translate for him, so he spoke loudly, hoping the force of his bellow would impart meaning. He pointed to the Marines who had routed the people and thrown grenades into the bunkers with his carbine, and said, "We are here to help you resist the Viet Cong. We know there are Viet Cong here, in this village. We want you to tell us who they are." But the crowd simply remained quiet, watching the big American from New Jersey rant the message they already knew by heart. It was the same old story, someone with a gun will kill you if you help the other one with a gun who will kill you if.

And right in the middle of the officer's speech someone on the periphery of the crowd saw something. A brown leg ducking behind a hedge, the movement of someone running. "If it runs, it's Viet Cong." A squad of Marines broke off from the crowd, and pursued the running figure, their rifles at the ready. They chased the Vietnamese man a hundred yards through the maze of paths and lanes before he broke into the open off a lane leading to the paddy land beyond the village. Then they were sure. He was running. He had a BAR over his shoulder. He was the one who killed Gonzales. The whole squad opened fire at once, their rifles on automatic. Two hundred bullets fired in less than ten seconds. They missed. They reloaded, plugging in fresh magazines. They fired again, some on automatic in a violent piss-off, some switching to semi-automatic and aiming more carefully. Another two hundred bullets. And they missed again. By then, the Viet Cong was gone. He had been running down the center of a shady lane and ducked onto a path, and vanished. The squad ran after him, located where he had ducked away, pushed through the bush and gardens, burst into doorways ready to blow that fucker away, and they couldn't find him.

Giving up, they slouched back to the company to report to their platoon leader. He called them a bunch of sorry mutherfuckers, one sorry-assed little dink, and you couldn't kill the rice-propelled zipperhead. You guys'll never live that down the rest of your lives, he said.

The gunfire effectively concluded the officer's speech, a demonstration worth a thousand words. He ordered us to sweep back through the village, and we separated into squads mulling over the day's events, many of us still furious that we'd failed to engage the enemy. What kind of jive-ass war was this when the Viet Cong got to kill you off one at a time and then got so slick you can't kill him back? In the distance we heard a chopper touch down to pick up Gonzales's body.

On the way out of the village a moment of sympathy broke through my well devised toughness when I saw a little boy with a fungus sore eaten deep into the flesh of his thigh. I got permission from the lieutenant to stop and treat him, "Yeah, Doc, go ahead. Hearts and minds, and all that shit." he said. So I took the boy aside and cleansed the wound, and balmed it with a fungicidal salve, wrapping the open sore with a pad and strip of gauze. His mother then came up and led me into a thatch house where her mother was moaning in a dark corner. Going in, I was soon joined by the lieutenant and several Marines.

The woman's complaint was readily apparent. She had stepped into a punji pit, and the bamboo stake had been driven completely through her left foot. The injury had taken place at least a year before. Scar tissue had formed ridges around the opening, but the wound was still open and oozing a purple pus. I looked around the little house and saw only the rope bed she was laying in, the cooking pit, and a short-handled broom. There wasn't even a crutch for her to hobble around on.

The lieutenant leaned over the woman and peered at her wound, then said, "Fix it, Doc," as if his power as the leader of men extended magically into my hands and knowledge.

There had been no wounded in my platoon to run to and save that day, and like everyone in the platoon this was the day to prove worth and manly conduct. Squeezing the old woman's hand I looked at the wound again. It was impossible, I knew it immediately, but my desire to please my superiors was so strong I kept trying to devise a method of doing a minor surgery before their very eyes. If I could inject her with morphine, then I could, debride the scar tissue, clean out the pockets of pus, close the inside of the wound with absorbable suture, none of which I had, then suture the wound closed and bandage. But the opening was too heavily scarred to close, and no, the light was no good, it would take hours, it was a filthy environment, there was dust and disease in the air, the water, on the very breath of the people, no it was impossible. I had already taken out my minor surgery kit with its forceps and scalpels, hemostats and 4.0 silk, and could see even in the woman's exhausted resignation the fear that this boy was going to do some horrible experiment on her and she'd have to submit at gun point to the pain and humiliation, maybe he was going to cut the thing off, so what, it was time for her to die anyway she could no longer work in the fields or even gain strength enough to warm the evening rice. It seemed ten minutes that I pondered the wound, and finally concluded that even if my reputation grew by leaps and bounds, the risk to her was much more profound. I'd have to accept the humiliation of incompetence. "Yeah, Doc couldn't do shit."

"I'm sorry, lieutenant, I can't do it. I'd like to help her out, but I just ain't got the tools. She needs a real live surgeon, I can't do shit with these instruments, and I don't know what I'd find once I got inside that foot. There's all kinds of tendons and connective tissue and stuff I don't know about. There's a couple of doctors at the Battalion Aid Station with nothing to do. Tell her to go there."

Then I turned to the woman's daughter and shouted, "BAS! Bac si at BAS," several times, as if she'd understand my acronym by aural osmosis. The old woman was visibly relieved when I folded up my canvas medical kit.

The lieutenant then mollified me by saying, "I'll see if we can get a pacification team up here next week. I'll tell 'em to send a doctor," then turned to the daughter and said, "Bac si come next week. Take her to see Bac si," and the woman nodded as if she understood, or perhaps just in hopes that if she said yes we'd go away.

As we left the hamlet no Viet Cong had rigged boobytraps at the hedge openings and we exited with rifles slung over our shoulders and held by the barrels, disappointed. Gonzales was no longer lying in the fallow paddy. The people of the hamlet were drifting back to their houses. The company walked back up our hill sadly quiet, and when we reached the top took up our night defensive positions.

Later, the Captain called me into his kerosene-lighted headquarters and asked me, "All right, you been there, what do those people need?" I'd never been asked so complex a question by a Marine officer before and it took me several moments to formulate an answer. I had to consider not insulting the Marines or our purpose of conducting war upon the Vietnamese, but was too tired and full of doubts to be much less than honest, so I blurted out, "What do they need? They need for us to leave them alone. Shit, sir, we go in and blow up their houses, scare the shit out of them, and tell them we're the good guys. What they need is to be safe from us. Safe from the fucking Viet Cong, too, I guess. What they need is hygiene, food, medicine, the conditions are appalling!"—a word I regretted using when I saw his lips purse in befuddlement. "They've got every disease known to man down there. They got diphtheria, yellow fever, tuberculosis, liver flukes, malaria, everything. It'd take ten years of missionaries to get those people on their feet. Most of them are emaciated, I'll bet you could buy their next crops of kids, if any of them lived, with a case of C-rations!"

I could see the age-old imperialist superiority stop him from listening, as if because they were poor and sick and unproductive, it was all right to kill them. "Soap and grease, OK, Doc. Thanks," he said, and dismissed me. Reductio ad absurdum to diminishing returns, plus echoes of Germany.

Wandering in a confused daze I joined up with some men of my platoon. We sat together making friendly noises, none of us willing to broach the subject of Gonzales' death. It was just something that happened, that we expected to happen, and he was so swiftly swept away, so quickly that only a few men in the whole company had seen him die or be dead, that his exploded heart and his death was effectively a rumor. He was gone, there was just no more Gonzales, the sweet boy from Yuma who had always tried so hard to be one of us. Gone, dead, gone forever, gone. Forever dead in our hearts.

◆◆◆◆

Sometimes in the long nights in the country of no maps currents like the battles for the Ashau Valley, Na Trang, Khe San, Hue, the hideous monstrosity of Tet, would whirl in from the future, wild flame knived tornadoes seizing you by the soul to brain suck you. So, when they happened, you already knew. Even though your body wasn't there anymore you didn't have to watch. The people fighting and being blown apart had already registered their souls in your own; as if all the horrible mayhem of the future that you were tied to was stored in the demon dreams of the generals, and was waiting to be unleashed and sent forth like slithering tongues lashing malignant through the living countryside, down into the middle of our ongoing centermosts, where the whirl and snarl of hell ties its knot. Big Bob Ortiz was cautioning me, "Watch out you don't get no shit on your boot, Doc!" and we'd laugh like crazy. It was our joke, and we said it every time we saw each other walking out into the bush with an E-tool to dig a cathole. Bob Hope was coming, and we figured it was a joke he wouldn't get, though we were also worried about how big the joke was being played on us. Bob had played to our fathers and uncles who had burned the Japanese out of the jungles and caves of Guadalcanal, had driven the Japanese plunging dishonored and suicidal into the sea off the cliffs of Saipan and Okinawa, had won Sarabachi, had pushed the savage Bushido back to his island and cauterized his national resolve with a nuclear blast to be carried forever in their mutating genes.

Vietnam was a diminutive nation compared to so formidable an enemy as the Japanese, even the Chinese in Korea. There were relatively few of us there at that time, but the build-up was underway, and it seemed to me massively criminal to persecute the Vietnamese, corrupt or Commie, just because we had the machinery to do so. That Bob Hope would be cracking his jokes to legitimize the prosecution of the war, make our futures less and less tenable, would add ruin to the World. The crowd of happy Marines laughing while Bob frolicked with untouchable sexgirls photographed for hometown papers would tell of mad world as normal, would sanction annihilation as divine will, like father like son, onward Christian soldiers. Ortiz and I didn't want to go.

When our battalion was docked in Bangkok, Thai fathers would bring their beautiful daughters in sampans to the ship's fantail, offering their young bodies to the Marines hooting at them from the rail. So superior and arrogant were we, so brutal, that when one particularly beautiful girl started crying in protest and fear, the Marines threw garbage on her tears.

To go see Bob Hope would be to elevate our conduct to the sacrosanct, would permit us to make the people we were supposedly saving for democracy into disposable lives that could be crushed at a whim; Korea—the human wave attack, the millions of people willing to die rather than live in utter destitution and hopeless repression, were to become unilluminated meat, merely dangerous, heathen, Chinese, almost-people afflicted with the mental disease of Communism—an aberrant religion promising angel pussy and sweet grits for throwing yourself in front of a machine gun, so familiar. Unlike the victim peasantry, we took no comfort in knowing that the cadres bound their soldiers and civilians together at the neck with barbed wire, marching them forward into the scythe of tracers with .45s pointed at their heads. That the cadre were evil was enough to get us to both kill and die for the great sustaining mother, Freedom. Going to see Bob would be to deny the dignity of the engagement, the depth of the injury. So we didn't go.

HILL 321

At night in the moonless dark the frogs that lived in the paddies surrounding the old French fort would send up a steady million voiced croaking that would go on for hours, then abruptly stop. We'd listen hard then, knowing some shadow men would be sneaking toward our position, or a human wave would be forming to slaughter us, the cadres prodding the civilians forward with threats of a bullet in the head. Then the frogs would resume their calling, all starting up at once as if signalled by the passing of one star in front of another. But the fear of what made them stop would not be eased. We could feel the VC lying in the paddy mud with the frogs and leeches to learn our defensive positions, waiting to rise inevitable as the moon in the night to kill us.

Armed with the belief instilled from the earliest days of training that each Marine was worth any ten scrawny dinks, the thought of a team of VC sappers creeping toward your shallow foxhole could still pump the fear into your blood. When it came right down to it, to the fractional violent moment between life and death, it was just you and him, and the night was on his side. We were on his land, and he was insidious and cunning, a sacrificial warrior capable of slipping under our concertina wire, blending with the dark, finding our foxholes, waiting with noiseless breathing right beside us until a moment when we dozed, then slitting our throats. He'd had much practice. Generations had cloaked themselves with night to rid Vietnam of the foreign pestilence. Lore had it that he'd lie perfectly still in ambush for the whole long night, not even moving to piss, his finger on the trigger of his old M-1, waiting for the second you moved into his sights, blowing you away with one simple flex of muscle, then slipping away into his village to work his paddy the next day. The only clue he'd leave would be the dead man beside you who you couldn't wake when it was time to assume the watch, the rifle flash on your retina flagging into infinite black.

And though neither of those things had happened to any one of us the fear was a persistent feature of mind. Relaxing into peace was a posture we could not afford. We were ten thousand light years from home, a force of a mere twenty thousand, counting office pogues, in the midst of seventeen million, as foreign to the body politic as a withering disease. The company had been losing men to malaria, heat prostration, mines that blew off parts of their bodies, amoebic dysentery, murder, so there were twenty fewer of us after only a month in country. Not only was the grass out to cut us to ribbons, the jungle out to suffocate us, the rivers full of microbes, the insects full of fever, the people full of loathing, the heat and the long nights of watching for the shadows to become murderous men had driven at least one man to shoot his sergeant five times, three in the back, and two in the head as he was spinning, already dead.

It was into that state of fear that General Walt, USMC, descended, wearing his personal Cobra gunship. Generals didn't visit the troops, especially General Walt who personally knew Chesty Puller and was reputed to be the toughest man in the Marine Corps. Something terrible was going to happen, no doubt about it.

Seeing him come down I was taken by the feeling that this was just like when Kennedy was killed (by the mob, or the CIA, our guys in some arcane power struggle that left the little guys with more world to fight), and the whole weight of the planet shifted under our feet. The only time you saw a general was before things got more dangerous, as if they rode the history curl and could move you closer toward immediate death by implementing us as their dreams.

General Walt stepped out of his Cobra dressed in his just cleaned .45, his buttoned flack-jacket and his strac herringbone fatigues. He looked like a sentient bulldog. Thick neck, narrow hips, chest like he had lungs big enough to suck up the atmosphere barely contained by his personal body armor. He rested his right hand on his pistol grip, and made some guttural noise to get our attention. A lieutenant yelled for us to "Listen up!"

Nobody in the gathered group of eighty Marines was waiting for a battlefield promotion. He had our complete attention. If the world was going to go sour on us, if we were about to be ferried off to some huge battle deep in the Annamese Cordillera, it would only be a kindness to tell us first. We'd heard plenty of stories about Special Forces 'A' teams being wiped out in hand to hand combat, and how spooky it was to try to stay alive in the jungles with the tigers, snakes, Viet Cong and NVA. regulars, where it was just you and them, no confusion about who is the enemy, it was each other and they'd kill you outright if they found you.

When the chopper blades had slowed to quiet, General Walt first complimented us for all the patrols we'd conducted, and the night ambushes we'd sat on, even though they were unproductive in killing any Viet Cong. Then he said, "I don't want to alarm you, but the reason I'm here talking to you front line troops is to tell you that the government in Saigon has fallen, and we don't know…"

Which is the point at which we stopped listening. It didn't matter if we knew that the maniac Khanh had been deposed by the young maniac Ky and his dope smoking wife. Any indication of an unstable government, unstable leadership for the ARVNs and the peasants meant increased danger. It was an opening for the Viet Cong to launch preplanned attacks and, rallying their sympathizers, to turn on us protectors and murder us as we tried to leave.

For a long wishful moment I hoped that the CIA had put its own man in that government, again, and that everywhere in the world the governments were the same as ours—the will of the good people unshakable and inviolate, the shining mountain of God's heart predicated on the love of the law of life, the salvation of world order and peace residing in the generous American soul. But it was Vietnam, a corrupt opium whore, and it didn't matter who was at the helm. The constant injuries of war had maddened every being so that not even the purity of spartan Ho could revitalize its heart. Even in my nineteen year old's naivete I could feel the planet slip off its harmonious orbit, reeling deeper into infatuation with oblivion.

"We can expect increased enemy activity, so keep your eyes peeled and keep your powder dry," the general said. "Our mission is to protect the people in our area of operations and to defend our airbase against attack." And some men grinned at each other like now we were really going to get into it, but my fear just deepened and the dream of the safety of the World grew more intoxicating. The general finished his speech with, "Good luck, men, and good hunting," then boarded his helicopter like Paul Revere.

We weren't going to be moved up to Khe Sanh or Pleiku, thank whatever forces that control destiny, but were going to increase our patrols and double our ambushes, maybe now we'd catch some action. The B-52s were stepping up their bombing of the Ho Chi Minh Trail and Hanoi, infuriating the people who suffered under the exploding death from the air, the wretched cries of their children ripped open by shrapnel, carrying them the six weeks of arduous sloughing to deliver their rockets right down the throat of those murderous arrogant bastards who presumed to save a people by killing them.

So we patrolled. We explored every road and every path off every road, sweating under sixty or seventy pounds of gear, filling our canteens from every stream, halizone and Kool-aid to cut the halizone, four gallons of water a day, plus salt and still dehydrated. Memory: Captain Frankle, thirty-five, rawboned blond, sweating under his helmet, consulting his map while screaming into the radio handset, "Fuck if I know where we are! I got a company of men stuck down this fucking dead end road, we're taking fire from the point, I need a goddamn air strike, and I mean fucking now!" We were inching our way down this dirt road that ran down a very narrow valley in bamboo thicketed hills, the vegetation so dense and dark only snakes and mongeese could tunnel through, and in there somewhere was a sniper or a squad of VC, we didn't know which, who would pop off a round at any man brave or stupid enough to poke his head around the bend and everyone was crazy to mount an attack, or flank them if they could find them, the point man crawling down on his belly and spotting the approximate position of where the last round came from, letting loose a clip of twenty rounds and crawling back, the Captain desperately trying to maintain military discipline, me saying, "We're gonna let one dink stop us! Let's go in and get him!" and the Captain looking at me and my caduceus like I was escaped from kindergarten, damned if he was going to let some noncombatant impinge upon his thought and get his people killed, and a squad of Marines led by then-Corporal Hurlock producing machetes and starting to hack their way into the jungle, making a tremendous racket and having to stop when a round went whistling over their heads, the Captain finally deciding that there was no objective to be reached by pushing through the tangles at the end of the road, and turning us around to take another route over the hills.

Sergeant Hurlock had made Corporal just a few days before. We were in the field, so his demotion was summary, a matter of postponed paperwork. And it wasn't the first time in his ten years in the Crotch that he'd seesawed between E-4 and E-5. This time he'd found a Honda-riding beer salesman and purchased his entire stock of twelve bottles of Tiger Piss. Which he neglected to share with his platoon—there being too many of them for them all to get a buzz on, it would just be a waste of good beer, and he wanted to celebrate his reenlistment with singular reflection, anyway. So, off in a corner of the French ruins he consumed the lot, and was a bit tipsy by the time 0200 came around. And, well, it was dark, and he wasn't absolutely sure where his fartsack and rubber-bitch were, but he was pretty sure and definitely had to pee before he hit the rack, and so he did. His lieutenant, waking at the sensation of warm wet on his head, tried to understand, but the symbolism of the accident would erode the men's confidence in his ability to command, so Sarge, kiss three years of hard work goodbye. The men loved him for it.

More and more patrols, most of them resulting in nothing more than exhaustion. Sometimes we'd find Vietnamese men on the road or working in the paddies, and would check their green identification cards, but they knew the rules and didn't run and therefore didn't get shot in the back. And sometimes we'd be graced by the fourth estate, hearty middleaged reporters who would attach themselves to our furtive wanderings, trailing tape recorders and television cameras, recording our leaps into the bush at the wrong snap of a twig, or point the camera into our weary sweat and anger strained faces and ask us foolish questions about the political reasons of why we were there and get, "It's the only war we got," or, "My daddy was a Marine, in the Big Deuce, I can't go home 'less I get me a confirmed kill," or, "Beats me, all we seem to do is bop around the boonies, these chickenshit mutherfuckers won't engage." And we'd see behind the eyes of the reporters their snarling desire to get down on the ground with the blood and the guts of a fire fight, people getting killed right and left, being there to get some violence on tape, get a little blood on their combat boots bought that morning on the black market in Da Nang, then go back to town with their stories, get paid and get laid, safe and sound, these guys would die for them.

"Doc, they tell me you are one humping corpsman," one said to me, pushing his microphone into my face. "How many patrols have you been on?" was his question, but it wasn't the question he was really asking. He could care less how many times any one of us willingly exposed ourselves to enemy fire, or how much courage it took just to get up in the morning and go at it again, or lose your sleep sitting out in the stinking rain all night on ambush just as sure that Charlie was waiting around the next bend to blow you away every time you took a step. What he was really asking was, "Have you personally engaged in hand to hand combat with a gook and killed him and did it feel good? Can I go with you next time, and watch?" But the answer to his real question too closely approximated my own question about myself, would I be able to, so I said, "We're short some Docs. Planter spiked a hundred-nine temp with malaria, I think he caught it on purpose, and Dione got killed by our own four-deuce mortar, you want to tell the folks out there in television land something, tell them that, tell them we're getting killed by Pentagon malfeasance, those mortar increments were from 1947 and wet, killed nine men, fucking bastards, yeah, I hump a lot, every patrol that goes out has to have a corpsman and I'm it."

Lieutenant Anderson, another football hero, overheard my for-the-public-record speech and told me to shut-up. I retreated to my bed-down and tuned in the *Johnny Carson Show* on Armed Forces Radio, Vietnam, who do you trust, like a child embracing a glimmering ray of home. It was shortly after that exchange with the reporter that I was sent up to Hill 321. Along with Hurlock.

Hill 321 was the observation point for the eastern-most sector of our area of operations. It was a red soiled barren hilltop that served as a landing zone for the brass who occasionally came up to have a look see. A high ground observation post overseeing the flats leading to Da Nang.

Our platoon humped up the hill from Dai Lai Pass. And when we got there we began digging in, stacking sandbags, burrowing into the hillside to make caves deep enough to sleep in and stay out of the rain. We cut roof timbers from the trees and stacked the sandbags three deep on top to protect from mortar attack. Hurlock and I fancied our bunker the best, the one most likely to be attacked because just a hundred yards below us was a fine staging swale bordered by dense trees, and the slopes on the other sides of the hill were too steep and brushy to allow easy attack. We built a mortar pit south of the landing zone, set up machine-guns in four of the bunkers, protecting all avenues of approach, then sat to watch and wait, kings of the hill.

And we sat and watched and waited for weeks and weeks. When the weather was clear we could see Monkey Mountain, the city of Da Nang swelling with military ships offloading tanks and trucks, amphtracks and munitions, its outskirts growing with the ramshackle of refugees. We could see the calm waters of Tourane Bay, a scatter of green hamlets and villages rising from the flat spread of rice paddies, the jets and choppers and propped transport planes taking off from the airfield east of Da Nang, and the slow sinuous expanse of the Tourane River. Behind us the foothills of the Cordillera held small narrow valleys, and Charlie.

He was down there, all right. Frequently during the day we'd hear a sharp exchange of automatic gunfire. Or the crump of mortars exploding. We'd hear the freight train roar of artillery shells coursing overhead, and exploding far into Indian Country across the Song De. Sometimes we'd hear just one rifle going off, a frustrated Marine, someone who saw something, recon by fire, the constant probe exercised to allay an overwhelming fear or to bring about a kill. Sometimes in the shimmering haze above the jungled mountains I could feel the Montagnards chanting their cannibal hunger, the unhappy union between the Special Forces and the CIA and them against the hated Vietnamese telling the secret gnawing at our centers, their same ancient voices muttering in us when we'd put on grease paint for night movements.

And it is all still there, stored in the aural spiral, registered in the retinal cells, contracted in the muscle and seeped into the marrow, the brain still spinning back to every moment alive there.

Like when Gunny Mead came up with the mail and the meals to check out why the black members of the platoon had refused to stand watches, and would gather in a circle around the mortar tube, defensive and afraid, their hunter eyes telling anyone of us dickless honkey ofay chucks to stay away or suffer humiliation and beatings, black men lived closer to the bone. Which incited LeFever and Hinton, two Louisiana boys, to say within their earshot, "Shit on them, man. We oughta get drunk some night and go insane, do them good and do them dead, say Mr. Charles snuck up here and did it, caught them napping, yeah, we fired on them but you know Charlie, he's slick, he don't leave nothing behind."

Sometime late into one of the nights up there, watching the flares drift down over Iron Bridge Ridge, some trooper said, "Check it out. We're here killing gooks right in front of the Splibs, so they'll know."

But Gunny Mead knew how to handle recalcitrants, and forcibly put a black Marine in every bunker, breaking up the clique, and precluding such murderous talk. Let them riot when they got home, one thing this outfit didn't need was dissension while it was surrounded. Then he stuck around for a few days to make sure his orders were obeyed. Hurlock received a browbeating for not being on the stick and keeping harmony amongst the troops. Gunny Mead didn't buy his rationale that if and when the gookers came charging up the hill, everyone would be unified against them. Men integrated with each other moment by moment was what made the world turn.

Gunny Mead was pure warrior. Craggy, gravel voiced, barrel chested, he had risen to the top of his profession, a Gunnery Sergeant in the United States Marine Corps. You could bury him in six feet of sand and still know what and who you were standing on. He had fought all through Korea and he knew men and what they could do if properly led. I gravitated toward him as student to teacher, and had pleased him that day by spotting six NVA regulars in a small village east of our position. He and I were having a last smoke before nightfall when something down below caught his attention. "You see 'em?" he said, almost whispering, as if even from a mile away his voice could disclose our position, and turn the violence he foresaw toward us. The night and the horrors it carried made you quiet. "Down there, on the edge of that tree line," he said, pointing west and down. And in the deeper shadows of the trees we saw darker shadows moving. "That's a squad, Doc, moving like a squad, maybe two squads. Experienced. Maybe those people you saw today, Doc. Hard Core."

"Maybe we should radio Battalion?" I said.

"Go tell LeFever to get his ass over here, and bring his radio, but don't sweat it too much. Ain't none of our people supposed to be out tonight."

"Maybe they're ARVN."

"Oh, there's ARVN down there, all right. But that weren't them." the Gunny said, and he chuckled. "Now, get moving."

By the time I got back with LeFever and several other curious Marines, Mead's attention was focused on the center of the village to our front. A kind of lightless electrical eddy seemed to be forming in the treed dark. In empathy with the living air I could feel hearts pounding into adrenal readiness, frightened souls preparing themselves to leave their bodies, safeties switching off with the creak of a finger joint, the rasp of clothing brushing against leaves. Down in the dark men like us were narrowing their vision, peering through the shadows for a glimpse of movement, sensing each other like long lost brothers coming home to ancient grudges and hatreds, the embrace of murder.

"Keep your eyes open, boys, down there about two o'clock, can't you feel it?" Mead said. "What's happening, Gunny?" one of the Marines asked. "A lesson for your young ass, Private. Watch, and keep quiet."

Another twenty minutes passed with us searching the dark bowl of the village. Then an insane arch of white rifle flashes and red streaming tracers tore through the dark. A pause, then responding rifle fire. By the time the sound reached us, like a chainsaw about to explode, the firing had stopped. They were reloading. A grenade burst in a bright yellow sphere.

"They're close, but they didn't wait." Mead instructed. "They should've waited, you watch, watch and see what happens next."

It was too far away for us to hear, but we thought we could feel the screams of men being hit by shrapnel and bullets, men dying. Another furious firing erupted, fewer guns than before, fiercely white sharp flashes. And again tracers sprayed out in a broad line, several more grenades exploding hot and yellow.

"Holy shit, Gunny, what's happening?" LeFever asked, chambering a round and putting his rifle to his shoulder.

"Nothing we can do anything about from up here, LeFever." Mead said, and motioned for him to put his rifle down. LeFever asked, "Are those our people? Do we have to go? I mean, shouldn't we go down and help them?"

"They're too far away, we couldn't get to them in time. And no, that's the NVA and the ARVNs. I saw the NVA setting up that ambush hours ago." Mead said, "Hold your water, boy, nothing we can do but learn."

Another twenty minutes passed with no noise or sound from the village. Then there were a few sharp single shots from the southern position that had been held and evacuated by the NVA. No prisoners. More time passed, then another burst of fire opened up, this time configured in a broad point, firing south. The NVA immediately responded, firing from a concave arc, green tracers, red tracers, sprayed thickly and furiously, the two groups breaking out into the flat paddy land, covering behind dikes. The chase was on, the distance between them growing. Again the firing broke off, and again resumed, the ARVN point becoming an intense fist of rifle fire, the NVA arc splitting into flanking wedges.

"Jesus Christ, a running fire fight," Mead exclaimed, "I ain't seen one of them since the Frozen Chosin. Those slopes got some guts. Don't you people forget this. Fire and move, fire and move. Poetry, Doc. Beautiful."

By then both platoons had expended most of their ammunition, and the fight broke off, a few rounds fired at fleeing shadows. "That is balls, boys, no medevac, no resupply, just go out and kill 'em." Mead said.

Moans of men wounded and dying that we could not hear resonated through us. Even hardening our hearts with the thought that they were just dinks, they want to die, failed to quiet their pain that spread through the night on the currents of our mixed lives. Our own futures were also laying their pools of blood and broken flesh. Mead was exultant, but the spirit of we immortal jungle fighting Marines was subdued.

In the morning, through field glasses, we could find no trace of the fire fight. We could see no trees blown down, no bodies, no severed limbs, no sears and chars from grenade blasts. In our inexperience and fantastic estimation that any one of us was as good as any ten of them, that two platoons of Vietnamese could come together in a vicious firefight and do so little visible damage made the effort of warring seem futile. Even totally confident that if it was us down there there would be no VC left, that our moral superiority would decimate and prevail, to find no proof of the violence was greatly unnerving. Not even the consolation that the villagers had come out later in the night, we'd seen their lanterns, and collected the bodies of their brothers and fathers, restored our invulnerability. None of us who had watched slept that night, spending the time constructing interior steel barriers to protect ourselves, spinning out resolutions to kill first. It was our only chance.

Maybe if we sent out patrols we'd find the wounded and dying NVA soldiers in their jungle hospitals, recuperating in hammocks made of sticks and vines. Then, at least there would be proof, evidential results to diminish the sting to our imaginations. But that wasn't to be. Our assignment was to sit and watch and radio in our observations. Battalion wasn't interested in our changes.

Still reeling from what I'd witnessed, I went with Hurlock for a walk down the mountain to the waterfall where we bathed ourselves in a quiet pool tucked into the hillside. It was a long hump down the hill, and scary with only the two of us for mutual protection. In the glade and resting on a mossy rock, we talked. "I've got the feeling that some of the men in the platoon don't think I can do my job," I said, more concerned over whether we would stand a chance if we got ambushed by the NVA, whether our bravado would stand up against men experienced in killing other men.

"Well, Doc, I'd say seventy percent trust you."

"This is a hundred percent outfit, I know that, I try to be a sadist and be cruel like they want, but it's hard, Boy Scout Altar Boy and all."

"Don't sweat it. You'll be there when the time comes. They got to pretend to be hard, and the peckerchecker's gonna catch the shit. Hell, that's half your job. The Gunny thinks you're all right, and if anyone knows, he knows."

"Well, I guess that's not what I'm really worried about. I mean, that shit we saw the other night. What the fuck are we doing here? Those people really like to kill each other."

"That they do, Doc, that they do. Puts you in a hard spot, don't it? All we gotta do is kill them first. You gotta save us and them at the same time. I know you ain't no CO, but to a Marine you might be just because being corpsmen is what COs do, and a lot of those guys aren't too sharp at distinctions. And that makes them think that you might be unsafe to be around. You know them dink mutherfuckers would as soon blow you away as pissing, and no one wants to think a man on our side would give them up for as silly a notion as peace. This is a full blown shooting war, baby, even if it don't look like it yet, and you gotta get hard, be hard and stay hard if you want to stay alive."

"But it's really them against them. Our ass is caught in the middle."

"Only way to beat it is bring your own grease. Be there firstest with the mostest. Stay alive."

The waterfall was pouring out its steady charge of purity. There may have been flowers blooming among the soft green leaf shadows, but I didn't see them. If we used that waterhole, so did Charlie, and I kept my awareness open for the hard sinew of he who was out to kill us. Hurlock's fear did not match my own. He had his muscle and wit, his confidence and his rifle. All he would need in a fire fight was stored coiled in a fathomless reserve of total violence ready to be ignited by the sound of a shot. Until that moment came he'd move through the war with casual muscular ease, disciplined, ready, his natural joy unsuppressable. Every fight came down to one against all, like the DI said, "You are surrounded by five hundred of the enemy. What do you do? Kill them, sir!" and he was the one.

"Let's take the long way back, catch the boys at the Pass, maybe get a Coke," Hurlock commanded. We put on our gear and started the trek back up the mountain. At the sandbag fortifications at the Dia Lai Pass the men on guard were happy to see our familiar faces. Hurlock gave them a hard time about letting the gooks get past them the other night, and a corporal countered by saying, "It was all planned. We didn't want to waste the ammunition on them. Let the gookers shoot each other, less work for us to do," and everyone laughed.

A Vietnamese woman and her sister, both carrying baskets on poles, had been hanging around the Pass, selling beer and Cokes. Hurlock motioned to them, and asked the corporal in charge, "She boom boom?"

"Naw," the corporal said, "Everybody asked her, says she's a good Catholic, married."

"You just ain't said the magic words, Corporal. You watch."

Hurlock approached her, bought a couple of Cokes, handed me one, then began bargaining with the woman and her sister, pointing to our hilltop position. She nodded yes, as though she was frightened and saying yes was the only way to get Hurlock to leave her alone. Hurlock then told me to follow along and we headed up the hill. "It's just a short distance," he said. That was his favorite phrase. It was, in fact, a long four hour hump through crackling briar and dust.

And I was amazed the next day when I saw the woman and her younger sister push on through the brush onto the landing zone, their baskets full of Cokes and beer, followed close behind by several Marines prodding them with their rifles. The women were panting heavily under their load and the long walk, and frightened that they'd been captured.

"Take it easy, people. They're just here to make a deal. Trade some rats, make a buck. We gotta help the local economy, you know," Hurlock admonished. And seeing that he'd invited them, the Marines who'd gathered around let down their weapons. Hurlock was teasing us, lording his power over us, taking chances with our safety, and there was nothing we could do about it but accept it. A lance corporal took a chance, and said, "God damn, Hurlock, you know better than that. No gooks inside the perimeter up here. They come up here and go home and tell their husbands and we get our asses waxed. Fucking dumb, man."

Another man said, "I ain't buying any of that shit. I don't care how far they had to carry it. They put ground-up glass in that stuff. Wood alcohol in the beer, too. Make you go blind. I'll be damned if I'm gonna let them take any C-rats with them, either. They'll just feed Charlie with them." Which gained the platoon's agreement. No one would trade with them. To do so would be aiding and abetting the enemy.

"Bunch of chickenshits." Hurlock said, "Don't any of you go telling the Gunny about this, or I'll have you building bunkers ten stories high." Then he took the older woman inside our bunker, stationed her sister to sit outside, and told us all to stay away until he was finished.

We heard the sounds of submissive whimpering and macho grunting come from the bunker for the next forty-five minutes. All anyone could say was, fucking Hurlock. To get in line would be to violate the platoon's integrity, and no one was willing to compromise the outfit or become subject to court martial.

By the next night the platoon's anger had been leavened by Hurlock's joking, but the paranoia wakened by the firefight down below, the forced integration of the night-watches, and the presence of Vietnamese, VC,—who could tell—in the perimeter, persisted. And corpsmen who are outside the shared secret of being combat soldiers are prone to commit stupid acts. Not only were we living in the midst of a civil war, trying to maintain our fighting edge with little support from Battalion, we also had rats to live with. Big ones. Rats big enough to put on a spit and roast for dinner, which, we believed, the Vietnamese did regularly. And these particular rats had been fattening nicely on our C-ration refuse, and growing bold enough to run across our sleeping bodies during the nights. More than once I woke with their tiny claws trying to open my mouth or scratching inside my trouser legs. One in particular was living under my bed, and though I'd tried to trap it with a Boy Scout snare, it had been too smart for me. In my hysteria, I decided on murder by gunshot.

Leaving several choice bites from my ham-fried in its can, I placed the can on the shooting shelf of the bunker, sat back, cocked my .45, took the safety off, and waited. It would be a blind shot. The night was completely dark and inside the bunker was even darker. I'd fire at the sound. Now, shooting a rat with a .45 is like hitting a fly with a hammer, but I was hardly rational. And irrational people tend to forget the consequences of their actions. I waited, feeling a kind of destiny dread hovering about me, which I ignored.

I could hear its little nose sniffing at the can. And in that moment, if we were an isolated outpost, I was even more isolated, my paranoia separating me from even imagining that the men around me could do me harm. My thought was that we were so completely attuned to each other that none of us could commit any act without the instantaneous knowledge of the others. The rat crawled up to the side of the can, sniffed, then began eating, no doubt thankful for this grand find. I took careful aim at his sound and squeezed the trigger. The muzzle flash blinded me for a moment, and under the gunshot explosion I could hear the rat squealing in agony. He ran first right, then left, then up my pants leg and across my chest. Finding the doorway, he ran outside. I could hear him writhing outside, trying to kick away the pain. I rushed out, and barely seeing him, shot at him twice more, the third shot tearing him in half but still not killing him.

That's when a flare shot from a M-79 burst into light above me. I was so intent on killing my nemesis I thought some Marine was trying to help me. I heard a Marine's harsh whisper say, "Fucking Hurlock left the gate open. They're down there man." I heard the clump of ten bodies hitting the deck, their rifle slings slapping against the stocks. Safeties were being clicked off. I was kneeling triumphant over my dead rat, and there were ten Marines a second away from killing me. They were ready. I looked up and faced nine rifles and the M-79's blunt barrel. The faces behind the sights were intent and utterly concentrated. They were all in prone position on the edge of the hill bluff aiming at me, the arrogant shithead who made them dig the slit-trenches.

Someone, Lance Corporal Mitchell, I think, was still more afraid of the chain of command and making a mistake, of even giving away our position, perhaps, than of the suspected hordes that might be gathering in the staging swale below the bunker. He called, barely audibly, "Who goes there?" saving my life with the fifth general order. At once fearing that during my preoccupation with the rat some VC had snuck up behind me and I'd be caught in the crossfire, that I'd infuriated the Marines by my callous disregard for their fears, that some hardcharger would shoot and set the others off in a furious firing, damn the torpedoes full speed ahead, I threw down the pistol and raised my hands in supplication, saying, "It's me, it's only me, Doc!" The flare was still hanging above us and I could see their faces relax, even though they were still pumped and angry. A long moment passed, me trying hard to smile.

"You scared the shit out of us, Doc. What the fuck are you doing?"

"Just shooting this rat." I said, bending down to pickup the exploded body by its tail, a trophy shown to gain their forgiveness for my stupidity. "You better stay away from Hurlock," someone said, "He's rubbing off on you."

Another Marine admonished, "Next time you think you're gonna shoot your weapon, let us know, Doc. Dufus dumbshit." And they started getting up and moving away from me like my idiocy was contagious. I spent the rest of the night sitting on top of the bunker trying to figure a way back into their graces, the voice inside me saying, "Dumbshit, that was close, that was so close. You just might get what you want."

A week later the platoon was relieved by a company of newly arrived Marines. The war was being expanded, the bombing of Hanoi increased, the number of operations increased, the Marine Corps was going on the offensive, and I was glad to be getting off that hill and back to the flat ground where we could move around again, safe from each other.

Hypnomemory

Hypnomemory, persistent, recurrent. Out the door for the first time. The grass is blown into writhing waves of silver green. Tree leaves are blown into a chaos of prop storm. The horizon is hot white blue and I'm hanging back with Gunny Mead, wild eyed, .45 drawn, ready to shoot anything I'm told to, anything dressed in black pajamas, any living threat at all. Eight more Marines are coming off the H-34 and spreading into a forward arc, nothing routine about it, pure armed instinctual attack-defense movement, our spreading circle bristling with death potential, automatically dividing the landscape before us into precise fields of fire, each covering his own and half the other man's beside him. Mead sees my state of terror and tells me in a firm gentle voice to put the gun away, I won't be needing it. Someone as frightened as I am could be very dangerous. But he keeps his own pistol in his hand and is trying to shout above the rotor wash for the men to keep spreading out, don't clump up, one grenade will get you all.

A moment before we are cruising at two thousand feet, wind hot and gasoline laced, crossing the Song De into Indian Country, hearts in our throats, and there in the chopper is Mead, Mitchell, La Fever, Gerhart, Washington, Orrick, Anderson and the door-gunner who sees the sharp yellow blips of a daring VC firing at us from a treeline and he lets go a few bursts from his M-60, but we're moving too fast for him to find him out with a line of tracers. He's talking into his headset then he petulantly slams the machine-gun down with the heel of his hand. Then we're descending in a slow circle, the ground looks foreign and hostile, trees and ditches, fallow paddies, stretches of elephant grass, abrupt rocky hills rising off to our north and east. The only things alive down there are the vegetation, the vermin and the snakes. There are no people or draft animals or pigs, just ground that had been used for a thousand years then abandoned to the war.

A thousand yards south of where we're about to land lies a dilapidated village. Charlie knows we're coming. We told him, we know he knows, some fool in G-2 dropped leaflets announcing our intention. The objective is two thousand yards south, the village bordering the river across from our French fort position, and our tactic is an aerial enfilade. A weapons reinforced company of Marines to be set down behind the village, get on line and sweep through, engaging any enemy suicidal enough to show his face. The big guns back at Regiment are suppose to soften the area between our landing zone and the village with a half hour long barrage.

The ground is coming up fast. Looking out the door I can see other helicopters disgorging frantic Marines. It's the first time for all of us, the first offense against the Viet Cong in a Viet Cong stronghold, and everyone is scared down to their bones and quiet. Then we're on the ground and the door-gunner is pushing us through the hatch, he wants to leave, to get back up in the sky where he can play god safely. The whole backed-up murderous slaughter dream impels us out of the choppers. But the zone is cold, someone throws a green smoke, and the choppers take off, leaving us to our own devices.

It's almost worse, the anxiety and trepidation building up during the hurry-up and wait, the mental preparation to come out of the door firing into the dark treelines is still a charge with no place to be executed and so is stored as a readiness, still churning like an unconquerable nightmare. If Charlie wasn't waiting for us here, where he knew we were going to set down because we told him, then he was surely waiting further on, perhaps in well fortified positions, in better advantage because we would be walking on his ground into his sights, slick fucker.

Mead and I catch up to the Captain and his radioman, the skipper is calling Regiment to tell them we're in place, start the barrage. This operation has been planned for weeks and should go off like clockwork, except it's the Marines, and nothing ever happens like it is suppose to. Snafu is normal, even the helicopters were late this morning and instead of mounting the operation in the cool of the morning we are rushing into the thick heat of midday laden with enough equipment to stagger a mule. The Captain is calling for platoon leaders up, and when they get there, earnest pinched faces, white knuckles gripping their carbines, he tells them to get the men lined up, we're going to make a two thousand yard on line sweep toward the village, wait until after the barrage lifts and wait for his word on the radio. And they run back to where the platoons are facing back to front, sure an attack is about to come from either direction. The barrage is going to scare the shit out of the wily little fuckers for sure, get this war off the ground, let them know we mean business.

Moments later we hear the sickening crump of a five hundred pound shell exploding in front of us. A red brown geyser of earth and weed clots rises. Then comes the round barrel sound of its travel behind it. We wait for more. There should be a hundred more. But none come. Just like the whole military mechanism, I think, renege on a promise that might save your life and get you killed just so it can continue justifying its existence. The radioman reports to the Captain that Regiment says the barrage has been cancelled, the 155s are broken or something is haywire with the artillery computer, it won't work in this heat.

The Captain gives the word and the company starts to move out on line. It's only a matter of minutes before the line starts breaking up from running into dense brush and deep ditches. The men are struggling to keep up, sweating, cursing the razor cuts made by the elephant grass, slapping at the mosquitoes and flies, every step we take growing more and more difficult, an hour into the operation and most of our canteens are empty.

The heat is unbearable. We'd gone less than five hundred yards when men started falling down gasping for breath. Word came from all down the line for corpsmen up, the men were out of it, going into hysterics, turning white, their skin hot to the touch. The advance had to be stopped.

The Captain ordered all of the men suffering from heatstroke to be brought to his central position. Other men improvised stretchers from rifles and ponchos, and fifteen men were brought in. I'd been promoted to company corpsman, so I directed the company's canteens to all be brought up. We corpsmen then stripped off the heat victim's gear, and cooled them down as much as possible with the remaining water, fanning them with shirts and helmets. One man was turning fishbelly white, his eyes dilated into blue starbursts, his skin temperature easily over one-oh-six. I had the radioman and a couple of Marines build several poncho hootches for shade.

The rest of the hardchargers seemed relieved to not have to go any further. The Captain, a black mark on his record for sure, had to call for choppers to take the prostrate victims out. The operation was going to hell in a hand basket, and the brass had so counted on its inevitable success. The Captain kept asking me when the men would be ready to get on their feet and get going, fucking malingerers. And I had to keep on insisting that they'd take a week to recover, if we could get them back to Battalion soon enough that they didn't die right here, not a shot from Charlie fired. He didn't need to. He'd been here for 10,000 years, and we'd only been there a month.

Someone back in Regiment was thinking. Before sending the choppers out to pick up our heat victims they commandeered the pogues' lunch, packed the whole roast beef dinner along with some trays and forty jerry cans of water and sent us a resupply. Hot chow, the first in weeks, freshwater to refill our canteens. The corpsmen passed among the troops, distributing salt tablets by the handful.

The sweep resumes, but the going is tough, getting worse, more men are having to stop to catch their breath and the mortar men are bitching about having to carry these goddamn base plates what the fuck for, for Christ's sake, then the right flank finds a footpath under some trees that looks like it leads to that abandoned looking village, Jesus Captain, there ain't no Gooks out in this shit. So the Captain relents, what's one more change in plans, and we trail off to follow the right flank squad down a shaded path bordering the rocky hills adjacent to the plains. I'm amazed that for being in the midst of an economy based on water and muscle that the only stream we crossed was a narrow rivulet that served as the benjo for the village. Vile, wriggling with disease, we waded through it avoiding floating feces, feeling microbes enter the pores of our skin, feeling disease enter our blood from the double mouths of leeches.

Still in the middle of the column with the Captain and Gunny Mead I hear the skipper ask the lead squad by radio what's the hold up, and the squawk over the handset says they're checking out the ville, don't look like nobody's home, and we push on through. The village is comprised of ten thatch houses scattered along a widening in the path, and their walls have been kicked through, their roofs caved in, it's been searched many times before, and there is no sign of recent human habitation, even the dogs have been eaten. The dust kicked up by our feet lingers in the heavy air like stunned moths. Everything is hay yellow or light bright green, being poked through by Marines with rifles and bayonets. No enemy is waiting for us, the point man thought he saw the flit of a black clad leg, he fired at it, but no one could find a blood trail, he was pretty sure he missed.

Another five hundred yards down that trail, sweat murky eyes, when is this shit ever going to stop, if there is any good in God at all he'd give us ten days of rain and a way home, why do those idiots have to keep up this kind of a pace, there's going to be plenty of war to go around, what, we got to make an appointment with the choppers, nine to five warfare, the officers have a date down at the club? Half a canteen left and all day to drink it, hope there's a well in that next ville. Hey Sarge, next time we do this can we bring our golf carts? Parasols for you girls. Keep your interval.

Then the shade ends and we bunch up in clumps of men looking across another flat plain of dried up paddy land. There is a sheer jungle-covered rise of rock on our right flank, and the VC village lays drawn along the edge of the river. Under its trees it looks cool and inviting, tropically restful, still in the strongest heat of the day. The Captain calls his platoon leaders up, again, and tells them to deploy the men in a sweep formation, and the Marines stretch themselves into a long broad line facing the village. When everyone is in place, he gives the order to advance. We start marching forward, a Marine fires a single round that skips over the hard paddy surface, recon by fire, shoot and see if someone shoots back.

My mind is extending into the village, feeling out the hiding holes, searching the trees for snipers, contacting the people living there, sensing who is peaceful, who is dangerous, who is there to kill us, and I feel a tight squad of Vietnamese men hiding behind a dike just at the edge of the village, but can't tell anyone my mind feels the presence of the enemy among the silent sobs of women and the pitiful cries of breast held babies. I tell the Captain to watch the right flank, but he doesn't hear me, intent on getting the men to conduct the sweep in a coordinated military fashion. Looking right and left I see the men around me are tense, fearful, the front of the village is ringed with low hedges and dikes, there are plenty of shadows and trees, it is a perfect aspect from which to defend your home against the invaders. They could fire and take a third of us out in the first volley, then run for the river behind them and vanish forever. I'm scared, but there is nowhere to run to, nowhere to go, there is only this situation, this condition of walking forward possibly into deadly enemy bullets with armed men who rejoice in killing, or so they insist, and there is nothing to do but accept it, it would take a miracle to stop it, or a radio call from Regiment saying they changed their mind, and that would take an even bigger miracle. The President, the Commander-in-Chief, said that the honor of America was at stake, no matter that it might cost every life in the world.

Someone sees movement in the village. It is furtive, like someone watching and running to tell someone else. The Captain tells the company to hold up. We're now fifty yards from entering the village and we're standing in a wide arc, still as targets in a sideshow. One last swig before we go in, they're in there, we know. Word is passed to not fire unless we're fired upon, we don't want to hit any innocent indigenous personnel. Everyone is ready, the sweat is streaming now, fingers have worn grooves in the riflestocks, get this thing over with, if Mr. Charles is going to start something, now is the time he will do it, and just wait until he does, indigenous personnel my ass, that whole fucking ville is gonna go up, goddamn gooners, get through this fucking ville and be done for the day, get back to the base, ham fried and peaches, maybe some sleep. Maybe the grave. Strobic fury the only thing that keeps one foot stepping in front of the other, the connection of man to man, he who is walking next to you is you. You are both the centers of the war, each and all, moving forward now, they're in there, you can feel them sight in on your chest, snap that fucking flack jacket closed.

Three men in the middle of our line fall like a giant has thrown them down. Spurts of quick dust fly up around them. Then the crackle of an AK-47 whips through our ears. I'm confused, I didn't see any rifle flashes from the front, and the sound is coming from behind us, up and behind us. I see Doc Scanlon dive on top of one of the men who went down. More crackling sounds of a rifle on automatic reach us, the dust is kicking up around the downed men. Several tracers spin off red hot into the village.

It's hard to say if I saw the muzzle flashes with my eyes, turning to meet the sound, or with my mind. Mind is so expanded during a fire fight it touches everywhere danger might arise. They were behind us, all right, shooting us in the back, chickenshit mutherfuckers. My own realization was simultaneous with every other man in the company. There is a flurry of legs and diving bodies at the center of our line, heads turning to spot the source of death, locating the blue yellow muzzle flashes left suspended in the air, as if the air itself is living and retaining whatever force passes through it, the retina is plugged directly into the ear, the brain throwing off scalp and skull, opening directly to the whole world, the sound of a gnat as significant and memorable as the sound of the bullets cutting past your ears.

Three rifles are firing at us, spraying the whole span of the company. We are hitting the deck, bullets are slicing overhead, we can feel the hollow tunnels of vacuum they trail. I'm down in the dirt, clawing to get a purchase to turn toward the fire. That is the only chance, face the fire and shoot. The Captain has found himself a safe dike to hide behind and is raising his carbine. Gunny Mead is holding the radio handset. Anderson and Orrick are beside me, swinging their rifles into their shoulders. I am persuading myself that the clumps of paddy clods are sufficient protection to hide behind. I am completely exposed, I can calculate the angle between the VC shooting at us from the rocks behind us and my own body lying prone in their field of fire. It is a precisely perfect angle and I can feel the bullets impact behind my feet, sending tight tremors through the ground and through my body. My pistol is in my hand. I am not afraid anymore.

No one had to tell any one of us what to do. Every single man in the company opened fire at the same instant. We released a tremendous volley. Rifles, machine-guns, bloopers, all firing as fast as they could be fired. Thousands of bullets focused on the outcropping of grey rock where the VC fire had come from. The event was clear and absolute. The backshooters had fired on us and it was the perfect catalyst to transform us from green trainees into men ready to fight back to the death. Theirs.

The range was two hundred yards. We blew out enough lead in the first minute to turn the face of the rock to dust. It was stunning to realize just how powerful and formidable a force a trained rifle company is, all firing at once, with vengeance and skill. The long arc of rifles firing made a furious growling sound, the intense flames of the muzzle flashes creating a wall of impenetrable energy.

There was only one thing for me to do, and that was fire my pistol and hope I got lucky. There was only one goal to accomplish, and that was to kill the enemy. It was my and every man around me's singular intent. The clarity of my thoughts at that moment still astounds me. I recall tracking the path of my heavier bullets, calculating to shoot at a higher angle than the men with rifles, thinking I could arch the bullets to their mark. I remember thinking I could see the blunt dumb slugs leave the muzzle of my pistol and track their path and see them smashing into the skulls of the VC who were hiding behind the rocks, thinking I could see their exposed forms as easily as they could see mine.

Our fire stopped as abruptly as it had started while we all changed clips. The sergeants were shouting at us to control our fire, but no one was listening. We were looking at each other, as happy as we'd ever been in life. Vindicated, released from childhood, the same body joined at the soul like a strand of violent pearls, suffering a kind of delirious ecstasy, death flying over our heads shouting its hollow black we'd long to know, our own heart beat the same as the man's next to us, exquisitely fearless.

Then they did it again. The VC opened fire again. Three or four thousand bullets fired at them, seven of my own, and they opened up on us again. They'd waited for our first blood ejaculation, patient, knowing, playing with us, insulting us, humiliating us, waited until we were plugging in new clips, and opened fire again. The callous disrespect, the foolhardy effrontery, the inscrutable bravery. Two hundred yards away and invisible but I could see their exultant confident faces, imagine, three VC taking on an entire Marine Corps weapons-reinforced rifle company. We let loose another furious volley, this time some of the men firing on semi-automatic, aiming their shots, the vectors of tracers converging in a four foot circle at the rock face. M-79 rounds exploding fifty yards short. Machineguns coughing off short bursts. Noncoms shouting hold your fire, hold your fire, like commands could penetrate the ecstasy of our exchange. A mortar team had set up its tube and were dropping rounds above the VC's position, none exploding directly where they must have been standing. And just as none of our bullets had stopped them, none of theirs had wounded any more of us. After the company had expended its second volley the Captain began to apply military strategy, classic fire suppression, ordering sustained withering fire from both flanks to keep their heads down while he dispatched a squad with two M-79 men from the center of the line.

And the Marines did it. They stood up and walked forward, pausing every few steps to fire their rifles, the men on the flanks keeping up a steady staccato of shooting. There was no point in my continuing to fire my pistol. I looked over at Orrick beside me to confirm my decision, and he smiled at me benevolently like he'd seen me for the first time in his life. There was no hope or dread that I'd killed someone, some enemy, some VC, some human being, with my pistol shots. If they were dead or wounded their death could have come from any one or any fifteen or any one hundred of us. If there was a prevailing emotion it was that of loss for not knowing you were the one who had killed them. The attacking squad kept moving forward, ignoring the possibility that the VC, in a spasm of courage would rise up from behind their rocks and cut them down, trusting that their yearning to live was as strong as our own, not even they were as courageous as Marines willing to walk right into enemy bullets, willing to stand up and die, trusting that the flanks would keep their rifles firing to keep the gooks in their place until they could gain enough ground to kneel and fire the M-79s and send the exploding rounds right down their throats. Fight and win, or die. No right or wrong, us or them, me or you, final and absolute, no yield getting philosophical.

Fifty yards out the squad fanned out, took kneeling positions and while the riflemen fired at the rocks, the two men with grenade launchers laid in a steady barrage of exploding shells, peppering the whole of the area where the VC could be hiding with at least twenty rounds. Then we waited, the wash of adrenal exultation fading back into exhaustion and fear, there was still the village to sweep, there still might be VC waiting for us in there, there were the practical considerations, like how much ammunition was left, how quickly could we get this job done and get back on the helicopters and back to base camp, and would these patient sneaky wily ballsy little gookers wait until we were loading up and open up on us again, a bad end to a perfect day.

Smoke from the M-79 rounds burst in quick succession, and the flanking riflemen ceased their fire. And we waited, feeling an odd sympathy for the men who'd so daringly attacked us, and still wishing them dead. Still feeling the tremors brought on by the bullets coming so close to me, the fear of how close I'd come to being shot began to rise in me like bile, churning through my contorting organs. But it was over. The V.C. failed to return fire, had been killed or wounded or ran away.

It was with sadness and frustration that the company got out of its hiding places behind dikes, bushes, tufts of grass, quarter inch depressions in the hard ground, and turned toward the village to continue the sweep. "That'll teach 'em," Orrick said to another man in his fire team, "Man, did you see that, everybody was firing. Shit, even Doc was firing." And he grinned at me like his mere presence had caused me to violate a sacred tenet. He was a happy man.

The Captain assigned the mortar team to protect the wounded men, along with two corpsmen, telling them we'd pick them up on the way out, he was changing the landing zone to the fields just behind the village instead of humping back to where we were deposited that morning. The threat of attack had not diminished. The three wounded men were in no immediate danger of going into shock and there wasn't time to risk a medevac.

We cautiously kicked through the brush surrounding the village, entering on line, keeping our eyes peeled for tripwires, for the glint of sunlight on a muzzle, a face twisted in telltale hostility. But there was a meditative calm emanate. A seizure of spirits making themselves as small as possible to escape detection by demons. The faces of the men around me were still flushed from the exhilaration of the fire fight, and still convinced that there could be more fighting to do. It made sense that the fire fight was a diversion that would allow the VC in the village a chance to escape, had there been any. To face such a formidable force as ours on flat ground in close quarters, with our options of death from the air delivered by Phantoms would be foolish, suicidal, pointless.

We entered the hootches, finding most of them empty. The stock was penned, chickens and ducks hidden under thatch baskets, the pepper gardens tended, the courtyards swept clean. When we did find people they were women who were younger and healthier than the people living in Le Mai, the children healthier too, and taller. The people were still defiant, still engaged in ruling their own lives, still hating and fearing us, and not taking us as their savior benefactors. We searched through their goods like cops looking for stash, trying to find weapons and explosives, rice caches, documents, propaganda. But what we needed to know was being transmitted to us from the villagers' eyes. It was pointless to badger them into betraying the whereabouts of their men, probably the same men who opened fire on us, the same men we were sure slipped out the east end of the village, the men who would wait until exactly the right moment and later kill us or maim us. VC di di?, have you stopped beating your wife, who pays them to shoot at us, who steals from you, profound futile despair an opening into the maelstrom of the violence we'd brought to bear. They were richer because they still had the resolve to fight back. They acted as if our furious fusillade was so common it bore no significance. They ignored us. I could see the Vietnamese women's cold disregard grinding into the Marines. Not this time, maybe, but soon, soon, we'll teach you to give sanctuary to the enemy, Commie symps.

After we finished searching the village, our fury expended and hence not doing much damage, the Captain organized a detail to search the rocks from where we'd received the fire. I cajoled my way into the detail, saying they had to have a corpsman with them, regulations, besides, they might still be up there, you never know. We followed a trail that led back into the jungle bordering the ville, and then back up onto the hill and to the rocks.

It was too hot to be too cautious, everyone wanted to get out of there, back to the base where we thought it was safe, so we humped up the hill not really expecting attack. The V.C. had gone. We couldn't see them or feel their eyes tracking us. When we got there we found nothing but a tight bundle of clothes, some brass and a pair of sunglasses. There were no bodies. No blood trails. No body fragments. No victory. A Marine said, "That's Charlie, Skipper, he was just shaking hands." The Captain looked disappointed. After the exhilaration of the firefight, after expending thousands of rounds of ammunition, taking three wounded, even after realizing that we did not hate or loathe the enemy, even thanking him for blooding us and letting us in on the secret that to defend ourselves against death in whatever form it took was as natural as breathing in your sleep, the anticlimax of finding no evidence of our enemy taking an injury spun us into further fearful apprehension. From curiosity we untangled the bundle of cotton clothes the VC had left in a hurry. Among the shirts and shorts, Da Nang wear, the clothing of cycloriders, was a bra. A woman had been firing on us. Odious thought, to kill a woman. Frightening that a woman was courageous enough to take on a Marine rifle company, and hence we were further diminished. Our mothers had bred us to defend the nation.

The three wounded men are slung on poncho stretchers to be taken aboard the waiting helicopters. They are smoking and joking, morphine turning the pain to dream. They have noble wounds. They are going to Japan. They are happy. And I'm jealous that Doc Scanlon was the one to protect the life of a wounded Marine with his own body. Luck, instinct and courage brought him a Bronze Star. And though we each and all say medals are for the pogues and the brass, I'm like everyone else, I want one too.

WILKS

We'd go out, checking out the territory, looking for VC suspects, parading our armed might in replication of the French patrols that had been used so unsuccessfully to subdue the Viet Minh. We were demanding identification cards from the peasantry, though we were sure that the NVA in their duplication of the social infrastructure, readying themselves to assume political power by eliminating the current office holders, could as easily replicate the laminated plastic ID cards as could the Saigon government for which we were warring. Though, admittedly, by then the World was but a dream held fast by hope, Saigon but a rumor, there was really only us and them.

We'd also been told that the rules were changing again, that if a peasant was running from us he had reason to fear us and was therefore fair game. And also, that we were at another disadvantage. The Viet Cong had just received a resupply of new weapons provided for them by the Russians and the Chinese, endorsing terrorism by the gun, and that although our ammunition would fit their barrels, their ammunition would blow our weapons up in our faces. It was a matter of a silly little millimeter, so, boys, don't lose your ammo and don't use theirs.

The morning that Lance Corporal Wilks killed the woman I was out with Lt. Anderson and platoon, a daytime patrol, easy in the morning cool, the air clear and clean from monsoon washing, no sense of being dry-sniped or vehemently hated riding the psychic currents. The countryside looked almost peaceful. A work crew of Vietnamese men was repairing the road that ran to Liberty Bridge, we could see fishing sampans working the mouth of the river. Another patrol of Marines was walking the dikes beyond the hamlet. Across the Song De women were planting rice and boys were plowing paddies riding the backs of water buffalo. Green and lovely, ancient rhythms stretching back thousands of years, for all the disease and warfare, persistent order generating life upon life.

Just below the French fort, in the flat expanse of paddies reaching down to the river, the platoon came upon twenty or so people working knee deep in water, old men and middle-aged women yoked to the task of planting rice. A runner would bring bundles of rooted rice stalks to a team of four who would bend and walk, planting the young plants in even perfectly measured rows. Even though the people looked familiar, the same people we'd see when we swept the village or went down to the marketplace, Lt. Anderson ordered a squad to flank them, a squad to hang back to block any chance that the Vietnamese might escape, and a squad to go with him.

The column broke apart, one squad following Anderson. The people in the paddies seemed to ignore our presence, continuing the rhythm of their work. Plant four left, step, plant four right, step. Anderson shouted at the workers, and motioned with his arm for them to come to us. They stopped their work and talked among themselves for a moment, selecting an emissary to go talk to the Marines. There was no point in interrupting the work, in expending the extra energy necessary for all twenty of them to wade all the way back to the road.

An older woman with betel blackened teeth approached the platoon. Reaching Anderson, she bowed, shading her face with her hat, as if she dare not chance looking into the Marine's demon blue eyes, or try to find mercy in the clouded displaced souls of their brown brothers. It was best not to provoke them, the big friendly Marines were easily irritated and unpredictable, never seeming to know whether to help or destroy. She had been through this procedure many times before, with the ARVNs and the French and now with the Americans. She produced an ID card from her shirt pocket without being asked. The rest of the workers stooped back to their work.

Staff Sergeant Thurgood stepped forward to ease the task of inspecting the ID card from the lieutenant. It was her picture on the card, her name, why was he shouting at her? "Mamasan, you bring all the people here. Chopchop, moshgosh, you savvy?" he shouted, using whorehouse pidgen as if our occupation language was shared by all of Asia, and being that we were there to save them, it was their obligation to understand us. He pointed with his rifle, and motioned for all of them to come to us.

But something wasn't right. The Marines were on the alert, perhaps thinking some fool Viet Cong would reach down into the paddy mud and produce a rifle and start shooting us, protected by a wall of innocent peasants. The workers ignored the beckoning signal, and that was uncharacteristic, their usual behavior compliant to our armed demands. They seemed to be shying, looking for a way out. The sergeant kept the old woman's card, telling her again, as loud as he could, to go get the other people. She understood, turned and walked toward the workers.

Lance Corporal Wilks, a gangly, intense Tennesseean, was particularly agitated. He was pacing back and forth between the clutch of men that had gathered around Thurgood and the old woman. "This is hinky, Lieutenant, something is fishy," he said, and Anderson ignored him.

Reaching the others the old woman explained something to them, then they started filing out of the paddy, climbing up on the dike and heading toward us. One water buffalo was standing in the field, but four people remained to tend to it. Seeing the group broken up, Wilks said, "Watch those people, Lieutenant, them people are VC, sure as shittin'." The rest of us were merely curious, taking advantage of a chance to rest in the rising heat.

As the file of sixteen peasants approached us, Thurgood pointed his rifle at the remaining four, shouted, "Hey, you, assholes! Come 'er!" The sixteen people started gathering around Lt. Anderson, effectively cutting off his view of the other four. Three of the remaining four women looked at the younger, more beautiful woman, as if awaiting instructions.

"Those people are VC, Lieutenant. You watch." Wilks insisted, aiming his rifle.

"Hold your horses, Wilks, we have to give them the benefit of the doubt. We can't shoot these people just because we want to. Put your weapon down," Anderson said, preoccupied with checking the offered ID cards of old wrinkled men in wispy beards and aging women.

Three of the remaining four women started walking toward us, but there was something slower in their walk, they were wary and suspicious, as if they could they'd vanish into thin air at any moment. The Marines around Wilks backed away from him, instinctively avoiding his murderous intent. Seeing the last woman turn and sprint in the direction of the river, Wilks shouted, "She's running, lieutenant!" and without waiting for Anderson to recover from his confusion, Wilks quickly aimed his rifle and squeezed the trigger.

She was dead in mid-stride. The bullet hit her, throwing her forward like she'd been hit by an invisible truck. She splashed into the paddy water.

The three people who'd lingered to protect her froze where they were standing. The rest of the Marines, hearing Wilks' shot, readied their rifles, not sure who or what to shoot. Several women in the group around Anderson started screaming and wailing, tearing at their hair and kneeling in the dust of the road. Another one of them had just been killed outright and there was no recourse, there was no possible immediate revenge.

Anderson was completely perplexed. Responsible for every breath his men took, he was the one who'd have to explain why Wilks had killed the woman. A grin of immense pleasure grew on Wilks's teenage face.

"Now you've torn it, Wilks!" Anderson croaked, barely able to control his fury.

"She was running, lieutenant, sir," Wilks said, his voice cold and contemptuous. The three women remained frozen on the dike.

106

The others kept sobbing and wailing, one of them clinging to Thurgood's trousers. Thurgood kicked her loose, saying, "Better keep an eyeball peeled on them others, sir. Wilks might be right."

If you could strip away Wilks's skin you'd find a wide open tracer hot current of war, a willing killer ready to goad the war itself into action, damn the consequences, VC were the enemy, it didn't matter that no one in the paddies had raised a weapon against us.

"What do you think we should do, Thurgood?" Anderson asked after he'd cooled down enough to start considering how he was going to explain what had happened to the CO.

"We oughta round up that bunch that was with her, take 'em in for interrogation, shit, they're all VC, sir, leave the cunt for Charlie to bury," the sergeant said, spitting the words out like the lieutenant and the women were something awful clogging his throat.

Stunned, I'd never seen anyone shot down in cold blood before, backshot, anathema to the American code of fair play, a woman, I stepped into the mix, saying, "We don't know if she's dead. Maybe we can do something for her."

"That was good shooting, Doc. The bitch is dead, all right," Thurgood said. "Center shot. Right on."

A flicker of hope faded out of Anderson's face. He ordered the flanking squad and me to go out into the paddies to certify that the woman was dead, and to round up the other three women. "You stick with me, Wilks," Anderson said as we moved out down the dike. Anderson wasn't going to allow Wilks the pleasure of gloating over his kill.

The squad reached the three cowering women with their weapons leveled, ready to shoot them if they made a wrong move. The women's faces were beseeching us not to kill them where they stood. Half the squad circled around them and began herding them back to the road. The rest of us walked further down the dike to where the dead woman's body was sinking into the mud.

Then there she was, a black and brown still form, hair spreading away from her head in a black swirl. Pretending I could handle anything, I forced my hand down to turn her over by the arm. A sucking sound rose when the mud gave up its clutch. She floated over easily, slow, like a solid ghost rising in a nightmare. Her eyes were wide open, glazed, still, unseeing, dead. Like she saw me in my own dead future. A ragged clot of bruised offal floated nearby, separated from her body when the bullet tore out her heart and breastbone. Leeches had already settled around the gaping hole in her chest. Foolishly, I checked for a pulse, saying some sort of silent sorry prayer.

"She's dead, all right," I told the sergeant in charge.

"Leave her, then," he said, not wanting to look. Some other Marine said something about her being young, she'd have been a lot better off in a Da Nang whorehouse. But I was too ashamed to hit him.

We left the dead woman and followed the dike back to the road. Moving out, the three other women were being led by two Marines each. They were clutching the women's arms, half dragging them along. The other people just stood and watched us leave, the burning fury in their eyes cutting through us.

On the walk back, Wilks could hardly contain his self congratulation, coming up to me and saying beneath his maniacal grin, "That was sure some shot, huh, Doc? Did you see it? Scratch one Victor Charlie." And I said, yes, I saw it, but I refused to give him any more, refused to fuel his homicide with the gory details of what his desire had wrought. I was sick down in my soul with his weight and the recognition of his undeniably clear understanding.

By the time we reached the French fort, Anderson had solved his perplexity. Greeted by the CO, he turned over the prisoners, the three middle-aged women, and said, "Three VC captured, one killed." Good for the unit, good for the lieutenant, good for the captain. The women were held near the wire until a truck was dispatched to take them into the ARVN compound in Da Nang.

Ops

Friendly fire was what the brass called Lt. Griffen's accidental killing of Doc Dione and eight other Marines. And to prove it, they left Lt. Griffen to man that same mortar for the rest of his tour, and to live with the buddies of the men he'd killed. He was totally ostracized, masturbating himself to sleep in his poncho hootch each night, cheery and smiling at us as we went through the wire to leave on patrols and ambushes. He was an officer, empowered to send us into the scything fire of the enemy, and as an agent of those we'd volunteered to serve, the same corps of men who'd supplied Griffen with the faulty materiel that brought death to us, deserved whatever treatment devolved to him. Or so said our collective regard.

We were leaving him behind on this operation, like always. Griffen would serve as fire support for the Regimental sweep of the entire main line of resistance, and our company was getting ready for the big one. We could tell it was going to be a major operation. The news teams were milling around among us, trailing microphones and spawning fear, unarmed noncombatants possessed of a special naive neutrality whose presence angered more than one man. "Where do these fuckheads get off? Man, they ain't even got balls enough to carry a weapon. What am I suppose to do when the shit gets thick, jump on a grenade to save their film for the evening news?" Every issue of *Stars and Stripes* had carried a story about a Marine who'd sacrificed his life for the other men in his outfit by throwing himself on a grenade they'd been playing with, and such self-sacrifice was the expected course of personal conduct.

The company staged in the paddies below the fort, awaiting the helicopters. Rumor had it that our mission was simply to look into every nook and cranny the Viet Cong could use to hide himself, weapons and foodstuffs, that we'd be searching through villages and back into the hills in a kind of Viet Cong round-up, taking all the ground for ten miles around and herding the fleeing enemy toward an awaiting company of Marines who would slaughter them. It had been continually reported that a Viet Cong battalion was operating in the area, though we'd heard no evidence of it for weeks. Our latest casualties had been boobytrap victims, and as far as we were concerned, any Vietnamese was capable of setting out the little bombs that would blow us up. You didn't have to be a Commie cadre to want to rig a trip wire.

The urgency to turn the war from guerrilla harassment into conventional warfare, forcing the enemy to meet our massively destructive machinery, combined with the pogues in the puzzle palace never venturing out beyond their own wire and therefore not knowing the complexity of the abominable terrain, set up the conditions we'd be living through for the next few weeks. While the SeaBees were building the four foot thick reinforced concrete bunkers for the general staff, oh yes, we were going to stay, we'd been living in sandbag holes eating C-rats, dressed in rags, and our resentment was mounting. While they were looking at the maps and logistical lists, we'd be the ones hacking our way through jungle until some VC took a quick chance and shot the point, then ran away, live to fight another day. *Catch-22* was more popular reading than *Sgt. Rock*.

The other and more distinct possibility was that this was going to be just another huge operation that would exhaust us, get a few of us blown away, wasted, disappeared so there was only a hole in our collective soul where Barns or Stephens or Gonzales had vanished into leaving us not even grief to maunder. Grief covered by callous toughness, well that's the way the cookie crumbles, if he'd been on the stick, can't afford to get too close to each other, might hurt too much, blunts your edge, it just as easy could have been me. Just like all the other operations where we'd go out into the bush expecting to be hit at any moment, expecting to be attacked by well organized companies of NVA in set-piece battles only to stumble through the endless humps from village through treeline, through paddies and back into the jungled hills, yielding nothing but jungle rot or immersion foot or malaria and the anguish of not fulfilling your purpose of engaging the enemy until he was defeated and dead.

Everywhere beyond the line of fortresses from the Dai Lai Pass to Highway 1 to our French fort and the Le Mai hamlet, and west on to Da Nang was considered a free fire zone. Any Vietnamese in the free fire zone was a potential enemy, a potential target. We loaded on the helicopters, the reporters recording our movement, the movie magic on us, making our mouths more dramatically grim, running toward the open hatches crouched a little lower. Then we were in the air again, heading somewhere dangerous, fast.

Every helicopter in northern South Vietnam must have been being used. Looking out from the door I could see strings of choppers spreading out through the sector like geese lifting from a lake, cumbersome from our weight in the turgid air. Seeing all that machinery was at once awesome and frightening, carrying our destructive potential and scaring the VC into the posture of terrified animals. Hide or fire, try to knock us down with small arms, the bounty on a helicopter could feed a Vietnamese family for years. Open season on each other, throwing our lives in front of each other's deaths, each life spin drawing in another life, the rotor whopping announcing our arrival.

Lt. Anderson, Gunny Mead, Gerhart, Orrick, Marshall, S/Sgt. Thurgood, some reporter from *Time Magazine*, and I are sitting in the web seats of the H-34, and the inertia and fear are pulling at our faces as we start the inevitable spiral descent, no one daring to admit to fear or apprehension so it gets frozen inside, but the zone is cold and we clamber out of the hatch at the head of a narrow valley of paddies that haven't been worked for several years. On both sides of us and ahead of us are steep ravines of impenetrable jungle leading out onto a dirt road that connects with another road that leads to Le Mai five or six miles away. We've landed in a perfect ambush site. But there are too many of us, and the sky is cluttered with too many helicopters to invite attack. Chalk one up for luck and guerrilla sense.

The platoon leaders are called to the tactical command post and deployment assignments are handed out to the company. The same thing is happening in a ten mile arc around us, but when the helicopters leave we feel very much abandoned and alone. Now it's us and them, if they're here, and they surely are. There is a brief exchange of automatic rifle fire a mile away, but there is nothing we can do about it. It would take two days just to cross the hills between us, the jungle is so thick. The first platoon, Anderson's, is given the point, and we take off walking further into the ravine, Gerhart taking our point, the lieutenant, Marshall the radioman and me following ten men behind. The monsoons are about to start soon. I can see the great grey thunderheads building up on the teeth of the Cordillera.

We march for a few hours, the fear never ceasing, the tension in our muscles aching for ease and release, until the point man calls a halt. The ravine had momentarily ended at a clearing overlooking a bend of slick brown river. It is an upper tributary of the Song De flowing out of the hills. Across from the clearing there is a village standing on a spit of land. But Gerhart has heard something and calls the lieutenant up.

"Fucking dinks ain't got tanks, do they lieutenant?"

"Not that I've ever heard of, Gerhart."

"I heard some big engines, for sure. Listen tight."

And I'm looking into the village across the river and see the mind haze of men gaining defensive positions rise like a curtain of sparkling vapor. Beyond the edge of the river foliage the village is as still as an object in a vacuum. Then the churn and thrum of diesel engines reaches our ears. And we spot them, two Amphtracks backing away from the village, crossing the river with their tracks spewing murky water.

There is a squad of Special Forces men on top of each Amphtrack yelling and screaming, and they open fire on the village, shooting their rifles in wild abandon. At the sound of the rifle fire the platoon instinctively backs away and crouches, even though we are out of the line of fire.

The Viet Cong hiding in the brush at the base of the village fire at the retreating Amphtracks, four rifles shooting ragged bursts. Which causes the men on the Amphtracks to break into hilarity, and insult them, some of the Special Forces men standing up shouting, "Shoot me, mutherfuckers, shoot me!" then firing back, spraying the brush with hundreds of bullets. Their faces are portraits of exuberant invincibility. The following Amphtrack opened up with his twin-thirties, expending a thousand rounds in less than a minute. The brush is cleanly mown. "That's right, that's right!" we hear one of the men yell, "Git the muthers!" And another burst of fire came from the brush across the river, but only from one rifle. Again the men on top of the Amphtrack opened up, aiming their shots, completely saturating the place where the white hot blips of rifle fire came from, still yelling, still glorying in their frenzy.

The Amphtracks slipped up the muddy grass on our side of the river, dislodging some of the Special Forces soldiers, a few of them still firing at the bank across the river. But there was no return fire. The VC had either been killed or overwhelmed. The victory was decisive and clear. S/Sgt. Thurgood stepped out in front of the lead Track, held up his rifle for them to stop, and addressed the men on top. "Any more over there?" he said, almost longingly.

"Well, whatayouknow, Jarheads. You girls out for a walk?" the Special Forces sergeant jeered. And the other men on the track laughed. "Naw, Sarge, we got 'em all. Four for us, none for you, ha ha," he said, then banged on the track's hatch for the driver to move on. They passed by, waving their rifles and smiling, talking amongst themselves like boys who'd just won a football game, leaving us in their dust. The Special Forces sergeant had made his claim so casually, so matter of factly, like it was their daily activity to ride around on the great lumbering machines shooting Viet Cong and they were used to it, while we were still hunting hard to make our first kills. We were stricken sick with envy.

There was no way to cross the river to inspect what damage had been done. The dead or wounded VC would have to remain a mystery. And even though their threat was gone, we crossed in front of their field of fire with crouched caution. The village seemed possessed by a great blackened sob. We pressed on up the narrowing dirt road, the steeps of the ravine growing closer and sharper, the road moving away from the river, the daylight permeated with dank green. Attack could have come from any point along that road, and moving down it was like sloughing through a nightmare, except in this one you didn't wake up.

We took ten at a small flat at the bottom of a narrow pass between two of the hills, reclining into the foliage, slapping at the constant mosquitoes, burning leeches off our necks and legs with cigarette coals. The lieutenant consulted his map and radioed in our position, then received instructions that we were to press into our left flank, and find a trail that was indicated on the map, then work our way back toward the landing zone.

"Impossible, lieutenant," S/Sgt. Thurgood admonished, "the day is most gone, we'll get lost out in that shit sure as shootin'. No way we can make it back to the LZ by nightfall, sir."

"Orders are orders, Sarge," the lieutenant said, as tired and resigned as the rest of us.

"Charlie catches us out in that shit, and we're grease for sure," Thurgood protested. "No way a chopper could get into us if we need one."

"We don't have a choice, sergeant. The skipper says go that way, we go that way. And no, we aren't going to bag it. This is a big operation. We're not going to be the ones to fuck it up." The lieutenant was adamant.

So we pressed inland, entering a bamboo and sapling forest where the plants grew in half light and the air was so stagnant the only things that moved it were insect wings. There was no sign of human passage, not a footprint, not the smell of urine or sweat, not the trace of a living soul. We were heading for an opening between two hills, and the lieutenant, being in a hurry to get to the coordinates given to him by the Captain, told Gerhart to pick up the pace. We clattered and clumped, stumbling over roots and vines, cursing the fetid atmosphere, sweat pouring off us, our water supply nearly exhausted. Every breath caused us to inhale tiny winged creatures. We crossed over a hump, heading toward high ground, and found the path we'd been looking for. It joined the small pass from the east, and was only one man wide. Judging from how overgrown it was it hadn't been used in years. We trudged on for hours, going deeper and deeper into the jungle, our fear mounting with each step. We'd lost radio contact as soon as we crossed over into the hills.

The path led us into a deep bamboo gallery, a cleft between two hills. Dead bamboo and rotting vines cluttered the pathway, and we slipped continually, finding it impossible to maintain our balance while carrying all our gear and trying to gain a footing amongst the rotting vegetation. The sides of the gallery were steep, climbing a hundred feet on both sides, and falling another hundred feet down, so that the only possible movement was either moving ahead or having the tail end Charlie take the point. We followed the cleft through its winds for another hour, the yellow light fading into near darkness. Finally, we reached the cleft's end. A sheer cliff of bamboo rose before us, impenetrable and impassible. We were lost. If that trail had been used by anyone, it was by the mountain people, the ones who hunted heads. They were the only people who could stand being there.

Lt. Anderson concluded that we'd followed the wrong trail, and ordered us to turn around and head out. We'd radio in as soon as we got to a place high enough to permit transmission. But there wasn't one until we went back through the bamboo gallery, and that was at least a three hour trek. It was now dark. The passage to that point had been so hazardous we were lucky we didn't have several broken bones and twisted ankles. To try to traverse that same ground in the dark would have been impossible. Our only option was to tuck ourselves in under the fallen bamboo like grubs wrapped in our ponchos and wait out the night, hoping that we hadn't been followed by those who would destroy us. We kept a twenty-five percent watch all night, though no one slept much.

If there is a place in nature where the angry spirits abide, where the souls of soldiers ripped out of their bodies by bullets and shell fragments linger to haunt and conspire, that was the place. We could hear them rustle among the bamboo leaves like breezes of moon luminescent gauze, their thousand voices muttering in our deeps their violent stories, looking for an opening within which to gain a purchase, to be carried back to the brief world of the living, inhabiting our souls, hungry for sense.

When first light finally filtered through the leaves, no one bothered to eat, and we headed back to the road as fast as we could walk. That night's dream kept recurring; a boy was given a nautilus shell and a thin gold chain. His task was to thread the chain through the apertures in the shell, and if he succeeded in reaching its spiral apex he got to keep the shell, to add it to the Thai balance scales of life. The boy could have been Vietnamese, or me, it didn't matter.

Lt. Anderson was on the radio as soon as we reached the dirt road, explaining where we'd been, receiving the Captain's admonition and forgiveness, but surprised that no one had been sent to look for us. His instructions were for the platoon to rejoin the company, and continue the sweep down through the draws, flushing Viet Cong along the way. I couldn't tell if we were hunters or bait. Our fates seemed to matter little to Command; either we got into a firefight and won, or got ambushed, or found the Viet Cong and annihilated him, what really mattered was how many of the enemy we killed. The war wealth was immeasurable, and as the Marine Corps joke went, we were expendable, and as volunteers we'd each agreed to be spent.

The heat and weariness of the days' march churned within to become cafard, a conglomerate depression made from exhaustion, lack of purpose, lack of role and definition, heat, dysentery, nightmares, apprehension of the real truth of one's situation, put one foot in front of the other, keep your nose open, your eyes peeled, try to remember that there is lethal danger everywhere, be a man, death is just a shot away, maiming just a slight mistake, lying that you weren't actually looking for that punji pit to step into, hack it, maybe getting blown away would be a blessing.

We searched up into jungle draws, climbed vine covered rocks, cut through bamboo thickets, always pressing on toward the company position, finding nothing. No sign. The Viet Cong were scrupulous in covering their presence and their tracks, Apache. Several miles down the road we came to a waterfall coursing out of the hills, and stopped to fill our canteens, and bent to drink from cupped hands. The water was cool, clear, pure, genuinely refreshing. But there seemed a taint to it, something unidentifiable, a touch of the ocean. As a water source for us it was also a possible water source for Mr. Charles, so we started the climb up the hill to its origin.

Gerhart saw him first. He stopped in his tracks, awed and uncomprehending. He signalled for the lieutenant to come up, and I followed behind. And there he was, lying in the middle of the falling water, the first dead Viet Cong we'd seen.

On the barren hillside, in the clear daylight, in the clear water, lay a very young man who was very dead. He was slight and sinewy, and his blood had leaked into the stream, leaving his skin sallow white, and his feet bruised purple. His eyes were open, sun baked marbles. His arms were twisted in flailed open contortion. The water had covered the large bullet hole in his chest with his black shirt. He lay very still, empty, the water waving his hand at us. Flies had eaten his eyelids and lips away.

"Careful, Doc," Anderson said as I bent to take a closer look, "he might be booby trapped." A caution that didn't make much sense. True, if there were VC around, and a dead one proved they were, and one of our men had killed him and left him to lay where he fell as warning that we were intent on their destruction, come out and fight like men, the only way he could be boobytrapped was if his comrades rushed out and put a grenade under him expecting our curiosity to turn him over and let the dead kill the about to be dead. But we all listened to the warning, and passed by the body, taking a good look, registering the fascinating fact of death, so very much closer now. His friends could be just beyond that next draw, in the

117

bush, waiting for us to come on line, surely they would have missed him by now. Anderson radioed the find into the TOC and heard back that yes, the point from second platoon had shot the VC, one round when he was running away, twenty minutes before, no weapon, no documents, maybe sixteen but you can't tell with these gooks, if he wasn't VC why'd he run from a platoon of Marines in a free fire zone?

We spread out on line, the presence of the Viet Cong very real now, they could be anywhere ahead, hiding behind the rocks and trees in the jungle and brush ahead, watch out for trip wires crossing into the shade. Anderson told Gerhart and Wilson to take the ridge line, get up there quick and no noise, don't fire unless you are fired upon, this is strictly recon. If the dead VC was a scout there was no telling how many of the enemy were lurking in the bush. Caution was the better part of valor. We pushed on through the brush, entering the strangling jungle, expecting to receive fire at any second. Not ten minutes had passed before Anderson's radio hissed, "We got 'em, lieutenant."

Anderson talked on the radio, then held up the line, calling for the squad leaders. When the squad leaders reached him he told them, "Gerhart and Wilson spotted at least a squad of V.C. on the top of the ridge. The CO says, don't attack, so we're going to head back down the hill and join up with them."

"What the fuck for, sir?" a Marine demanded, anxious to get into a fight.

"CO's going to call in an airstrike, is what the fuck for, trooper, do as you're told."

Gerhart and Wilson joined up with us looking frightened and beaten, as if they'd been ready to engage the enemy, but unsure that they could have prevailed and didn't want anyone to think them cowards. We slunk off the hill and down to where the Captain was waiting for us, quiet, furtive, knowing something momentous was about to happen. The Captain called Gerhart and Wilson to him, asking, "Now, exactly what did you see, Marine?"

Still breathing hard, Gerhart said, "Right up there, Captain, at the end of that ridge, we saw eight, maybe ten Gooks. They all had rifles. They were eating lunch or something, sir."

"Did they spot you?"

"No way, sir. We were real quiet. We didn't know what to do."

Another trooper, listening in, said, "Why didn't you shoot the fuckers?" engaged in the ten to one superiority delusion.

"You weren't there, you don't know," Wilson said, glaring defensively.

"You did right. I'm calling in an airstrike. That way nobody gets greased but them. No point in taking chances if the flyboys can get the work done easier," the Captain said.

Vindicated and forgiven, Gerhart and Wilson rejoined the platoon. The Captain consulted his map, radioed in the coordinates, instructed a sergeant to ready a smoke grenade to mark our position, then stepped back, keeping his field-glasses on the ridge where the Viet Cong had been spotted. By the time the Captain was off the radio word had spread throughout the entire company that the jets were coming, get ready to take cover.

Hot, sweaty, anxious, ignoring the possibility that the Viet Cong had spotted us and would start shooting into our midst, men clumped together waiting for the show. The squad leaders were telling us to keep quiet, the racket we were making could warn the targets. Targets, men like us, peaceably eating in their safe hiding.

We saw the jets before their sound wave struck us. Three silver wedges glinting in the sunlight to our north, moving as fast as our eyes could track them. Purple smoke grenades bloomed at either end of the strung out company, telling the pilots where we were.

"We see you, six actual," the Captain's radio said.

"Gooks on the ridge directly in front of us," the Captain said, sweating profusely.

"Standby for a hot one," the lead pilot radioed.

Then the jets were upon us, diving so close to the ground their shadows rode directly beneath them. Heat-cone blue and silver fuselage crossed over our upturned eyes. A silver canister of napalm tumbled from under the plane and exploded exactly where the Viet Cong were hiding. A great swell of orange flame burst and swelled into the air, sucking the surrounding air into its thick heat, conflagrating every living thing within fifty yards. The two other jets followed right behind, dropping their napalm. Two more great bursts of orange flame congealed with the first.

In stunned silence we heard the the sucking gasp of the napalm above the roar of the jet engines. I could feel the lives of the VC being ripped into the upwelling fire, but couldn't hear their screams over the roar of the bombs. The smell of charred flesh was masked by the familiar odor of gasoline. The radio crackled again, the lead pilot saying,

"Coming around again, six, just for drill."

The jets sheared in again, one after the other, tearing through the sky and releasing their second canisters of napalm, silver tubes of contained fire, heat from the jet flame cones flushing our awed faces, the bottom of their dive directly above us. The canisters accelerated from the Phantom wings, impacting before they could be heard coming. Enormous orange flames immediately consumed the hilltop. The Viet Cong didn't have a chance. If, by some miracle of grace, one of them survived the first strike, running until he tripped into a deep bog or stagnant mosquito pond and clutched at the bottom mud until the flame fuel expired, the second strike would have evaporated even that lucky cover.

"I think that got 'em, Phantom leader. Six out," the Captain radioed, shaken to his bones at the power he'd just brought to bear.

Many of the Marines cheered when the Phantoms made their passes. They exulted in killing the enemy, however that was done. The fewer Viet Cong, the better, done and done again until they were no more. The idiot fantasy persisted.

But it was unfair murder, and we knew it. The captain stood looking at the hilltop with sweat streaming down his neck and chest, eyes fixed upon the diminishing flames. He was, after all, simply a man, a good man, not a monster, simply the agent of monsters, but it was his soul and conscience that would bear the weight of those lives just extinguished. Lives burned down to grease and ash, blistered flesh, one breath of napalm cooking you

120

from the inside, your eyes exploded, your tongue choking you to death, your cock and testicles a bright leap of vanishing heat, your nerves spasming brain panic until the black barrel of merciful death swallows you. Times eight. Times ten. Times the rest of their platoon maybe just beyond where they were spotted, rising in the black flux of smoke. Killing sowed dragon's teeth. The news crew was filming it all, sending it all back home to the minds that made it.

"Buddhist priest," some grunt said, mockingly. "Crispy critters, you mean," said another. The tough innocence receiving spatters of laughter, but mostly awed shame, all of us, each of us, complicit by wish and witness. The true and actual code of conduct for combat infantry men is to shoot each other in mutual conflict. One man, one fire team, one squad, one platoon, one company, against all odds, using whatever small arms are available including knives, rocks and choking the enemy to death with your hands. He has the same chance to kill you. But the Viet Cong had no air support, no napalm, no willy peter that clung to your skin and burned a hole through you burning hotter when you poured water on it. So dropping napalm on a self-declared armed enemy, though it was the extension of the ambush ideal, his and ours, even as massive retaliation for his boobytraps, was a violation of the combat contract between men. Fear was a luxury in the face of such venal cruelty. Cut off your cock and balls while you watched and have them stuffed in your mouth until you suffocated was gook justice, gook amusement, and was invited. To drop such massive bolts of hell on men, on women and children, no matter their crimes against each other, seemed tremendously unfair, an indication of a sickness of the spirit— unholy vengeance designed by maniacs posing themselves as agents of fate or history safely murdering millions from their drafting tables. Part of us was also sucked into the flames, the lives they consumed still burning in our hearts. We would have preferred to kill the VC in open battle, our fighting skill and courage against their determined will. To issue hellfire and brimstone, the German ovens containerized, Teddy's big stick, the bully's bludgeon in the form of napalm to discourage the population from banditry by murder so conflicted with my ideals of Jesus and the good of my nation that the world changed from shining peace to banal slaughter, and I was part and parcel with it, the collective shame.

Bald barbarity, a current coursing through the mind-century and thus through us, me, twisting into the human helix precisely mechanized, the clean valves and guiding circuitry of planes and bombs distancing the makers from the blistered flesh, living like an embolism of self-absolution; evil. Oh mother world, what a number to hang on your boys. Were I a villager engaged in the lifelong struggle of raising food and children and caring for my ancestors, and even defending my ground against those who would come to rob and kill me or them, what could I know of the balances of mechanical destruction wielded by civilizations bent on vaporizing God? How could I, standing underneath the blooming flames with my pistol and my medical kit, shout peace, freedom, compassion in the long dream loudly enough? Or should I retreat behind the Maya wall, adding the brick of my mind, accepting the turn and turn again of men ordering each other's annihilation and do my best to stay out of the crossfire?

I went and found Gerhart and Wilson. They were sitting with the point man from second platoon, the man who'd shot the VC scout. "We're in a world of shit," I said, and they all three looked at me like children about to cry, and nodded their agreement. I could feel their grief and commiseration flowing between them in their silence, each of them knowing their small everlasting part in what had just happened. "No big thing, Doc," Wilson said, "Just the way it's always been," expressing the wisdom of despair.

The Captain told the XO to get the men moving, and the XO ordered us to saddle up. The company shifted under the weight of their packs, and began moving further down the dirt road, still talking like brave boys about the airstrike, but subdued too, like for even the least of them dreadful apprehension had taken place.

Six months to go, one hundred eighty days and a wakeup, four thousand three hundred twenty hours, two hundred and fifty-nine thousand two hundred minutes, one million five hundred fifty-five thousand odd seconds, it takes three seconds to breathe one breath,

122

two seconds to take a step, there was a long way to go, a long time! and no way out that didn't invite enormous pain, enormous regret. The dead scout's blood was our own.

◆◆◆◆

The operation went on and on for days and days, sending us through paddy and treeline, up hills to clear landing zones and dig in, only to abandon our positions the next morning, then into the jungled ravines to find where the VC had cleared fields of fire in anticipation of our arrival only to not be there when we came upon them exhausted and furious at our condition. We found tunnels and bunkers, small caches of food and propaganda, but no weapons and munitions. Sometime during that operation we hooked up with the ARVNs, who seemed giddy and eager to please their benevolent American brothers.

We went into a decaying village together, on line, Marines in front, ARVNs trailing behind. Finding no people living there, finding no one to fight or capture or intimidate with saving grace, were about to leave when the ARVNs decided to leave their calling card, produced their gratuitous Zippos, and set the shacks ablaze, laughing like they knew their futures lay in American cities and sparking conflagration was permissible rural renewal.

Seeing the flames recalled the napalm attack, and I remember worrying that so much fire so uncontrolled would soon turn into a great forest fire, spreading through the whole mountain range, the scorched earth policy consuming the whole Asian peninsula. It was the end of the hot season and the sun seemed to have sucked every drop of moisture from every living thing. Six, eight canteens a day, brought in on resupply choppers or scooped from stream trickles, halizone and lime Kool-aid from home. But the neutral ground seemed as capable of drinking fire as blood.

Then, finally, it was over, and we were ferried back to the French fort to rest for a few days while the brass tallied the results. If they called our weeks in the field a decisive victory, or a policing of the main line of resistance or said we had Charlie on the run, it made no difference to us. It was clear, even through the paranoia and attack lust, that Charles had us wired, figured out to the least footstep, and he would choose when he would attack, who and where. We were hunting, search and destroy, invade and force the issue for the time we were each going to be there. But he had a long term plan. Any people capable of withstanding the mechanistic violence of jet planes bombing you with napalm, then resolving to cling to our belts while killing us had the advantage. Seeing our willingness to commit companies, battalions, of heavily armed men to the ferreting out of merely a few enemy belied a wanton squander, a deep seated fear that cost little to exploit.

Pinning tiny flags demarking VC positions to their maps, the regimental officers must have discovered that we were surrounded. Charles was everywhere. He was in Le Mai, in the village across the river, in the hills behind the fort, in the hills behind Iron Bridge Ridge, saturating Da Nang, in every village and up every draw in the hills. Small groups who only met briefly to plan their harassment and set out their mines and booby traps, who openly bought weapons from the black market, who came in through our wire to cut our hair and mark our bunker positions, their loathing and their promise of our destruction flowing into us directly.

Though we were never officially notified, obedience being the only requirement of our tenure, the scope of our patrols was being cut to the immediate area, no more than two thousand meters out from our most forward positions. There would be fewer and fewer company sized patrols, more and more platoon sized patrols and squad sized ambushes. Our vulnerability had just increased.

Along with those changes came the announcement that in the effort to win the hearts and minds of the villagers in the Le Mai hamlet, that even if we were fired upon, we weren't to return fire. There was too much chance of hitting non-combatants. "You mean we're supposed to tromp through that ville and let them kill us without a fight?" some Marine protested. "Not a chance, sir. No fucking way." A consensus among us all. The brass was constantly altering the rules of engagement, keeping us undermined and off balance, thus inviting individuals to exercise their own set of fatal rules, divorced from the authority of the Corps.

The rains started, and I spent my days passing out pills, or once a week joining the pacification medical team down at the main entrance to Le Mai. The people would bring their babies and we'd inject them with penicillin, or salve their ringworm, or distribute vitamins to check the rickets and beri-beri, or pull abscessed teeth.

Our losses were light. Owens tripped a grenade on Iron Bridge Ridge and his leg was shredded below the knee. A whole squad had been swept away by a flash flood in the hills, resulting in broken arms, ankles, legs, a fractured skull. The squad's sergeant was so proud of his losses he boasted about it to anyone who would listen, the weather and terrain nearly as formidable an enemy as the Viet Cong.

Intelligence, G-2, would hear a rumor that the Viet Cong were going to be moving some night, and a platoon would be deployed to intercept them, ambush them. The sergeants would line us up, check to see if our dog tags were taped, paint our faces with night fighter grease, shake us to be sure our gear didn't rattle, and we'd go out through the wire into the total cloud covered dark, so dark that if you lost sight of the man five feet in front of you you might just as well sit down and wait until first light or until the Viet Cong found and killed you. We believed he could see in the dark better than we, that he could see by sense of smell. And reaching an ambush site, some hillside somewhere above a path, we'd sit and wait in terrified silence, as afraid that Charlie would sense our presence and come up behind us and shoot us before we had a chance even to react, as having to execute the ambush, letting loose our impacted rage on men dead before they knew what hit them, as they would us. Mutual murder, routine.

G-2 didn't have to tell us that the Viet Cong were moving around at night, we could feel them. Someone on the hill would have a hallucination of hordes of armed men massing at the gate, and illumination rounds would float down around the perimeter for hours, casting eerie mercury vapor light, our eyes scanning the brush and shadows for any movement, any sign. And who is to say if they were or weren't there, none were foolish enough to stand up in the broadcast light inviting quick death and a thousand rounds of copper jacketed bullets. It felt like they were there, all the time, all around us, watching every move we made, knowing who was sick or wounded or sleeping on watch, timing when the listening posts were set, how many men and their state of exhaustion, counting the number and directions of the night ambush patrols as we tried to sneak unnoticed through the wire at dusk. It was their terrain, they knew every likely ambush site, every path leading to it, they'd been living down in the dirt war for ten generations.

Every squad going out at night needed a corpsman, and being the platoon Doc, I went out on every one. My paranoia became so advanced that I thought I could generate the will to live through the thick night air, that because Charles knew every likely ambush site he would surely avoid us because he could sense my generation of the love of life. My desire to engage him in battle had vanished when I apprehended his poverty and disease, when I could find so few women pregnant. My only concerns were lasting through the remainder of the tour of duty and keeping my friends alive. Supposing the Viet Cong's senses as acute as my own, surely he could hear the rain plopping on our rubberized ponchos from fifty yards away, and rather than risking life by tempting an ambush would skirt the site and live to fight at a time of his own protected choosing.

One night, when we were waiting to ambush them, I know they were there, just out of range. Incredibly dark raining, we could not possibly see them, but when I closed my eyes and looked into the distance I could see a Viet Cong squad leader cautioning his men, feeling us perhaps, his intuition an effective weapon of survival, and I could feel the panic of the Marines start to mount in them, stripping away the darkness in burgeoning veils, oh shit, this could be it, then could feel the VC ambush team turning away on a current carried through the rain. But I said nothing, betraying our mission to kill Viet Cong. The sergeant in charge was gung-ho enough to want to hunt them down, but not being a hunter-killer I wanted nothing to do with such a perilous task. The entropy was upon me, the strobe of live or die constant. I could feel the men around me relax, their medullas easing the adrenalin output. There seemed to be no disappointment.

And so it went for weeks. Across the river where we found a group of military aged Vietnamese, part of a road repair gang they said, but we couldn't afford to believe them, and trussed them together at the necks and wrists with comm wire, tagging them with medical tags like they were vectors of mental illness, to be sent for interrogation by the ARVNs or the CIA, to be released or reeducated or executed. Into Le Mai for the twentieth or thirtieth time, to ransack the houses and frighten the women and children and catch a case of amoebic dysentery, once coming out of the village and encountering paddy water so deep and wide it was over the dikes and we had to hire some of the village men to ferry us to the road in sampans fashioned from teak planks. Dumb Americans, come to a country that is underwater half of the year and they don't even bring boats.

The monsoons would come in at ten after four everyday, and it was the only time during our tour there that we were regularly clean. The rain would start in silver torrents, and we'd strip and shower under them, wild with converting an adversary to an aid, laughing, scrubbing the mud and dust out of our fatigues, soaped and rinsed in minutes. Then the night would come and if I wasn't out on ambush I'd lay in my once-a-grave bunker contorting into a sleeping position that could avoid the leaks and get some of that half sleep where you think you might be asleep, you even dream, but your eyes are wide open, your boots still on, your pistol beside your hand, and maybe for a minute or two during the long waiting you don't think about blowing your own brains out and getting this shit over with. Ira Hayes, the Pima Indian from the Iwo Jima story, said in profound Marine Corps metaphor, "You don't go to war to get killed. You are already dead. You go to find your life." Central theme of every man around me, turned and differentiated into various lusts for valiant battle, discovered courage, spiritual unions with other such men in friendships that would last a lifetime, or like the corporal who had money sent from home so he could take advantage of the black market rate on converting dollars to MPC to piasters to dollars, or just slugging through, satisfied to simply survive, the future would take care of itself whether you were there or not. Light another Pall Mall, and another, maybe today's hump won't be so bad, self-destruction a father's piston fist named thick-skinned character, later in life you'll thank me for this, boy.

Corporal Dale comes to mind, the kind of young man injured early in life who would be your best friend at school, like me, the boys who knew the deep wounds and willingly protected each other from humiliation. He was blond and had tried to grow a fierce mustache, the fashion generated by the sergeants nervously twisting the hair-ends into Scottish points. And no matter how hard Dale tried to be gruff and intimidating his face always showed a frightened gentle boy eager to please. He was assigned the ambush the night we got to see our first Viet Cong, close-up, alive, and in our hands.

Dale got his squad together, nine men with rifles, one man with an M-79. They left the perimeter just after dark, shoulders hunched, whispering no talking, no smoking, lock and load. The assignment was to go out a thousand yards through the dark, toward the river, and set up the ambush beside the path that ran along the river's bank, any likely spot they could find in the starless pitch. Besides their weapons they took their flack jackets, two canteens, mosquito repellent (wear it and Charlie can smell you a mile away, don't and slap and itch all night), ponchos and a radio.

We were all friends, at least buddies, and had been together in that same horrible circumstance for months, so our spirit went out with them. Watching them leave the unexpressed sentiment was that we were glad it was them, not us for once, this once, there was some extra electrical charge to the molecules of the air. Connected, gathered around the lieutenant's bunker waiting to hear them radio in that they had reached their ambush site safely, we could feel them threading their way over the paddy dikes, slipping on the slick mud, stifling their fear and curses, following the soft clump of the footsteps in front of each other, minds fixed on the flame of life alight in each other, senses stretched to discover any movement, any anxious breathing of men waiting to kill them; like each one of us too many times before. A click is a long way in the dark, the fear makes you sense what might not be there and sends you hiding into clumps of brush or down into ditches or sliding silent as an eel into the paddy water, no sense in telling Mr. Charles where you are before you are ready to engage him. So an hour passing before we heard from the ambush squad was expected.

When we heard rifle fire erupt we knew it was them. The sounds of three rifles firing short bursts reached us first, followed by several single shots of return fire. Then the three rifles fired again, several short bursts. Knowing the terrain like the inside of our brains we could tell that the fire was coming from three hundred yards this side of the ambush site. It meant trouble.

Lt. Anderson was shouting into his handset, "Dale, this is Two, what's happening, Corporal?" But he received no reply. The squad firing into the dark was far too occupied to answer. Marines firing into the dark was nothing new, everyone had an overwhelming moment of fear when the shadows assumed murderous proportion, but receiving return fire could only mean either the squad had found some Viet Cong, or some Viet Cong had found them. "Dale stepped in the shit," a trooper offered, trying to sound like he'd personally gone through this before and any Marine as good as he could handle the situation, you betcha. "Check the listening post, Lieutenant," another man offered. Doing so, Anderson heard the men on the L.P. whisper that, no, they just heard the shooting, nothing more, no, no one but the ambush team had crossed in front of them. They sounded scared.

By then the four or five of us who'd been waiting around the radio had become the rest of the platoon. We were closest to the road, the first line of defense, and it was the other men of our platoon out there in the dark, surrounded by Viet Cong for all we knew. Illumination rounds popped in the air on the far side of the hill, out over where Dale's squad had been firing. The shooting had stopped. Someone on the hill had been listening in on the radio and ordered the rounds. In my panic I named the illumination premature, there was no telling if Dale's squad had found cover or were exposed. The hill cast a long shadow over us. My imagination insisted that the ambush squad was hunkered down in a line behind a paddy dike, and sneaky men in black pajamas were closing in on them slow and easy, dope enhancement brightening their vision.

"We gotta go get them, lieutenant," I said, seized by an urgency to bring my friends back from danger and a desire to act bravely.

"Hang on, Doc. We don't know who or what or how many," Anderson said, exercising prudence. No point in sending out men to be killed unless the ambush team was in deep trouble. There had only been a brief exchange of fire, and no word for ten minutes. Everyone around the radio was smoking, checking their weapons, fidgeting like if it weren't for gravity they'd flit off the planet. Fear sweat, fear funk, teeth grinding, jaws tightening, organs shrinking, getting ready.

"Lieutenant," the radio whispered, "we got two prisoners, wounded. We're out here, somewhere, fuck it's dark, we can see the hill. What do you want us to do? Should we kill these guys?"

The remainder of the platoon around Anderson and the radio looked at the lieutenant expectantly, while he looked back at us as if seeking our wish. "Yeah, kill 'em!" a grunt shouted. The Captain on the hill broke into the radio exchange, commanding, "Two, this is Six, have your men bring those VC in. They're worth a lot more alive than dead."

At that time the moral standards of the Geneva Convention were still a saving grace to be honored, elevating us above the terrible carnage perpetrated by the VC upon their own people. In our persistent war fantasy taking no prisoners, giving no quarter and expecting none, was the code of self preservation. But reason superseded our blind infantry rage.

Maybe the skipper could see through his field glasses from the hilltop, finding the ambush team gathered around two skinny prone bodies, afraid in the flare light, and seeing no other VC around. Maybe his intuitive knowledge of guerrilla warfare eliminated the possibility that there were other VC lurking in the dark. But I felt no such assurance. To me the flare light swinging down on nylon parachutes only further jeopardized my friends. I could sense in them the impulse to ensure their own safety by killing the two wounded prisoners outright, then heading for safe hiding, expedient and practical. Their fear was my own. If there were two, there were many. Any second could be the last second to take a breath, to feel the night heat sucking the blood out of your skin.

"Dale, the CO says bring them in. Forget the ambush, bring the prisoners in," Anderson ordered over the radio. Confusion and bewilderment crossed the faces of the gathered men. Those were our friends out there in the nightmare dark and the CO didn't seem to give a shit about them at all, all that asshole ever did was sit up on his hill drinking our beer, he never went out on ambush, he didn't know.

With cunning arrogance, taking the chance that even if there were more VC waiting in the dark to kill some rescue squad foolish enough to venture out just like the VC knew we would, my role and my love for them compelled me to tell the lieutenant, "I'm going to go out and get them." It wasn't a request, or a command. It was so foreign to his hearing that he had no response. "Who's with me?" I said to the men around me. Until then I'd been a good follower, but now I was taking the bit in my mouth, and there would be no denying me. Without waiting for permission or assent, I grabbed up my medical kit and headed for the wire. I don't know if the lieutenant nodded his permission to the rest of the platoon, but the squad followed, frightened, trailing behind a determined non-combatant, ill-trained and ill-equipped. Maybe they figured I needed their protection as much as the ambush team needed to be reincorporated to our mutual safety. Nevertheless, they came behind me, passing the sentries at the gate, down the road in front of the hill, slowing at the halt who goes there from the listening post, and skirting the hill silhouetted against the road in the flarelight, trotting, rifle slings rattling, canteens bouncing, fuck, if they're out here they got us in their sights for sure, hoping that the lieutenant had foresight enough to warn the ambush team that we were coming and they didn't shoot us as we came up on them.

My rationale was that Dale was my friend, that in the dark, frightened, holding members of the enemy forces, vulnerable because he was occupied with bringing the VC back in instead of watching for attack or ambush, he would be able to recognize my voice above any others. We'd all heard the stories of the Japanese and the Germans imitating American phrases then killing the unsuspecting GI dumb enough to answer them. Every fifty yards or so we'd stop and maintain silence, listening hard, hearing nothing but the sound of our own labored breathing and our rapid hearts.

Two hundred yards, two hundred years, down the road we stopped, kneeling to catch our breath, eyes searching through the gloom for movement, muzzle flashes, any sign of danger, then we heard the wheezing of the wounded prisoners. Thirty yards in front of us. Then we could hear the Marines who had the VC in their clutches harshly whispering keep going you mutherfuckers, keep moving.

I took a chance. Calling out to the ambush squad could invite them to open fire on us, or let the enemy know our position, calling out could get us all killed, but there was no other way. A platoon had a better chance than two separated squads. Calculating the distance between us, I threw my voice so it would just reach Dale, like lobbing a stone. "Dale, it's Doc. Go easy, man."

"Doc?" came the reply, disbelief and fear dripping from the sound. "Doc?"

"Yeah, it's me, it's me and the rest of the platoon. We're here to get you." Sensing his relief, we moved forward. Reaching him, he almost embraced me. "We got two prisoners, wounded, I shot them both." Expecting him to be proud, if afraid, I was surprised to find him nearly crying.

"The prisoners can walk?" I asked, in a hurry to get out of there, to get back, to leave the exposure held in the horrible dark.

"Yeah, the fuckers can walk. Let's get moving. These fuckers might have comrades." And no one had to give an order to turn around and head back for the hill. The last man set a healthy stride, leading us back, careless of stopping to listen for approaching enemy, the lure of the supposed safety of the perimeter our beacon.

Coming in through the wire the sentries were envious, stepping out of the dark to pat the ambush team on their backs, and to catch a glimpse of the Viet Cong. In the flare light I could see that their hands were bound with belts, and blood was coagulating on their wounds. Their injuries didn't seem serious enough to warrant allowing capture; a facial gouge on one man's left cheekbone, the other man with two superficial flesh wounds, shoulder and hip, like they were sacrificing their lives to wound our souls, knowing we would know their deaths forever. The two troopers walking behind Dale were carrying the captured weapons, two M-1s from the long ago war.

Lt. Anderson approached out of the dark, and without congratulation or welcome, told Dale and his squad to take the prisoners directly up the hill to the CO, the rest of us to stay down near the bunkers, there wasn't anything to see. Nothing to see? The protest was immediate. These guys could be the ones who shot Gonzales, or blew up Stemper and Owens and maybe they were the ones who shot up the company across the river, or laid the booby traps that would take one of us out tomorrow, and dropped the mortar rounds on us, no one hit, finally caught in the act, and we had them.

Even though the fear that there were more VC out there kept our voices quiet, the Marines gathering around the VC were sounding like they wanted revenge, like if given the slightest pretext, one bolting away, one spitting in defiance, someone would level a weapon and dispatch him, tough shit. But the CO wanted to view the trophies, and even if some of the men could barely remember Gonzales and Owens and the others, so quickly had they vanished, and it was such a curiosity to actually see real VC, they looked no different from any other middle aged Vietnamese men and most likely weren't, that a mild relief over not having to tear them apart or shoot them came over us as the ambush team took them up the hill.

We gathered around the radio at Lt. Anderson's bunker, waiting for word on the VC's fate. The .81 kept up a steady outpouring of illumination rounds, a new flare popping every four and a half minutes, keeping their heads down if they were waiting for a chance to move closer to the wire and if indeed there were more of them out there. The rest of the company was keeping an eye out while the squad that I had so arrogantly led out to rescue our friends told the story back and forth, still in a heat of accomplishment. It didn't matter that we'd encountered no enemy action. What mattered was that we took the chance. We'd ventured our lives for the lives of our friends. It was enough. No thanks, no good job was needed. No one could expect more from us, not tonight, anyway.

But the skipper had a company to run. He had told headquarters that there was going to be an ambush team at such and such coordinates, and he would not renege on his word. He sent a runner down the hill to tell the lieutenant that since the ambush team was going to be occupied being debriefed, the other half of the platoon would have to go out and take its place.

"The fuck we will, all due respect, Lieutenant," burst out of my mouth before I could regain my military compliance. It was spooky scary out there, I knew, I'd just gone out and I knew that the two VC weren't the only ones out there. Full of my defiance like a boy who'd finally had enough of his father and said, all right old man let's get to it, not even caring if he got knocked on his ass, letting him know was enough, I stood back from Anderson's eager gaze and said, "No way, Lieutenant. That would be the dumbest thing we could ever do. Straight suicide. Don't you think they know we'll be heading right back to that ambush site? Don't you think they'll be waiting for us? Just 'cause the CO has a hair up his ass doesn't mean we have to walk into an ambush, Jesus fucking Christ! what can that idiot be thinking?" In for a penny, in for a pound.

Anderson was calm, that was how you handled enraged enlisted men who were ready to kick your ass, total assertion of quiet power, brig, chain of command, gunnery sergeants who would take the defiant punk out in the dark and give him a lesson in military decorum. Refusing a direct order in a combat zone was punishable by firing squad. "You don't have a choice in the matter, Doc. What the skipper says, goes. No questions asked. When he says shit, you say what color. Now get your gear and get your dumb ass out there.

Saddle up, people," he said, waving his hand at the squad of Marines watching our exchange. I sensed that they were with me, that they didn't want to go back out into the horrible dark, that they had already spent their portion of courage for the night.

My own idea of the powers of the VC at the time was that they could communicate with each other by thought osmosis, that they could send messages through the air without aid of radio, that a current of kill the Americans, here is where they are going to be, interconnected each and every one of them at the brain like an electric tendon.

A corporal, a friend, said, "Doc, you're fucking with fate, man. We gotta go. The lieutenant's right." Receiving his message I made an impassioned speech to the whole squad, saying that it made no sense to throw ourselves into the meat grinder, nothing good would come of it, that if the Viet Cong wanted to do battle with us, here we were, that sending out another ambush team would be just plain stupid, if Charles wanted to move around out there in his paddies let him, there was no way in fucking hell that we were going to win this fucker tonight, no point in getting shot up or killed just because the CO doesn't have the balls to call Battalion and say we cancelled the ambush tonight. An ambush one way or the other, what difference would it make in the long series of fuckups those people called a war?

Seeing that my arguments were finding acceptance, Anderson tried the reasonable approach. "If you're chickenshit, what do you think about us sending out another squad from another platoon?"

"They shouldn't have to go, either, and I ain't chickenshit, Lieutenant. Didn't I just get back?"

But Anderson wasn't listening anymore. He radioed up to the captain on the hill, saying, "The corpsman doesn't want to go out again, Captain, and the troopers sorta feel the same way." I had implicated us all in a mutiny. Refusing an order in the face of the enemy, the fear of the repercussions huge compared even to going out and facing the enemy who might or might not be waiting for us to step into their sights. The monster of the military machinery was most certainly there, impinging upon every utterance of every officer. Court-martials, Leavenworth, Portsmouth, years of brutality to endure. It didn't matter if my fears of who awaited us in the dark beyond were imagined or paranoid delusions or real. My defiance was real, and there was no way to retract it.

"Tell the Captain, if he wants us to go out again, we'll go, but only if he comes along," I said, which was tantamount to calling him out to a gun fight in the street. It just wasn't done. To challenge a superior in any capacity, but especially to challenge his courage, was like sharpening the headman's ax for him. And I knew all that, but was too tired and too crazy to stop myself.

I stepped back, finished, the challenge had been delivered and I was waiting for the glove to be thrown back in my face, for the Captain himself to come thundering down the hill and personally kick my ass out through the wire calling me a chickenshit mutherfucker malingerer fucking up the morale of his troops, think you're a leader of men, asshole, get out there by yourself and don't come back in until you kill every one of those little yellow people, goddamn corpsmen. The men were agitated, torn between the sensible argument of a certain loony, their own absolute fears and the need to surmount them, and the duty of being a Marine, which meant complete obedience. They were shifting and fidgeting around, not sure of whether to pick up their weapons and head back out through the wire or to go to their bunkers, let some other squad do the deed, unfair as that might be.

But the Captain had bigger fish to fry than punk corpsmen and lazy troopers. The Marine Corps way was to demand and expect complete effort all the time, the only relief ever permitted was in death. Handling young men full of the fire of the fight required the application of history, though, so he solved the problem I'd generated by giving me what I wanted. First he said, over the radio, "Tell those people we ain't got a democracy here, we got people to kill, Lieutenant." Then he paused, and said, "Cancel the ambush."

Hearing the good news I looked at the rest of the platoon for approval, thinking that in the test of wills I'd won. But I'd violated the code, even if I'd expressed their deeper desire. By going along with me they'd stepped out of the normal chain of command, and by agreeing to the implicit refusal they'd broken with the natural order and the discipline that defined them as Marines. They looked back at me like I was poison, guts or no guts. I'd lost my bid to gain their trust and confidence. I retreated to my bunker to conduct an inner feat of denial, the sour flux of endless entropy warping through me, trying to get some of that sleep.

At first light the company corpsman came to take me up to the helicopter landing pad, the brass was coming down the hill with the VC prisoners and we were to inspect them before they were transported to Da Nang. We had to certify that they hadn't been beaten and brutalized while in our custody, before they were sent off to be executed. We joined the gathering clutches of men waiting at the pad.

The whole headquarters group came sauntering down the hill, beaming with pride and swaggering elan. The two VC were trussed in their midst, hands bound with comm wire, battle dressings loosely tied to their wounds. Reaching the landing pad the Captain pushed them both down to kneeling positions while fingering his .45.

The faces of the headquarters were uniformly flush with taking dexedrine to stay awake during the arduous interrogation, though none of them spoke Vietnamese. They'd spent the night poking the VC, examining their ancient weapons, probing into their barren pockets for documents and identification cards, threatening them with summary execution, heaping humiliation upon humiliation until it got light enough to land a chopper.

The VC were crying. Drawing close to them I saw they were peasant men, worn down to long muscle and bone by struggle, half their teeth gone, the soles of their feet wide and thickly calloused, salt tear trails caking their brown leathery cheeks. The Marines were teasing them, calling them gutless wonders because they were crying over being sent off to be executed by the ARVNs, if it were them they'd stand up and take it like a man, never give the enemy the satisfaction of knowing a weakness. Mud coated their black hair. Both men were probably in their forties, tending their fields like the men of their village had for a thousand years, defending

137

their families and their livelihood and their land like men everywhere. And in a few hours or in a few days they would be dead, dead after the ARVN beat their confessions out of them, or applied electrodes to their balls and sent jolts of concentrated anguish through their bodies until they wished to escape by dying, by being shot in the head or dragged behind an Amphtrack or thrown out of a helicopter, anything to make the pain stop.

Even clinging to my warrior shell, I was appalled at the delight being shown in the headquarters men's faces over the future of the two Vietnamese. I was reluctant to give my certification that they hadn't been brutalized, as if by withholding it I could somehow save them. At that moment the men were simply Vietnamese soldiers. I had no knowledge that they had committed acts of terrorism against their own people. They had been out last night to shoot us and kill us in an ambush, like we them. And that made us equals. But to allow them to be human I would have had to allow myself and the men around me also to be human, and I'd never learned how. In the pure fury of survival moment by moment there were really no past deeds done, only you and him, only now. It was exceedingly difficult to hold the Saigon government an entity of civil law.

Amid the jeering, the company corpsman leaned in close to me and said, "Lets get it done." And we lifted the battle dressings to determine the extent of the wounds. The wounds had been cleaned and dressed, though a bit sloppily—a concession to the pressure to afford the enemy no aid or quarter. We were, after all, Marines dedicated to killing the enemy, and that meant corpsmen too. Looking into the furrowed gouges made by the bullets I could see purple muscle netted with coagulated blood. There was no fat visible, no bone, no swelling. The men could have been made of leather. I caught one of their gazes for a brief moment, secretly giving him a breeze of compassion, both of us knowing it would do nothing to save them. It was just man to man understanding for a soul wrenching second.

"Yes, Captain, they're OK for transport," I said at the company corpsman's prodding. The Captain smiled. He had won. Now we were all in their death together.

After the helicopter settled in for its landing a Marine major accompanied by two Kit Carson scouts and two Marine MP sergeants, all dressed to the strac nines, stepped off proud and officious, like couriers of civilization, like it or not. Handshakes all around, the headquarters group by then completely responsible for the shooting and capturing of the two VC. That a third had escaped wasn't mentioned. The MP roughly grabbed them up, and forced them squirming into the hold of the chopper. The doorgunner never relaxed his grip on his gun. More handshakes, these officers knew each other, were in this deadly game together, then the chopper flew off, leaving us co-conspirators in the prop wash. The headquarters group turned and headed back up the hill, patting each other's backs.

Dale had only been watching from his seat on a nearby rock. When I approached him after the chopper took the VC away, he hardly nodded to me, even though we were tight. For a moment I thought I'd fallen from his grace by my refusal to go out and get ambushed, but soon saw that he was occupied mulling his own soul. His eyes were vacant, as if he'd retreated far back in his body and his time, and his shoulders were humped like he'd been sobbing.

"Hey, man, why so down? You did good," I said, already knowing the depth of his trouble. "You shot 'em, you caught 'em. That's what we're here to do."

"The gooks are going to kill them, you know."

"I know. Hey, man, it's their war."

"Then why do I have to be the one to carry it for them?" Dale said, the words choking in his throat.

"You ain't alone, Dale. We all carry that weight."

"I was going to kill them myself, last night. Damn I was scared."

"But you didn't. We're all scared, man, we'd be fools not to be."

"Man, I'm tired of this Mickey Mouse shit. I mean, what the fuck are we doing here? Did you see the look on those ARVN gook faces?

I mean, they were absofuckinglutely delighted to get those VC to kill. And the brass wasn't much better, talk about pigs in shit. I gave up heaven to give those shits a good time? I feel like a whore who can't even give it away anymore."

"We're living with monsters whose dreams are coming true, Dale. We got no choice but to go with it, even when you win you lose. Let's just stay alive, man, until we're gone, nothing better to do."

"I'm not so sure," he said, quietly, like the extra weight of those two soon dead men had bent him into a decision he'd kept in abeyance for years.

I could feel the sweet boy crying inside, the whole of the world a fist in his face, the promise of the land of the big PX had vanished, there was nothing more to expect but more of the same and it was going to get worse before it got better, no relief in sight. Lore had it that once you had the experience of shooting the enemy you acquired his power, that you became stronger, as strong as he and you or you and how ever many men you shot. But it wasn't true. I could feel the two VC feeding on my friend's heart.

"Why don't you try for a gig as driver, or go back to Battalion, hump a typewriter or something."

"Wrong MOS. Bravo 211, and that's it forever, shit, you know that, Doc."

"Sandy still writing you?" I asked, just to get his mind onto something, someone else When someone would ask me that same question I'd answer that, no I didn't have a girl back home, it wouldn't be fair to come here to Vietnam to maybe die and leave one behind, noble and fatalistic, and lying.

"Naw, she hooked up with some college clown. Fucking cunt. Shoulda known she was after officer material."

Double whammy, in a world of hurt. I handed him a few Robaxin to ease the tension, telling him, "Go zone for a while, I'll catch you later." There was nothing more I could say to him but to tell him that I'd be there for him when he wanted next to talk. I didn't know you could win heaven again.

140

Three days later he was somber, self-contained, but still alive when he and I and the whole headquarters group went out on an ambush. Apparently my challenge had gotten through, after all. For the first time ever the Captain, the XO, a new gunnery sergeant, the weapons platoon lieutenant, two staff sergeants, Marshal the radioman, and four other privates who I didn't know went out on an ambush.

Having to redeem myself in the captain's eyes, I volunteered to take the company corpsman's place on the adventure. Being in no heat to get his ass shot off and liking his sleep, Doc Broad gladly gave it up.

Swaggering down the hill with their carbines and rifles freshly cleaned and oiled, the group looked dangerously foolish. I had to stifle a snicker when I saw the old fat and forty sergeants gaudied up in night fighter greasepaint, wearing their most gruesome expressions. It was a hot night, but there was no sense of danger in the air, there'd been no repercussions from Dale's capture of the two Viet Cong, and no enemy activity reported in the entire sector. Charlie was probably taking the week off.

"Ah, it's the green machine," I said to Dale, and he laughed, but out of hearing of the officers. "We better watch our asses, these dipshits could get us greased," he said. At least he hadn't lost his sense of humor. It was better to not forget that the first thing an enlisted man learns are the consequences of not taking an officer, any part of him, seriously. Gunny Mead wasn't among them, and it's doubtful that he would have committed such a self-indignity to appear in front of the troops so outlandishly. To indicate to them by laugh or gesture that we didn't regard them as utterly complete warriors would have made them touchy, though, and touchy officers could be vindictive. We stiffened to attention at their approach, and at the motion of a hand signal, fell in behind them.

But they had it all wrong. They didn't wait for darkness to fall, or for the listening posts to be set, before going out through the wire. We left the perimeter in full view of the villagers who were then starting their cooking fires and readying their lamps. Neither did we hold close to the side of the hill when walking down the road toward where Dale's ambush team was to have set up their ambush. Nor did we pass much further than fifty or seventy-five yards down the road, settling just twenty or thirty yards beyond the apex of the hill where the CP was located. It was as if the Captain could not bear to be separated from his radios and his maps.

We deployed in a lazy line along the ditch that ran along the side of the road, still completely visible to any Vietnamese who happened along. I couldn't tell if the captain had so cleverly thought this ambush out that he wanted the Viet Cong to know where we were and how many we were, or if they had conspired to only show the rest of the troops that they were indeed as courageous as them, and were as willing to expose themselves to enemy attack, thereby negating any complaint that the officers ordered, the troops died.

The Captain put the sergeants one each at the ends of the line, took the center, and stationed the rest of us at twenty-foot intervals. He told us to take our safeties off, and to remain silent, which we did, reserving the observation that it was still near daylight and any Viet Cong worth his salt would be waiting until at least 2200 before venturing out. As soon as it got dark the mosquitoes began their foraging, and to ensure that if their were any Viet Cong about, they should avoid us and the trigger happy mob of unproven officers, Dale and I started slapping on insect repellent as loudly as we could, our only resistance to the absurdity. If the tenor of a voice could strangle, the Captain's order for us to quiet down us would have pinched our heads right off our necks.

So we quieted down like good little soldiers and we waited, watching the pale stars rise in the moonglow, and feeling the tension and anxiety boil in the headquarters group. They had a lot more to live for than we did, a lot more to lose, and had had little experience in mastering their fears. To Dale and me the signs just weren't right to expect an ambush or to encounter foolish VC loping down the road. We relaxed and waited. The plan was to stay out all night and, of course, to kill anyone moving around at night, girls home late from a tryst with their VC boyfriends, children taking home the buffalo. If the night belonged to Charlie, anyone but us moving around at night was logically VC. And if our sense of self preservation heightened every shadow, the headquarters people's fears were the same as ours, and manifoldly increased by their compulsion to prove themselves worthy. Even above the insect repellent scent I could smell beer and suet, fear and muscular tension. Eyes turning red-rimmed from peering and searching, jaws clenching at the distant sound of a bamboo gate closing, fingers spasming at hearing a burst of rifle fire a mile away. I guess I just couldn't believe it of the officers, but we were bagging it.

I'd been sitting between the Captain and the XO, and by the time midnight came around had developed a tremendous headache from absorbing their mounting tension. I could feel their muscles flex and tense, hear their breathing increase in labor, feel their hands clutch their riflestocks until the wood sweated oil. At midnight the Captain looked at the radium dial on his watch and whispered fiercely, "Enough is enough, we're heading back in."

"Thank fucking God," I said, though not so as he could hear me. "Nothing happening out here tonight, Skipper," I said, to congratulate his decision. My headache vanished.

We walked back in, silhouetted against the hill by the moonlight, Dale and I glad the short ordeal was finally over. The sergeants grumbled that we should have stayed out longer, hell, the gooks are all over the place, right? It was the last time the CO went out on ambush.

BAS

I'd been rotated back to the BAS, pulled in from the field to run sick-call while the ranked corpsmen looked busy with their clip-boards and their inspections. I felt demoted, unworthy of being a field medic, somehow responsible for my company having not come under much enemy fire. Back at the BAS I would be unable to prove that I would be there, down on the ground and right there with the wounded men, dragging them to cover and injecting them with a dose of perfect painless unknowing uncaring, be there to staunch the gushing gore, saving their young lives from being burned down to sacred mud and ash. To lose one's status, one's potential to become heroic, was a kick in the balls, no matter that the change was standard rotational routine.

And just to let me know that military humility was a character trait to be cultivated by teenage delusionals like myself, the chief corpsman handed me a M-14, two magazines, and assigned me to lead the garbage detail. So, five Marines and I rode down Highway One to the dump adjacent to the Da Nang airbase in the back of a six-by filled with refuse from the battalion tent-city.

Arriving at the dump we were swarmed by a gang of forty to fifty Vietnamese, fighting for any usable scrap. We had been warned that the peasants could use anything we threw away as a weapon against us (bury your cans), and we were outnumbered by the unarmed people yammering and banging at the sides of the truck. There was no way to peaceably stop them, but the Marines started yelling and shouting at them, just to get them away from the truck so we could unload the garbage and leave. Just throwing away trash created a life and death dilemma.

The yelling got louder and more abusive, hands and arms reaching and grasping at the trash as we shoved it off the back of the truck. A Marine fired some shots into the air to quiet the crowd. They were only momentarily subdued. Years of war and utter destitution had deadened their fear. Seeing that none of their crowd had been wounded by the rounds, they resumed their scrabble for C-ration tins and expended syringes, damaged military equipment and used bandages. The Marines were scooping the garbage off the back of the truck with their riflebutts while two men swung their rifles at the clamoring people to force their grasping hands away from the garbage as it fell. The Vietnamese faces were contorted with shame. If one's whole body can be reduced to an anguished sob, that was how the Vietnamese men looked, so debased, so humiliated. The Vietnamese women were tearing at the Marines and at each other with desperate greedy sorrow. The children, some wearing only shirts and cutting their feet on the open tins, were crying and rushing in at the edges of the growing pile like scavengers at a kill.

"Can we shoot these people, Doc?" A trooper asked, not joking.

"No, man. Let's just get this done and get us out of here," I said, and the Marines kept scooping. One Marine had finally had enough, though, and struck a Vietnamese man in the forehead with a solid buttstroke. Blood spurted from the gash, and the clamor died down.

The Marines finished clearing out the truck bed and the people milled through the garbage more quietly, hiding finds under their shirts or making little piles away from the main heap. I jumped down amongst them and took the injured man aside. I applied a small dressing to his forehead, securing it with adhesive tape. He needed antiseptic, and sutures to close the gash, but I had no antiseptic or even a clean place to work, so I could not stitch him closed. He was so sad and pitiful that it was difficult to remember that these were the people we'd come to wage war for and against. The Marines chided me for abetting the enemy. By way of an apology to the Vietnamese from my breaking heart, I got into my pack and produced some chocolate chip cookies sent from Mom, and passed them out. With all the wealth of the world at our demand, with all the fervor of our national compassion at hand, all I had to offer was a cookie.

◆◆◆◆

When I was running the BAS sick-call two MPs marched another Marine in for me to give a physical examination. He was under arrest and the exam was required to assure that the man had not been beaten, that he was physically able to undergo a court-martial.

He wasn't frightened anymore. It was a forgone conclusion that he would stand the court-martial, that he would be found guilty, be dishonorably discharged, and that he would spend the next eight years in Leavenworth Federal Prison.

"This is just a formality, Doc. I mean, I did it. I shot the sonuvabitch," he declared.

"Who?"

"Sergeant Collins."

"I can understand. He is, ah, was, a real shitheel."

"Aw, he was all right. He was just doing his job. You know, it just sorta happened. I was pissed to the eyeballs. He'd been on my case. We'd been out patrolling five weeks straight, on full alert five nights in a row. He told me to take the LP I told him, bullshit, I had the LP last night. I was pissed. He was pissed. He thumped me on the chest and walked away. I put three rounds in him. I tried to do right by him. I tried to get him to face off with me man to man, but the shithead wouldn't believe me, so I did him anyway. The cat was always down on me. Giving me shit details all the time, dig the slit trench, hump the ammo, get his rats, like I was his personal slave. Said I wouldn't shoot him in the back, like that makes a difference when you're gonna kill a guy."

I looked for sadness and regret in his eyes, but saw only resignation to the wind of the system.

"Fucker just fucked with me once too much."

We continued with the examination.

"They thump on you much?"

"Naw. They want me. They ain't gonna fuck it up."

I took his pulse and respiration, certified that there were no visible bruises, lacerations or broken bones, then signed the papers.

Everything was settled for him. He could hypnotize himself into zombie compliance. There would be no more decisions, no more fear in the dark, no more invisible invincible enemy, just the half life of prison.

"Don't feel too bad for me, Doc. It was bound to happen. I mean, shit, what can you expect when you give kids weapons? I'll be out by the time I'm twenty five. Semper Fi, Doc. Eat the apple, fuck the Corps."

◆◆◆◆

Bledsoe was screaming something incoherent in my ear. He had my shirt front clutched in his trembling fist, pulling my ear down to his mouth, because, even though he was screaming only a harsh whisper would come out. Heat was pouring off his body, his breathing was labored, his eyes wild with fright.

From what I could make out he was afraid that the medical men taking care of him considered him expendable, a disposable unit, that they were going to kill him with neglect. He said he knew there was no ice in this fucking country except back at the Regimental Officer's Club, and he was afraid that his brain was going to cook in its own juices, leaving him a child forever, or the fever would make him sterile, or maybe kill him. He hoped so. He was sweating profusely, and smelled of laterite, bile and salt. Because of his nausea no one would give him any water, even to soothe his throat.

Bledsoe was my man, a man from my platoon, and the cohesion between men in a platoon is so compelling that to not do my utmost for him, even going as far as sacrificing my life for him, was unthinkable. He'd been suffering chills and fever for two days by then, and I was telling him that he was going to be all right, malaria was no big thing, I'd get him some water, that I would be there with him and for him as long as he needed me, I'd get him over to Regiment at first light if I had to hold a gun to one of these pogues' heads. The doctor and the two NCO corpsmen were standing off in the tent shadows watching us, evaluating me. They called me away from Bledsoe.

"Why can't we give him some quinine? Let me wet him down. Start an IV, get some fluids into him," I challenged.

"Just stay away from him, Doc. We've done everything we're going to do for him. He just wants some sympathy," one of the NCOs said, scratching at the scaly patch of psoriasis that had taken his hair.

"But he's my man. You don't leave your man."

"You do as you are told."

"You don't have to do anything. I'll take care of him tonight, until we can get him to Regiment."

"Just leave him alone. Let him quiet down."

"He's afraid. He says you don't give a shit about him. He's afraid he's going to die."

"You better learn how to leave him alone," the doctor interjected. "What if you are out there in the field with a bunch of wounded? You'd have to leave him alone, then."

He was demanding that I abandon my duty, to deny the needs of a sick man.

"This ain't no firefight. There's no reason not to give him whatever comfort we can give him, sir," I insisted.

The chief corpsman stepped into the argument, saying, "If you don't leave him alone, he'll just get to expect it. We don't have time to molly-coddle this boy," he said, even though Bledsoe was the only patient in the tent. The throngs of wounded had failed to materialize at the tentflap. Taking care of boils, immersion foot, the creeping crud, crabs, clap, syph, dysentery, and a panoply of mysterious tropical diseases had undermined their dreams of being omnipotent surgeons valiantly saving shattered bodies at the front. Not even doctors are immune from being ruled by William Holden fantasies.

Bledsoe was still moaning, then he'd start screaming oaths and promises, warning that he would murder every single one of these rat-assed mutherfuckers that wanted him to die so bad. He grabbed me again, demanding that I give him a shot, put him under, knock him out, end his suffering, he didn't care how. "Do me a huss," he pleaded.

I slipped him a drink of Lister-bag water from my canteen, for which I was immediately admonished by the doctor.

"Get away from him. He is not your patient," the doctor claimed, and the corpsman dragged me away by the elbow.

"Get your gear and get back to your unit," the corpsman warned. "Get out of here now, if you know what's good for you."

I'd crossed too many lines, again. And it was night, I'd have to find a rack in one of the hardbacks or sleep in a fighting hole on the perimeter. I left the medical tent in a huff, disgusted, shaking with frustration and anger. The next time I asked about Bledsoe I was told he had been shipped over to Regiment a day later, and that he had died.

◆◆◆◆

I met a man who looked like he was easily fifty years old, and had worked hard all his life, catching the lash too often. He carried his weight as if one more speck of dust landed on him he'd collapse like he'd been hit by a bullet.

He was a squad leader, a demolitions expert from the engineer company. I asked him what was making him look like he was being crushed from the inside. He told me he was in charge of the mine sweeping detail. Every morning he and his squad would walk the road outside the Airbase, sweeping for mines, risking their lives and bodies with every breath and step.

"Charles puts them out at night, and we dig them up in the morning," he said, "Ain't no big thing," trying to be casual, like getting blown apart was just a natural thing to do. He could take anything if there was a time limit to it.

"Haven't I heard of some kinda special truck that does that? So you guys don't get your balls blown off?" I asked.

"Yeah, but it's back in Virginia, or somewhere there ain't no mines."

"Just like the big green machine," I said, in sympathy.

"There it is."

GUNNY MARINE

Gunny Marine wasn't satisfied to sit out on a sandbagged ambush with the CO until the CO couldn't stand it any more, coming in without even firing a shot. Gunny Marine had been waiting all his life to get into combat and such a paltry exposure to the enemy was demeaning, even perhaps, ridiculous. He'd just missed The Big One (by four years), and had missed Korea by a fluke of fate that landed him passing out blankets at Camp Lejeune, and no matter how often he requested transfer to an infantry line outfit there was some vicious pogue who didn't want him to gain rank or combat experience and kept losing his chits until the war was over and he was sent to Okinawa where he distinguished himself again as a supply sergeant. Being on Okinawa he missed the brief police action in the Dominican Republic, and was despairing of ever becoming a combat Marine, until Viet Nam began its internal conflagration.

No one seemed to know what his name was before he convinced someone in headquarters that combat outfits needed old Corps discipline and zealous leaders, like himself if he only got the chance. When his orders to Viet Nam, 26th Expeditionary Brigade, MACV, came through he was so ecstatic with his personal internal self image of mow-'em down courage that he had his name legally changed to the ultimate personification of manhood, Marine. He was a short clumsy dumpy fourteen-year-old in a forty-year-old body, but no one could argue with his name. He wore it like a shield over his heart.

He was one of the best equipped soldiers we'd ever seen jump off a helicopter. He was wearing his brand new flack jacket, new helmet, jungle fatigues, a .45 pistol, an M-1 carbine with extra taped-together clips, a K-bar, an extra battle dressing, four canteens, new boots, a morphine styrette taped to his dog-tags, a maniacal grin and a gleam in his eye like he was in love with each and every one of us.

He was assigned to weapons platoon. And other than sitting around shmoozing with the brass in the CP, his job was to keep track of supply. Daily, he'd inventory the number of mortar rounds stacked at the .81 pit, check the remaining 105 rounds for the six-barreled Ontos, order the rations and heat tablets, the bandoliers and rifle rounds, halizone tabs and replacement uniforms and boots. He saw his duty as a way to keep the Captain's ear, and badgered him constantly for an assignment to get out into the field with the men, sweep, search and destroy, recon, ambush, anything please, Skipper. He would monitor the radio net for clues of VC activity, interrogate incoming patrols, call acquaintances in other outfits, always the same question, any action out there. He was sorely disappointed when a platoon from 1/9 was ambushed and wiped out, not hearing about it until it was too late to go and save them. The Viet Cong were teaching us a lesson, they'd methodically gone into the ambush zone putting a round into each head, making sure. But for the grace of God go we, my brothers dead, my friends dead, oh aching heart.

But this was during the time of small unit patrols, no call for weapons reinforced company sized operations, and therefore a stall in his ambition to become a hero. During the battle for the Ia Drang Valley I was hunkered down in my bunker praying to any god I could name that we would be spared, that new in country Air Mobile Army pride would prevent them from calling in Marines to rescue them, but Gunny Marine was needling and cajoling, calling us all a bunch of pussy mutherfuckers if we didn't demand that Regiment send us over to help the poor Army guys, you know they couldn't fight their way out of a paper bag with a K-bar. We didn't go, so I guess my gods were in a better mood than his. And though there was still plenty of desire to engage the enemy, the look on the faces of the other men in the outfit when we heard of the long slow slaughter being suffered by the Army was that of stricken shock, that could be us, there was no way out, it was merely a matter of chance, some ambitious general deciding whether we'd live or die as units in his experimental crusade.

We were put on alert, ambushes cancelled, no patrols, a kind of rest while we waited and gathered courage in abject resignation. Every time a howitzer shell would freight train over we'd look up, as if its sound trail were a road that would lead us through the sky toward Pleiku. There was also definite movement in Le Mai below us. The night lamps stayed lit longer, there was more cooking smoke in the air, the people's shoulders were more deeply bowed as the women and children and old men bent to plug the rice sprouts into the manured mud.

Gunny Marine was in a frenzy. He could sense there were Viet Cong, maybe even NVA regulars, down in the hamlet and he wanted to mount a patrol to go in there and flush the little yellow bastards out in the open and kill them. When the word came down from Regiment that, no, the Marines would not be going into the hamlet but would remain in a defensive posture in the event there was a ground attack on the fort, but that the ARVN troops operating out of Da Nang would be, Gunny Marine was given his chance. He would join with the ARVNs as an advisor, a recognized and acceptable role.

Receiving his permission at noon, he spent the rest of the day strutting around the hilltop, his pudgy face contorting into fierce grimaces, his pockets bulging with hand grenades, stroking his carbine, saying to anyone in his path, "Yes, yes, I'm going out tonight! Gonna get some. Damn fucking straight. Going out with the zips. Chickenshit fucks. They're gonna see how a Marine can kick some dink ass." There was a determined homicidal gleam in his eye, and we all sort of shied away from him, lest his charge toward self destruction whirl us into its catch.

He waited with the sentries at the gate, fidgeting, cupping his cigarettes in his helmet, until the platoon of ARVN soldiers arrived at midnight. "That fucker is crazy, man," a grunt said as Gunny Marine went through the wire to join with the Vietnamese platoon.

His walk toward them was strong and casual, as if he carried with him the entire might of all the arms borne by the whole of America. This was his chance to become Chesty Puller, a man respected among men, maybe his chance to win the Congressional Medal of Honor, a Navy Cross at least. He advanced directly to the ARVN commander, a jovial young officer with a Mike patch on his jungle fatigues, and the troop moved off toward the hamlet, vanishing into the cloudless dark and the darker gloom of the village.

The platoon marched right in through the main gate of the village, just past the concrete ruin of the house from where Gonzales had been shot and where we spent the sandbagged ambush nights. They weren't gone twenty minutes before small arms fire flashed its death from the denser tree-thick dark.

The ARVN platoon had been discovered, ambushed, shot at, maybe killed. The snarl of the rifle fire was quick, fierce, expertly executed, a short burst from ten to twelve rifles on automatic. Several minutes passed, we on the hill looking into the village hoping to see or hear some sign that our allies hadn't been massacred, fervently hoping that we wouldn't have to go after them, and surely walk into the same trap. Another burst of fire opened up, but this time from the opposite direction. The ARVNs had survived the ambush.

In the dark, the rifle fire opened up again. Both sides firing directly at each other, fierce, absolute, violent yellow flashes in two spreading lines like a mitosis of lightning. We could feel the bellow of murderous intent swell like a shock wave as the ARVNs and Viet Cong shot at each other, the pent energy of their thousand injuries focused at the muzzles of their guns. A ball of white-yellow heat exploded, then another, grenades thrown from the ARVN platoon. Another furious fusillade erupted, several more grenades exploded, we could hear the muffled crump and the ripping tears of bullets rending the air. Then a pause. A few shots from the ARVN platoon, the VC were turning, running. Fifty yards away the VC took position and fired back at the ARVNs, and the ARVNs, waiting until the firing tapered off, were then up and running after them, viciously pursuing them, firing on the run, until the VC squad split apart and vanished.

And there we were sitting on our hill, already primed to run down and enter the village and go after the VC, scared but willing, and fascinated. There was a whole other war going on in which we could find no interlock in our own lives. Those men out in the dark, the ones searching through the brush and hootches, probing with the flashlights and grenades into the bunkers under the houses, shouting to each other in screeching Vietnamese that they'd found a wounded one, and then we'd hear the hollow cough of a .45, were so frightening in their intense mutual murder that I could feel them only as relishers of death, mutual ritual conspirators inviting the bullet that would end this wretched existence and release them into the next, certainly better one. Out in the night I could feel their dark breathing flames, their eyes piercing into the holes where their loving brother enemy lay moaning and trying to push his intestine back in, how did this happen?, oh Amita take me into the light! life pulsing and flickering out, sudden black, the last face hovering in consciousness mother crying. Mad nation, mad mind, mad men.

But it was their war and the deaths belonged to the Vietnamese soul, and we weren't about to risk good Marines to help the ARVNs mop up, it was over anyway. Like they say, it happens so fast. So we waited, even though it was more than likely that one of our own was out there, dead or wounded, merely sending up illumination rounds to help them finish their gruesome tasks.

At dawn the ARVN platoon ambled toward the gate, Gunny Marine striding along with them in a bubble of ecstasy. The platoon was all accounted for, though dirty, exhausted, some wearing battle dressings. None of them had been killed. It was a clear victory, though there was no exact count on how many Viet Cong had been killed. Six, maybe eight, they only found two bodies, and two more in holes, even after searching all night. Gunny Marine dispatched one of the sentries at the gate to fetch two cases of C-rations, then waved good-bye to his comrades in arms, floating up the hill as loose and spent as after a three day debauch in a Thai skivvy house. His face was flushed red and he was smiling, carrying his carbine over his shoulder by the barrel. His pockets still bulged with grenades.

Young Marines gathered around him asking, "Got some, Gunny? How many'd you get?" or saying, "Chesty Puller rides again, eh Gunny? Shit, Gunny, you sure look good, you going out again tonight, take my squad with you, we'll kick some gook ass for sure." But the sergeant wouldn't talk, just looking back at the admiring coterie with his benevolent tolerance, implying that he had killed many many enemy himself and there was no way to reach his exalted plane of being except by doing the same, damned if he even had time for such clamoring punks, we could go out and earn it like he did.

By the time we reached the top of the hill and the gunnery sergeant received the handshakes and congratulations from the officers waiting there for him the sun was up bright and hot. He was nearly stumbling from fatigue, but still smiling that secret smile, and still not answering anyone's questions, including the CO's. Marines drifted in and out of his atmosphere of the conquering hero, willingly basking in its bloodthirsty warmth, a way to absorb some glory, some courage. And just as awed and attracted to mythman action as everyone else, I approached with my medical kit, saying, "You OK, Gunny? That was some fierce shit you were into last night. You catch any shrapnel?"

"Naw, they never touched me" he said, puffing out his chest, invincible. But I saw a trickle of blood oozing down the side of his nose, and looking more closely I saw a quarter inch tear.

"Well, I'll be damned. I knew you couldn't go through that shit without getting some on you." I said, ebullient with the notion of men braving all odds and suffering all blows to their bodies and minds without flinching, good Marines. "You got a Heart, Gunny. A tee-tee Heart, but a Heart." And making a show for the group of men around us, I took out my surgical kit, took out the forceps and probed the nose wound, extracting a tiny piece of shrapnel. I handed it to the grinning sergeant, saying, "There you go, Gunny, a souvenir." Then I filled out a medevac tag to certify my finding and wired it to his flack jacket. Date and time of wound, nature of injury, place of occurrence. "There you go, Gunny, one Heart," I said. I was doing my part for unit morale. I caught a look into his eyes though, expecting to see an enviable realized man, hungry on the warrior trail, his determination to fight and win shielding him from accident or death, making him sure and confident, a man to follow and respect. But what I found looking in there, looking past his grinning tired veneer, was a knotted worm of self doubt, a brutal convolute confession that he'd never be able to reveal. It was so strong I was embarrassed for him as a man, shamed that I'd looked in and discovered his cowardice, and I backed away blubbering something kind.

To shame him by exposing what I thought I saw would be the same as casting contempt on every man in the company, on the Marine Corps, a truth that could not be tolerated in a body of men whose lives depended on the belief that we would always win. I don't know what actually happened to him out there with the ARVNs. He may have valiantly stood up and blasted away, mowing them down, tossing grenades, screaming after the Viet Cong in a state of violent glee, finally realizing a lifelong ambition. Maybe.

But I never saw him much after that. He never went out with us, content to stay up on the hill with the officers unless the whole company was called upon for a sweep, content to let us believe about him that he had performed well with the ARVNs, that he had killed many many enemy and now he no longer had to prove himself to any man, least of all us kid grunts, a man completely satisfied and hence intractable to orders or ambition. I do know though that he never turned in his medical chit for his Heart.

FLAG DAY

It was Flag Day. The newly hired emissaries of the Saigon government had arrived on a day when we had gone out on a company sized patrol, showing force, emulating the French tactics of conquering by sheer size, as if even a half million dedicated soldiers somehow magically outnumbered 17 million Vietnamese, poor as they might be, hostages to each other's murderous intent When we returned, the shady green of Le Mai was fluttered over by at least fifty bright yellow spanking new flags, streaming south in the breeze off the South China Sea. It was a splendid show of the government's concern for its citizens, a clear statement to the Viet Cong of just who was running the show there, a trifling matter that its landlords were living splendidly in Da Nang on their four hundred percent a year rents. The ARVNs had occupied the hamlet to insure that the celebration would go on uncrashed.

On seeing the grand display, Private Palmquist flew into a rage. "Just who the fuck do those people think they are?" he was complaining, exercising his version of the truth, "That ain't no more an ARVN village than my mama lays eggs. If any flag flies over that place, it ought to be American. We're the ones dying for it!" Another Marine patiently explained to Palmquist that, "We're not really here, man, there hasn't been a formal declaration of war, we're not here to occupy or take over this shithole. We're just here to help these people out whether they like it or not. That's why we don't even fly our flag over our positions. This is their country, not ours. I mean, who'd want the place?"

But Palmquist wasn't satisfied. "Any place an American is, is America." He was emphatic, certain, the essential truth of his statement supported by an entire rifle company, a battalion, a regiment, the Seventh Fleet. Palmquist was the Marine who had kept bugging the Captain to build an observation tower at the foot of the hill so he could man it and shoot invading gooks like a prison guard. He could see himself alone and aloof, singularly protecting the camp, wiping out the enemy with his machine-gun, screaming his rebel yell. "I'm gonna see the skipper. If we can't fly the Stars and Stripes, by God, we can fly the Stars and Bars. It ain't official, but it'll let 'em know who's here."

And even though Palmquist produced a Confederate Flag from his sea-bag, the Captain could not permit it, citing the argument that even though we might feel we were still in America, it really was Vietnam, not Korea, or the Philippines, or Japan, and that is why you can't fly the flag or marry some girl you find down in the skivvy houses, or buy property, or vote, you are in service to your country, it's gotta be that way, private, hang your flag up in your bunker if it means that much to you.

Which is what he did, generating a fist fight between him and a black member of his squad, and the ultimate confiscation of the flag by his lieutenant. Confiscation was the only way to achieve peace in that section of the perimeter. But the black men of the company knew the story, and knew that the Captain had granted permission, the fact of that sentience compounding their desolation.

But it was a pretty day, weeks since a shot was fired or someone had their leg blown off by a booby trap. Conditions were safe to take the mile walk down to the new village built by the pacification program, modeled in two-by-four and corrugated tin, to buy a Coke and pick up our laundry. Nearly a quarter of what remained of the company began drifting toward the market stalls, carrying our weapons and military script. An easy day, an easy walk, a day off.

With the war so large in our heads, it was surprising that daily village activity never ceased. Approaching the marketplace we saw Vietnamese women carrying their goods for sale and trade in suspended wicker, dressed in black pajamas and conical hats, nearly indistinguishable from each other, peasant women with sharp eyes, sharp tongues and precise money minds. Reaching the market they'd set out their goods of vegetables, hats, sewn clothing, black market cigarettes and military rations, kapok pillows and rattan tatami, kerosene lamps and cotton wicks. Services offered were laundry, boot-shine, haircut, lice picking; even authentic Vietnamese meals—rice, fish sauce and fish served in one of the corrugated tin stalls that comprised the refugee housing behind the marketplace. Affectionate bodily contact between Marines and the local indigenous population was forbidden, though. But bodily contact was not denied to the ARVN soldiers who were also availing themselves of the market that day.

At least two platoons of ARVNs had also shown up, snarly, boisterous, richer by far than the women living in the stalls, and richer than their husbands who'd disappeared into the war. As Wilson, Anderson, Marshall and I sat on one of the slat benches that stood in front of a Coke stand we watched the ARVNs amble in, some holding hands, or arms around each other's shoulders, laughing, yelling commands to the women in the stalls, gesturing with their brand new American issue rifles, proudly displaying their new starched fatigues with bright yellow patches and new jungle boots.

"Catch the vines on those dudes," Wilson said, expressing our resentment. "We're sitting here in garrison rags, still wearing regulation boots, I ain't been clean in a month, and there's Uncle Sugar giving our stuff to the dinks."

"If you want some of that good shit, Wilson, all you gotta do is buy it from the mamasans," Marshall said.

"No way, Jose. Marine Corps wants me to look like shit, I'll be glad to accommodate them."

"Catch that cat," Anderson pointed, "that ain't no gook." He was indicating the biggest Vietnamese we'd ever seen, well over six feet tall and two hundred pounds. His skin color was lighter, and the rest of the ARVN soldiers gave him respectful distance.

"He isn't," I offered. "He's gotta be Chinese."

Which confirmed our suspicions that the ARVN ranks were infiltrated with Chinese cadre, though why they would tolerate the obvious presence of an enemy in their ranks was beyond any other explanation than they were all waiting to see which way the war winds would blow or he was the adventurous son of a Cholon merchant class family.

As the afternoon wore on, the marketplace became crowded with ARVNs and Marines, the two factions naturally dividing to occupy either half of the stalls. The noise of chatter and bargaining rose in falsetto and basso, each side warily regarding each other, scrip, dollars and piasters changing hands.

A woman let out a shriek, then began wailing and sobbing, spitting betel juice and opening and closing a tin box, her eyes searching through the crowd. It was clear that she'd been robbed, the figure of something over a hundred dollars American, the equivalent of six months' labor in the paddies. She started rummaging though the wares in the nearby stalls, still wailing and sobbing, spewing epithets in emphatic Vietnamese. Another woman shoved her back, sending her tumbling into the big Vietnamese soldier, which toppled him into a gathered group of ARVNs. A Marine was caught in the middle of the tumble, and went sprawling, losing grip of his rifle. An ARVN put his foot down on the rifle, preventing the Marine from picking it up. His buddy rose up from his sitting position, and butt stroked the ARVN.

My friends and I didn't want to get mixed up in the melee. As far as we were concerned the money that was stolen was only going to be spent on weapons and booby traps to blow us up, the further gone, the better. But in the midst of our friendly joking and relaxation that old feeling like the world was about to end, that sensation of the impending fire fight like when you jump out of a helicopter or you are about to walk into an ambush zone or entering into an enemy held village, the sudden constriction of vision when the mind at once prepares to end and turns to electric mush excluding all else but what can be killed in front of you came over me. Ion storm swirl, every body cell alert and trying to leave, freezing brain panic, meth jolt, breath streaming flame, staccato nausea waves, bowels turning to water, the very atomed air visible, blue goldheaven haze muttering in your head. The sensation was there, I was feeling it, but I was confused because we were in a neutral place amongst our allies, among the men with whom we were to fight the Viet Cong. But the noise had stopped, all I could hear was heavy breathing and Marshall tugging on my shoulder saying, "Get down, Doc." He was bringing his rifle to his shoulder at the same time.

Startled, I looked around, and saw that the women and children had moved away from the market stalls, backing up hurriedly, and two walls of men were facing each other across the entrance aisle, their rifles pointed at each others' chests. Oh fuck, a sudden death stand off, each side-staring at each other with furious molten eyes. If you could see through the shade thatch the two groups of men looked like a cell's chromosomes dividing.

This is absolute assured mutual destruction, I remember thinking. There's no where to run to, no where to hide, the space is so confined that with that many weapons firing on automatic everyone is sure to be killed. It didn't matter if I had nothing to do with sparking the altercation. It only mattered that if someone pulled the trigger that I be there with my own weapon firing until the enemy stopped or I was killed outright. My medical kit and role would be useless until afterwards, if there was one. Without even thinking I found my pistol in my hand.

Everyone behind the two standing files of men was on the ground, primitive mind churning, rifles shouldered, waiting for the urgent seconds to turn to violence. Pride and honor were at stake, the two allies not allies at all, but enemies constrained by politics. There was no possibility of winning for either side. It would be slaughter, death to every man, equally armed and equally offended, equally resolved to live or die. Wisdom said run away, but the cohesion of men under arms is so strong wisdom had no chance to arise.

The stand-off went on for tense minutes, neither side of facing men daring to move or blink, safeties off, rifles held hip high, ready at the slightest twitch to cut the other side down. Then something astonishing happened. A young Marine lieutenant casually broke out of the rank and stood in the very center of the face off.

He smiled at the ARVNs, then turned his back on them, and began speaking softly and gently to the Marines. He said, "This is hopeless, men. The Marine Corps doesn't need you dead. A dead Marine is useless. It doesn't matter who started it, all that is way past gone by now. We have to show those people we have more balls than they do. We have to put our weapons down." Incredible bravery. The ARVNs could have used that moment of diverted attention to cut us down. It took a few more moments of mollification, subtle calming argument, but the Marine who'd butt stroked the ARVN soldier finally relented, and lowered his rifle. Slowly, still wary, the other Marines lowered theirs. When all the rifles in the front rank had been lowered, the ARVNs lowered theirs. And it was over. The relief was like cool air rushing in to fill a vacuum. Time to go back to the base camp and prepare for the battalion sized operation tomorrow. An operation in conjunction with the ARVNs. We drifted back with our clean clothes and a new respect for the lieutenant. He was the one who'd dropped the mortar round on the mess tent.

166

SERGEANT BOTTS

Our company had been held in reserve during Operation Starlight, the biggest offensive conducted by the Marines up until that time. There was a regiment of Viet Cong operating around Chu Lai, future site of a huge military complex and the purpose of Starlight, other than wiping the Viet Cong off the face of the earth and striking fear into the hearts of any Vietnamese even vaguely considering siding with the Commies, was to clear the surrounds of enemy activity, thus ensuring uneventful work days for the thousands upon thousands of construction men and new troops being shipped in to control the country. News of the construction project precipitated compounding fear that our original scheme of going in, suppressing the couple of thousand Viet Cong working the northern area of South Viet Nam and winning the hearts and minds of the grateful peasantry with our few battalions of valiant Marines was being superseded by ambitions of megadeath. The fabulous military machine was cranking up for a campaign of complete dominance, even bringing in Bob Hope and a bevy of sexgirls to make us feel at home, pizza and radio, creating a great concrete scab from which the various forms of exploding persuasion could be efficiently delivered. And every form set, every nail driven, every violent wet dream mentally ejaculated there manifested its equivalent back home in the World, times ten. Bad times were coming.

Out on patrol we had run into more and more Army units, and more and more Marines, all of us looking for the same enemy, suffering the same heat and muck, leeches and dysentery, the same contemptuous resignation from the people whose lives we'd walk through and maim, feeling their baleful eyes peering into us from under the women's conical hats, their betel blackened mouths involuntarily spitting, the kids clamoring for one cigarette, gimme number one cigarette GI, and imitating us as children with sticks for guns, their futures already recruited, but by which side no one could say for sure. And each soldier's desire to engage the Viet Cong also sent its mental message into the nationsphere, generating its same heat in the men filtering down from the north to meet us and eject us, body and soul.

Hearing that we were being held in reserve caused the captain to feel unworthy, as if even though we'd lost many men to disease, mines, and sniper fire, he personally had failed to find and engage and kill a large number of Viet Cong and hence was less of a commander than was expected. Terse, gruff, absolutely powerful, he wasn't going to let the biggest operation of the war so far pass by without some form of participation. A good officer knows when to take the initiative. He had a plan.

The limits of operation for the company were two thousand meters beyond the French fort, and as the Phantom flies crossing the Song De and going back up into the sharp hills beyond the river plain was within that limit. Every time we'd gone into the village across the river we'd taken fire. We'd captured thirty or forty Viet Cong suspects over there, including a few soft handed women who were certainly cadre, yet more VC kept arriving. Probably coming down the canyons and draws of the jungled hills to take sanctuary in the ancient lush setting of banana trees and pineapple bushes, paddies and wells. The captain would mount a routine sweep around the village, just to let the peasants know we were still there, we still had our eyes on them. It would be conducted as part of our daily operations even though it was to happen during Starlight. If there was need to mount up and go to the aid and rescue of some other Marine outfit, there would be ample time to regroup. But the actual purpose of the sweep was to act as a diversion. We'd cross the river in amphtracks, form up in a column and as the column crossed the small streams coursing out of the hills a few squads would sneak off and go up the stream falls to ambush any Viet Cong coming down through the cover of the jungle. Like Charlie couldn't count. We called the captain Skipper, Captain, the CO, but most often: Whitefang. Whitefang was the name of the dog belonging to a cartoon character named Dudley Dooright, and I don't know who first snatched the simile from our mental stratosphere, but the name stuck to him unshakably, reaching mutual perception among the enlisted men instantaneously.

He would lead. The initial phase of the sweep wouldn't take more than a few hours, and he could be back at the CP to monitor the progress of Starlight, no one the wiser. After all, risk and daring was the name of the game, men getting themselves killed and blown up was what they got paid for.

After the CO told us, "Find them! Kill them! Good hunting, men," we clambored into the steel boxes of the Amphtracks, shut in and riding above hundreds of gallons of gasoline, one rocket round in the right spot and we'd feel the pain too many Vietnamese had suffered from napalm. As a prelude to the operation Whitefang ordered twenty rounds of H&I to be mortared onto the village, the vacuums of the exploding rounds expected to draw the enemy or infuriate him into attacking.

The river crossing was endless, it's the not knowing what is waiting for you, another merciless hump through the blistering heat or the rain so thick you can't find enough oxygen to fill your lungs, or a machine-gun nest quickly set up to cut you down as you jump from the track ramp, sudden black, your brain asking who will help me now, go to everlasting sleep big baby, or mortar rounds that would send three inch chunks of burred steel searing clean through you, the fear always present, but this time it didn't happen, like last time and the time before that, but you never know.

Attached to one of the two squads detailed to slip away unnoticed by eyes busy hiding from a rain of mortar rounds, I was following behind Sergeant Botts, crawling low under the greening brush until we were far enough up the steam canyon to walk unseen. And if Whitefang was the behavioral equivalent of a dutiful dog, Sergeant

Botts fit perfectly our saying, "You know the difference between the Marine Corps and the Boy Scouts? The Boy Scouts have adult leadership."

Botts practiced isometric exercises, narcissistically converting pleasure to pain to become a hulking bulked onanist with his brains knotted down in his neck, a square protruding challenging jaw and a shelved brow, twelve years in the Corps and still E-5. While many of us had John Wayne, Aldo Ray, Captain Blood and Zorro running around in our imaginations, Botts seemed to have no imagination at all. He was diffident and slightly menacing, as if the Marine Corps Manual supplied him with ample guidance and food for thought. It was the only book I ever saw him read, sitting stripped to his olive drab shorts on top of his bunker, muscular, bronzed, and bewildered. It is fair to say he was uncomprehending of our situation.

Botts kept pushing the squad further and further up the narrow stream draw as if he was certain there were no ambushers waiting for us, and well past the two thousand meter limit. The rise was fairly steep, the canyon walls sharp and jagged. The constant rains had sucked the softer minerals from the rock, leaving a honeycomb loess that might hold your weight when you reached for a handhold, or might crumble in your grip. Bamboo and thorn bush grew in pockets along the draw, the hill slopes beyond growing teak and camphor. And if it weren't for the war churning through our brains it would have been a beautiful place, gurgling clear clean water, sunlit bamboo leaves, shade from the relentless sun, a place to stop and rest and think and dream of home.

Near the top of the draw, where the stream turned to the north and through another shallow valley, we found an open flat of stream bed, a hundred feet of quiet water. Sharply fractured rock littered the stream gravel, and the water was ankle shallow, gleaming and cool. It was as good an ambush site as we were likely to find and most of us felt we were way too far from home for comfort, anyway. Our mission was to ambush any VC coming down the stream bed, and in the interest of remaining undetected, and officially not there, we weren't to use the radio, at all. The VC out here in the Indian

Country hills could be monitoring our transmissions. "Goddamn, Sarge, how could they know where we are, we don't know where we are?" "Just do as you are told," Botts replied, and set us to work.

We set about clearing the flats of the bedrock basalt of stone fragments, using them to build low protective walls from behind which we could fire and sleep. It was work familiar from childhood, from ancient muscular motion that built parapet and wall, castle and moat. The walls weren't continuous or contiguous, but individual semi-circles of rock spaced every fifteen feet or so, starting at a small falls and ending at the bend in the steam. Each two man team could place their trust of life and limb in each self-devised protection, like neurosis. Soon we were finished, chinking the openings with pebbles, then sitting back to make a cheese and crackers can stove with a P-38, heat up some beanyweenies, eat, and wait.

So it is mid afternoon, and we ten are casually kicked back, rifles leaning against our impromptu balustrades, shirts and flack jackets off, helmets pivoting on muzzles, Jackson and Smith, me and Botts, two new guys, Washington and Palmquist, and LeFever and Ortiz. In the heat of the day the assumption was that no one but fools like us would be moving around, so we're telling Sgt. Rock stories, grab-ass and jive, then quieting down enough to hear the dragonfly wings hovering above the flowing stream.

Behind us rose a steep thickly jungled hillside, and before us, across the flat in the stream bed, rose another two hundred foot hillside. There were only two ways out of the box we'd framed for ourselves, one back down the tumble of falls and rock, and the other further and deeper into enemy territory. Overhead the canopy was too thick to allow for helicopter pick-up or resupply.

Feeling like we were fish in a barrel, I had to know what was beyond the bend in the stream, if it was a possible escape route or if a company of NVA were also having their lunch, or if any form of menace lurked there. The rest of the men seemed satisfied to simply wait for night and worry about what might happen then, but I felt compelled to go exploring, not completely trusting in the valiant confidence of my friends. Telling Botts I was going out for a look-see, he gave his permission with a lazy nod, like there was no point in trying to manage the corpsman.

Lapsing into childhood wonder, I stepped out into the shallow water, looking for likely stones that might be hiding fish or salamanders, hoping I wouldn't run into a habu or a krait, walking through the cooling water, and reaching LeFever and Ortiz interrupted their daydreaming by telling them I was going further up stream, I'd be back pretty soon.

"OK Doc, don't step in any shit," LeFever admonished, both of them returning to their napping.

The moment I left their line of sight I was overwhelmed with the sensation that I was completely alone in the middle of a completely hostile country, helpless and alone in the middle of the Viet Cong jungle. My skin was growing eyes. Insect brain, monkey brain, man brain calling back millions of years all alive at once, that feeling again, the enemy is afoot. Then there he was, standing right in front of me not twenty feet away. Young, wiry, black pajamas, no hat, a wicker ruck full of rice strapped to his back, Ho Chi Minh sandals, no weapon. There is a look of startled apprehension in his eyes, as mystified as I am over finding his counterpart staring him in the face. I see his hands move to pat his body to find a weapon, but there is none to be found.

I forget that I have my pistol strapped to my waist. He is just a boy, a skinny kid who I could easily break in half over my knee if I got close and mad enough. A hundred kinds of panic whip through me. What am I supposed to do? Shoot him, capture him, warn the others? If I shoot him will that tell the maybe ten or twenty or fifty other Viet Cong behind him that there are Marines in the area, mount the attack? If I don't, will, if they're out there, the extra few minutes it'll take for him to get to them, give us enough time to wake up and defend ourselves? Is it fair to kill an unarmed kid who was just carrying rice, probably under duress, everybody has to eat, what honor is there in starving your enemy to death, without him the warrior is a more dangerous character? If in this split second my dumbfoundedness provides a common mercy will the war be lost or won? If I don't shoot him will my friends call me a chickenshit dufus, will my soul forever be stained and torn with his young life driving me into helpless turmoil no reparation could erase?

My eyes leave him for the half second necessary to unflap my holster and reach for my pistol, and in that time he is gone. Flit up a trail beside the stream, into the bamboo shadows, and I can't see him anymore. I am relieved, perplexed, instantly knowing that even as a corpsman my duty was to have shot the VC courier, and brought his carcass back to the ambush site as a trophy, let the chips of the future fall where they may. Embarrassed, my shame mounting, a new larger set of priorities leap into mind. I turn and hurry back to where LeFever is still napping and Ortiz is spinning his helmet on his flash suppressor. I have to warn the whole squad, meaning I have to tell each one of them that I was standing face to face with a VC and didn't have presence of mind enough to kill him, as they are sure they would have. To be quiet about it, to cover my embarrassment, would be to invite further disaster, allowing any other VC thereabouts the opportunity to shoot us down without warning.

"Didn't you see him?" I demanded of Ortiz. At the urgency in my voice LeFever stirred.

"See who? I ain't seen nothing," Ortiz said.

"The gook, the goddamn gook, right there, I just saw him."

"So where is he now?" LeFever asked, my adrenal charge waking the same in him.

"He took off, just up the stream there." I said, pointing back up the stream, "I gotta tell the Sarge."

Passing the other positions I warned them, saying that there was at least one VC, maybe more headed our way, get ready. By the time I reached Botts the men were readying their rifles and eyeing the upstream reach.

"What's going on, Doc?" Botts said, laconically, like nothing bad ever happened, especially to him. If anything horrible happened to one of us, that was our problem.

"I just saw a gook. Upstream. He was carrying rice, no weapon."

"So?" Botts said, like the news was conflicting with his personal daydream. His eyes were glazed with self-absorption.

"If there was one, there are more. And now they know we're here. We better get ready."

"Why didn't you shoot him?" Washington asked, his posture reflecting my wild eyed anxiety.

"I wasn't looking for him," I answered, which didn't seem to satisfy him. His mouth grimaced in contempt for my sorry ass.

"Did Doc see a gook?" one of the new men asked, his mind jittering through his face, his eyes looking everywhere at once.

"It's too hot for this shit, Doc. Just cool out. One gooker grocery boy don't mean nothing," Botts said, attempting to override my mounting paranoia with oblivious calm, a man like Whitefang who thought he could wish the war into or out of being at his personal convenience.

"Sarge, you know these guys don't travel alone. They know we're here. They could be setting up an ambush right now. We better keep our shit together!" I insisted, my independence and status seeking leadership ambition once more rearing its untrained head.

"He didn't have a weapon, is that right?" Botts asked, further attempting to denigrate my finding, as if when the bullets started flying he and the Marines would be able to combat any force thrown at us, like our death or maiming wasn't possible.

"No, he didn't have a weapon. But that don't mean he was alone," I insisted. I could feel men moving around in the brush further up the hill, brain cells reaching into every shadow and under every leaf.

"Doc says he saw something, girls. So keep your eyes open. Pass the word," Botts finally relented. But it wasn't a strong enough warning for me. Usurping his rank wasn't possible, Marines are honor bound to obey the orders of their superiors, but I saw us in a perilous situation, and also wanting desperately to regain my acceptance among them, I said to Botts, "I'm gonna go find him," and unholstered my .45, thumbing off the safety.

One of the new guys looked at me like I must be nuts, but we'd all been there longer than they had so what I was doing must be the way the war went. It occurred to me that the only way to redeem myself in their warrior eyes was to do as they would do, to hunt down the VC kid that I'd seen and either catch him or shoot him. If he was hiding out there in the bamboo thickets, I could find him easily enough, and the only thing that might warn the other VC I was certain were about would be the tell-tale sounds of gunfire popping through the jungle. Maybe there would be time to get back to our positions before they could locate the body of their fallen comrade.

"Anybody want to come?" I said, but the gathering men looked to Botts for permission. It was stupid to go out looking to start a fire fight, who knows how many were out there, or how close they were. Chances of surviving an attack were better the closer we stuck together. To go off looking for some rice carrier, even if he was aiding and abetting the enemy, jeopardized the safety of the unit. No grandstanding, no cowboy bullshit, Doc, is what Botts should have said.

"Well, if you gotta go, you gotta go, Doc. You better take a rifleman with you. Washington, go with the Doc," Botts said, so casually I thought he secretly wanted to get me killed, and maybe a splib to boot.

"Doc here might have something," PFC Jackson interjected. "I mean, it ain't like they're gonna walk right up and let us shoot them."

"It's already too late to di-di." LeFever said.

"Me and Washington will take a look around over there, if anybody comes running out, be careful, it might be us," I said, filling with false bravery. The smart thing to do would have been to sit tight, and wait for the crisis to pass, or for the attack. But I felt impelled by shame to prove my courage.

So my shame led Washington and me to step into the stream, quietly passing LeFever and Ortiz, telling them to keep their noses open in case we flushed some VC, and back upstream to where the VC rice courier has slipped away, into taking the chance that we'd walk into an ambush and be blown to pieces with a grenade or shot dead through the head. The brush was bleeding bullets. I was so divided that I didn't really want to kill anyone, especially a conscripted boy slave, but I was still fused and flushed with animal pursuit, performing the complete follower's act of murder for the love of other men. My brain floating in adrenalin, my eyes melting through the glistening leaves looking for body silhouette, my nose mulling each breath for human sweat scent, my every hair follicle training on death vectors, each step passing through planes of fragmented topaz light, feeling that if I relaxed my will for a microsecond I'd fly apart into a thousand vanishing pieces, as if by sheer concentration I could form an impenetrable shield of adamantine mind around us.

Washington and I penetrated further into the brush. His eyes were wide with fear. "This is far enough," he whispered. He was resonating in me, and I in him, our lives chained at the soul. "A little further," I said, maybe leading him into death, further for the Corps, further to claim my courage, further to show a black man that whitey had some balls. I could feel three men sitting in the uphill shadows, readying their rifles, still as groundwater. I couldn't see them, or actually locate them by any sense. I could just feel them impacting my mind.

By that time we were nearly parallel with our own squad. It became tactically clear that shooting into the darker shadows in the jungle ahead could bring both return fire from the VC I was sure I could feel, and from the Marines. We'd be caught in the crossfire. So, even in my whirl of confusion I made a sensible decision, much to the great relief of Washington. We started backing out. Washington looked at me like I was some crazy chuck mutherfucker.

We splashed back to our positions, Washington circling his index finger around his temple and pointing at me. But it wasn't over; I knew. "They're out there, Sarge. I can feel them," I said, panting from anxiety, entropic paranoia pouring off my body like vaporized oil. "You didn't see them?" He asked, as if impervious to the reality confronting him. "No, no sign, but they are out there. You can bet your life on it," I said. But Botts discounted my fear, saying that the VC courier kid was frightened off, we didn't have anything to worry about. After twenty minutes passed the squad began to relax, still sunbathing at the ol' swimming hole.

When a hundred rounds of automatic fire shattered the rock and branches six inches above our heads, the squad buckled into the tightest crevices we could find, snaking out slow hands to grab our helmets, clutching our rifles to our torsos that the steel might deflect a bullet. Rock fragment and twig splinters rained down on us. Several men squirmed into their flack jackets, careful not to expose their movement above the rock walls we'd built.

Another hundred rounds swept over us, some ricocheting off the stacked rocks, making us cringe deeper behind our walls.

"That'll teach you girls to wear your helmets," Botts said, so sergeantly. But we were too busy praying and promising God anything, anything at all, if he'd just make it stop, to hear if Botts the leader had anything more to say. Our faces were stricken and ashen, twisted into grotesque fear masks, simultaneously wishing for someone, something, anyone to come and take us away, eliminate the enemy, whisk us back to the World, make this horrible reality stop, please, while also knowing there was no way out of this monstrous horror except by our own efforts. We were utterly vulnerable, knew so, Charles knew who we were, how many we were, what weapons we had, where we were (up shit crick), and because the firing had come from somewhere above us that we had no viable avenue of escape. Either way we chose to make a run for it we could be cut down in midstride. We would fight.

Several minutes passed. Even though I was scared to dash from low wall to low wall to check the line for wounded, I called out, "Anyone hit?" breaking the silence. It took awhile for everyone to come out of their beseeching stop, stop, stop, you asshole mutherfuckers, stop or I'll kill you. Word passed back to me that no one had been wounded except by flying rock.

No one had seen any rifle flashes, no smoke rose from anywhere on the hillside that any brave eye could see. All we knew about the attack was that it was concentrated somewhere above and in front of us. The crackling echoes of the AK-47 told us the range was about one hundred yards.

Still hunkered down behind our rocks voices constricted by fear aimed their hopes and confusions at Botts.

"What'll we do now, Sarge?" One man asked. Another said, "Let's split. Let's go. Let's get the fuck out of here."

"A little shit falls on you girls and you want to go home to mama," Botts snides.

"Let's go downstream. We hang around here and Charles is going to kill us for sure. We don't know where he is, but he knows where we are," the M-79 man says.

"Whitefang won't know shit if we don't tell him. Let's bag it downstream," LeFever shouts.

"We're on radio silence," Botts asserts, "The skipper has our coordinates, and we've got orders to stick, dumbshit. So we stay here."

"Charles knows we're here too, you just wanna sit here and die?" another trooper says, his voice cracking with sobs.

"If we stand up and walk out we'll make real fine targets, trooper," Smith admonished. "We got no choice. Fight or die."

Ortiz, sleepy and not too bright, had the best eyes in the company. He altered our confusion by pointing to a huge fig tree one hundred yards up the hillside, well within our line of fire.

"I think I see someone climbing out on a limb up there in that tree, Sarge," Ortiz said, like a child reporting an innocent fact. Peering up over the rocks we could see the great tree Ortiz was pointing at, the sunlight defining its branches, but only Ortiz could see the man. "I think he's got a weapon, too, Sarge."

Everyone in the squad was looking to Botts for instruction, but his gaze remained unthinking and fixed.

"What should I do, Sarge?" Ortiz asked, putting his rifle up to his shoulder.

But Botts still wouldn't answer. Six quick rounds hit just above our heads, missing the sergeant and me by inches.

"Did that guy up there fire on us?" Botts asked, like he couldn't believe anyone would have the gall to damage his beautiful body.

"Fucking 'A', Sarge!" Ortiz said, "What should I do?"

"What is he doing now?" Botts asked, his voice still calm and disbelieving, failing to grasp our peril, each moment passing further endangering our lives.

"Shoot the fucker!" I yelled. Corpsmen don't give orders, but to my mind the only man in charge was the one shooting at us from his tree perch. Petulant, exceeding my role, reasoning that to shoot back at someone trying to kill you is different than shooting a man in cold blood, self defense for one's own life and the lives of one's friends was righteous and honorable, I yelled again, "Shoot him, man. He's got us in his sights!"

"He looks like he's trying to tie himself onto that branch." Ortiz observed, still sounding like a child amazed at what was going on around him and capable only of doing what he was told.

Another trooper demanded, "What do you want us to do, Sarge, you waiting for him to pick his fucking targets?"

"He's aiming, Sarge," Ortiz warned.

"All right, all right, just Ortiz. If you can see him, shoot him," Botts relented, laconic, afraid of a command decision, as if he was waiting for one of us to be shot before he could rightfully take action. But before Ortiz could aim, three more rounds hit behind us, Botts and I were his targets.

"I think I see a couple other zips." Ortiz adds, like nothing dangerous is happening, at least not to him. He's still calm and curious.

I yell, "Shoot the fucker!" again, but Ortiz is busy reporting on what he is watching. "They're working on the rope. Sending some stuff up to him."

"Jesus fucking Christ, you idiots," I shout, "That's got to be ammo. Shoot them all!"

But Botts is still analyzing the situation. "Have they got weapons?" he asks.

"I don't see any, but they could have leaned them against the tree or something," Ortiz says. Two more troopers take the chance, crawling over to Ortiz and LeFever's position, peering up over the rocks, finding the tree, aiming their rifles in the general direction. Even if they can't see the Viet Cong they can keep their heads down.

"All right," Botts says, like he is more frightened of what he is going to say than of what might happen if he does nothing, "just shoot the one in the tree." Then he turns to me and asks, "He's the one who shot at us, isn't he?"

Suddenly I feel like I'm the only one awake in a nightmare starring malicious mental defectives. Only the two troopers who took the chance of going over to Ortiz's position and LeFever seem to have any grasp of what to do, but no power to exercise it.

Ortiz takes careful aim, his face implacable, concentrated, lets out his breath, squeezes his trigger, firing three times. Another spray of automatic fire slashes just above our heads. Again we buckled for cover, involuntary grabbing of rock and dust, wishing the rock of the stream bed would gently swallow us and give us shelter. "Missed him," Ortiz sighs, sitting back, seemingly ignoring the incoming bullets, a phenomena happening fifty feet away, not his concern. Fear sweat, stale urine, flyspecked ration cans, cordite, rock dust, shattered lead, scents in the turgid air.

The riflemen beside Ortiz commanded him to, "Put a tracer on him. We can't see him for the shadows." Their faces were contorted into grim desperate purpose. "He's right up there." Ortiz said, still calm, pointing his rifle and quickly firing five more rounds. A tracer marked the bottommost limb of the great fig tree. That was all the two riflemen needed. They aimed quickly, and let loose full clips at the crotch of the tree. It didn't matter if they had a clear target, maybe they'd get lucky.

Another few AK-47 rounds impacted behind me and Botts. Oh mama when is this going to stop?! The VC gunner's balance was too precarious to shoot at the four Marines firing at him. In my imagination I could see the boy I'd run into in the stream bed being shrilly commanded by his comrades, terrified, tied to the tree limb, ordered to fire on us under penalty of being shot himself, our bullets tearing at his living being, and I didn't really want him dead, I only wanted the shooting to stop, as if a thought of mutual mercy could save us.

"Are you gonna kill that son-of-bitch or not?" demanded one of the new guys. The boy sniper just wouldn't lay there and die like he was supposed to, and our bullets couldn't seem to find him, and the new guy was frustrated to the point of rushing across the stream and up the hill, rifle blazing.

With utter resignation Ortiz once more took aim. The rifle fired twice. Then Ortiz, resting his rifle, said, "I think I got him, Sarge. He's just kinda hanging there." The other three riflemen fed new clips into their M-14s and opened up on the base of the tree, not aiming, just firing in case the other two VC were in hiding there. There was no return fire.

Fifteen minutes passed, Ortiz staring at the hanging body of the boy VC Finally, Botts asked, "What about the other two? Can you see them?"

But Ortiz wasn't talking. LeFever stuck his head up over the rock wall, gathered in what he saw, and said, "Yeah, Sarge, I can see them. They're trying to cut the little fucker down."

The chance to kill the other two VC was upon us, but Botts didn't respond. And no one could or wanted to speak. Even if LeFever could see the other two V.C., our collective unspoken will seemed to be to ignore them unless they fired upon us, we were momentarily safe, extending a merciful disinterest like exchanging with them a chance for them to retrieve their dead in return for the same chance sometime in the future—to be remembered by their forces as honorable men.

No one talked for hours. There was no backslapping, no great shooting Ortiz, no congratulations. Perhaps sensing an opportunity for teaching the big dumb Marines a lesson in consequences the two other VC gave up trying to cut the boy down, and left him dangling from the limb to fill our eyes and hearts with the real fact of his death. Ortiz settled back into his cover with his eyes fixed on the hanging corpse, the muscles of his face tightening into a permanent mask. Maybe the other two were cadre from the north, too self important to risk taking on a Marine ambush squad, having perhaps another more important mission at hand, but willing, also, to demonstrate to us their callous disregard for the lives of their brothers in arms, I thought, not giving them the humanness of simply being afraid.

By then the squad had uncoiled from their grips on the rock, mind-scanning every leaf shadow and jungle chirp for any sign of more VC moving above us, but there was no sign. Toward sunset someone broke the silence, saying, "Fuck this shit, Sarge. They know where we are. They could easy just send out a platoon to fuck us up completely. We oughta move, man, I mean, let's split."

Heading down stream in the dark would be next to impossible, and could easily lead us into clumsily stumbling into an ambush, shot to shit in no time flat. We didn't know the ground above us, and even staying put we were in serious jeopardy. A couple of men with grenades could get within a hundred feet of us over in the bamboo thickets and blast us to pieces before we knew where they were coming from, oh Jesus what are we doing here? The only real best chance we had was staying put behind our little rock walls and praying.

Botts rose from his lethargy and said, "Don't sweat the small shit, Private," and, hefting his unfired carbine in mock defiance like he could take on any enemy strength single handedly, added, "You know our orders. We're staying here. No smoking after dark. Full alert tonight."

So we lit our tiny blue flame heat tablets, ate our beef stews and ham and eggs, had a last smoke, splashed on the mosquito repellent, and at full dark I passed out the dexedrine to fend off the mounting exhaustion.

We were quiet, ready, waiting. Weighty presences wired together in the ageless watch. The night passed slowly, each second recorded in the rush of water coursing downstream. Under the cover of the jungle the only light came from phosphorescent fungi luminescing the leaf litter rot. Near dawn I sensed a squad of black hollow men crossing slowly, so slowly in front of us, the water flowing around their ankles, their scent acrid, the smell of gun oil rising from the stream center, and I can still see their masterful faces in my memory. Maybe the others sensed them too, but no one else stirred. When the night was playing its tricks on you who could chance exposing our position. And who is to say that the other troopers weren't also sensing them and independently deciding each by each to let them pass without risking a fight. At that point we were only communicating by the medulla. And, they may have not been there at all.

At the first white haze of false dawn we simultaneously lit up, everyone but Botts, grateful for whatever form of reprieve the day would offer. We spent the next day and night the same way, quiet, nobody saying much, waiting, counting the seconds until we could leave, trying to avoid looking at the dangling corpse, impossible, hoping and praying to whatever force guided our fate or luck that we'd be left alone. Though no one ever said so.

At third dawn we headed back to the old French fort. We stumbled down the stream rock, shaking off the cold and cramps of the night watch, eager to get back into the sun where the heat and sky could lift the weight we'd acquired. Reaching the bottom of the hill Botts radioed for the amphtrack to come pick us up, mobile warfare ain't it a gas, and while we were waiting to be retrieved Botts ordered us to, "Keep your mouths shut about that gook," which dumbfounded me.

Crossing the river in the belly of the track I tried to figure Bott's reasoning; maybe he also sensed the black hollow men crossing in front of us and was ashamed to have not ordered us to open fire, or maybe it was too complicated a story for him to tell, surely he knew that the Captain had heard the hour long firefight, and surely the Captain would be proud that one of his diversionary units had bagged a bad guy, his strategy proven, his leadership vindicated. But Botts was morose and sullen, there would be no explanation from him, best to keep our mouths shut unless we wanted shit details for the next three months.

Coming out of the track we were a dirty, haggard, tired-looking squad, glad to be back 'home.' The Captain was waiting for us, grinning broadly, welcoming us back into the safety of the fold. "Good hunting?" he roared. And the rest of the men looked to Botts for direction. Botts shook his head no at them, then glared at the Captain defying any further questioning. The rest of the men stayed quiet, resenting losing a chance to boast about the kill. Seeing the Captain's expectant face, a proud father's face, and not having to worry about being put on shit details, I said in the best Marine Corps machismo I could wring out of my weary body, "Yeah, Skipper, we got one!" And the Captain's grin got wider, and he put his fists on his hips and laughed, pleased as punch. I thought Botts was going to hit me, so I drifted away toward my bunker, pulling Ortiz along with me. Whitefang dismissed the rest of the squad, telling them to get some well deserved sleep, hot chow for dinner tonight, and motioned for Botts to follow him up the hill for debriefing. "Aye Aye, Captain."

I sat Ortiz down on a rock. He'd hardly spoken since he'd killed the VC boy, slipping into self examination bordering on catatonia. Ortiz was the Marine whose life I'd saved with mouth to mouth those many light years ago on Okinawa, and we were bound.

"Why do you think Botts told us to keep our mouths shut about that gook?" I asked him. It took him a long time to come out of his trance, his poor not too bright self rising like a clouded veil.

"I don't know. Maybe he thinks it shoulda been him who did him instead of me."

"Look, man, you saved all our asses. You're the only one who could see him. If you hadn't of shot him, we all might be dead."

"He was shooting at us pretty good."

"He was shooting at me and Botts pretty good, I'll tell you."

"I wish they wouldn't have left him hanging there like that. I know he was just a kid."

"And I wish I hadn't of seen him in the middle of the stream. But here we are and what happens is what happens. You did good."

"It would've been better if one of us got hit."

"We would've been in a world of hurt then, think of having to carry a couple of us out of there, likely to get hit every step down that fucking stream."

"I know it don't sound good, just more fair, like."

"Ain't nothing in this pissant little war that's fair."

"Is it gonna hurt like this forever?"

"I don't know. I've never done it, and I hope I never have to. I'm sorry I didn't shoot him when I saw him like I was suppose to and you ended up having to do it." Oh sad aching heart, the burden

184

grows immense. "But a lot of men have, and they learn to live with it. We're here, we don't have a lot of choice in the matter. He was trying to kill us, it was self defense."

"But it took such a long time."

"Get some sleep, man. There ain't no way to change any of it. Get some sleep, and try to stay lucky. Catch you at chow." And Ortiz gets up and walks away toward his bunker. Not feeling too good about myself I head into my bunker, but I'm stopped by a friend who has more news for me to absorb. It's Ramirez, an extremely competent corporal who tells me,

"You hear about Orrick?"

"We just got back, I haven't heard any scoop at all."

"Well, I know you and Orrick didn't get along too good."

Which was putting it kindly. Corporal Orrick was my nemesis, a brutal tough kid from East St. Louis who habitually baited and humiliated me with challenges to fistfights, a gung-ho second hitch jarhead going on lifer, who took delight in cruelty and injury, taking on all comers of lesser rank, out to prove himself the baddest cat going, once telling me he was going to shove a grenade up my ass to see how fast I could shit and run, ha, ha, Doc, and all I could retort was an affirmation of role, better watch your step, a man like you is bound to get shot and someone like me just might not come out to save your feisty ass. Never happen he says to me—and I took it, so hungry for acceptance I sought to see a friend in every man I met but too often received injury and insult that by the code of men among men needed to be repaid by injury or insult, now if your jaws get tight, Doc, and you feel froggy, just leap. What a pitiful tedious stalemate to abide by. The enemy is more within.

"What about him? He catch the black syph and wants a shot?"

"No, man, I bet he wishes he did now."

"You mean he's dead?"

"You got it. We were down to Chu Lai, man, there were more fucking gooks than you could shake a stick at, and we had to cross this open field under fire, hairy fucking shit, man, Gooks everywhere, so we're taking this treeline and Orrick goes charging out there, balls, man, balls, and catches three right up the middle. Guts all over the place. Deader than a mutherfucker."

And at first I think I'm glad that he's dead. But he was someone I knew, and he gave me something, even though I didn't like it, and the sorrow wells up in me like a burgeoning sob, and I'm choking on the news, on all the news about all the men and boys and girls and women and children who hear the news that their loved ones are now gone forever to never be loved again or to ever give love again, but I am impelled by man-code to tough it out, to be hard, as if I'm just as ready for the ultimate finish as any man around me, and I say,

"Well, that's too bad. But he got what he came for."   Silly and cynical, trying to expose him even in death as a poser endangering us in his personal bid to end his own central wail, and warning the messenger roundabout that you get what you give. It was the wrong message at the wrong time, because for whatever reason he told himself, Ramirez was bringing me that news to discover how to accept it himself. And even if it is the oldest story in the history of the world, heard over and over again by generation upon generation, and even if we should be singing Orrick's spirit into the new life or the spirit world or simply to be alight among the burning stars and a whisper on a breeze, there won't be any taps blown for him—vanished by chopper to Graves—and we shall each find our own way to find ourselves in Orrick's death because there is no other choice, it might happen any second, it's just a shot away, to incorporate it in the moment by moment breathing as an extra watchfulness, or bury it, freeze it until twenty years later when you're strong enough by good works to look at it again, or just be sick in the heart with it, be strong and move on, all the wishing and praying in the world won't change the true facts of the whirling past or the future for which you've truly volunteered. No way out and a long way to go, like you wouldn't believe. Ramirez kept looking at me like I had some kind of answer, but all I could find to say was, "Thanks for telling me. Good luck," and I retreated into my bunker to toy with my .45 for the thousandth time, feeling far far from home. Later, at chow, hot-chow, roast beef and gravy to celebrate the kill, I suspect, I sat down with Ortiz, answering finally his question about how long it would hurt, saying, "Yeah, it does."

◆◆◆◆

Other memories: coming through the wire after yet another exhausting patrol I headed straight for my bunker and the illusion of private safety that it offered. Even though the monsoons that came in at four-ten offered a chance for a shower all I could really think of was sleep. My vision was blurred from fatigue, and my body ached from the marrow out. How you could be so tired at nineteen wasn't really a question. On patrol all that mattered was if you could hack it. Some men just flopped in front of their positions and were immediately asleep, fuck the rain, let the others defend us if the gooners wanted in.

I tossed my gear on the ammo crates inside my bunker and was about to fall into my cot, nearly asleep as I fell, when the part of the brain that is always awake caught sight of a triangle of bamboo green at the edge of the blanket. It was alive.

The triangle of green had a pink forked tongue and bright yellow telling eyes. Sacs of neurotoxin bulged below its eyes. My body recoiled in self-preservation, instinctually alert. Desperately wanting sleep, I had no choice but to capture the snake and kill it. For a moment, my paranoia so vivified by fatigue and dexedrine, I thought the VC who came in to haul our trash might have planted the snake. Either them, or my fellow Marines out for a yuck.

I quickly fashioned a snake-loop from a bamboo pole and a leather boot lace, surprised in my weariness that my fingers still worked. Then, for the next ten minutes I chased the snake around the crevices of the bunker, the bamboo snake is the third deadliest snake in the world, someone said, one boot on, the other off and exposing my naked foot to the snake's lethal bite. Once I had its head in the loop, but couldn't figure the next step to take, and it slipped away.

Finally, as frightened and tired of trying to escape as I, the snake made for the doorway and I grabbed it around its middle with the loop. It was writhing at the end of the pole, out of effective striking range, like Marines safe inside the wire.

I took the snake outside, holding it as far away as I could, warning the two men who came to watch to stand back. Then I smashed its head repeatedly with a rock, its pink jaws twisting grotesquely under the blows. When it was dead, and fearful of using a boot lace contaminated with poison, I hung the snake from the bunker's ridgepole as a warning to other snakes, VC, and perhaps my fellowmen. "That thing stinks," a trooper complained. "Third deadliest snake in the world," I boasted.

Some months after that, after being in the field for four months without sleep, liberty, or hot-chow, after dozens of ambush nights and blowing bunkers with grenades, being shot at by VC and our own helicopter gunners, after losing more and more men so that all those events became a blurred dream that registered only in the autonomic nervous system, I came in off yet another patrol and found what looked to be another bamboo snake occupying my bed. This one was larger though, its belly yellow as rotting fruit. It occurred to me that I might be hallucinating, deja-vu that could kill me. Would the poison from a dream snake kill my dream self? Which was more real? How could I tell? But I was too tired to test my thought. Not even my backbrain cared if the snake slithered in beside my warm body and administered its tender drowning. It would be merciful, I'd never know, I'd drift into the deep dark, died of natural causes like some savage in a heedless country. I half-heartedly swiped at it with my medical kit, then lay down to whatever sleep would take me.

We were also each other. In the long nights of mind alive with violent dread we'd smoke and recount the feats and the names of the men we emulated. We'd listen to the clatter of rifles and grenades exploding somewhere off in the distant dark, entertaining the American spy fantasy, the schizoid mental retreat that would give you two lives, one of which you didn't have to be responsible for.

There were plenty of examples around. We'd see the CIA spooks come out of the bush, haggard and lean, no insignia, strange weapons recently fired, arrogant, contemptuous of us mere grunts. Sometimes they would suddenly appear in a village we were sweeping, officer types, cool, in command, seemingly answerable to no one. They were always looking for someone, VC cadre, compliant elders, maybe one of us.

Like young Lieutenant Roman. The lieutenant was sure of what he saw. He was sure of his role in Vietnam, of the fact that the war was the ebb and flow of the constant future, the ultimate expression of man-spirit moving him with tireless grace through the Vietnam night. To prosecute the war in Vietnam was his destiny.

He had a reputation of being cool under fire, of being just gung-ho enough to inspire loyalty, and of being distant, like he lived deep within a tunnel clinging to the compact orb of his soul. He moved like he was possessed of a final secret greater than any that could be delivered by any mere grunt mortal. In his presence you felt that he only wanted to use you, who or whatever you were, and you were grateful that he could find suitable use for you. The spook recruiters spotted him right away.

One night a team of CIA men took over one of our bunkers, and we saw them invite Roman into their kerosene lamp light. He stepped into the bunker, reaching for an offered hand. I heard one of them say, "Come in, lieutenant. We know..."

And Roman's smile was the smile of completion, the smile of a man who had found heaven like he knew he always would. Entropy, black fear that keeps you awake for years, a well of lives ten million years deep—the real drug. You can see it burning back behind their eyes. Phantoms feeding on souls. Roman was home.

◆◆◆◆

A bigwig was coming, a significant public servant. He was to be choppered out from DaNang to inspect our fortifications and to see the effects of the pacification program on the people of Le Mai. We were placed on full alert, to guard the landing zone and his eminence.

The sergeants and officers were in a frenzy, conducting head counts, ordering us to form up in our units, checking for clean weapons, trying to turn us back into garrison Marines in two hours.

"Who the fuck is coming?" I asked my friend Marshall, the company radioman. "I mean, we didn't do this much horse and pony even for General Walt."

"You wouldn't believe it even if I could tell you," he said.

"Don't tell us then. I'll bet we got some senator's nephew lurking in our midst, and he's coming to see if the boy is getting plenty of hot chow?" Anderson offered.

"No, it ain't no senator," Marshall teased.

"It sure as shit ain't Johnson."

"The Supreme Commander? Get his boots muddy? Not on your life."

"Hey man, we're risking our lives, and he's a military kinda guy, let him come out here and catch some of this shit," Anderson again offered. "It ain't like his hands aren't already bloody."

"I know, Jim, It's MacNamara. He wants to see if the gooks can build Fords after we get 'em trained," I said.

"Damn, Doc. You're crazier than me." Jim said, adding, "Naw, it ain't MacNamara. It is a civilian, though."

"I got it," I said, "It's got to be the mayor of Da Nang. Anderson, he's coming out here to make you pay for that Guernsey cow you shot for trespassing."

"Hey, if I gotta pay for it, then I get to eat it. You can't tell me those people down there didn't have a big Texas style bar-be-que and dink hoe-down after I greased that cow." Anderson said.

"Helping our little yellow brothers, right John?" Jim said, still teasing.

"Fuckin' A, gotta teach 'em the American way," Anderson smiled, adding, "I could have used a rifle-grenade."

"So, it isn't the mayor. You have to tell us, Jim. I mean look at those people, they're running around like they were waiting for the resurrection," I said.

Anderson challenged, "Are you going to tell us or not, Jim. If you don't tell us, you ain't got a hair on your ass."

Jim smiled and smirked, and let us squirm for a minute more, then said, "Nixon."

"You got to be shitting me."

"Tricky Dick?"

"His own self."

"Then what is all this horse and pony? He's got no status. He ain't even a government employee," I pointed out.

"I know." Marshall said, "And it don't make no nevermind. Nixon is coming in on a bird, and we're are going to throw our lives away if Mister Charles decides to take a couple of shots at him."

"They can't make us do this shit for him. He's a civilian. An ex-congressman, and ex-VP The key word here is ex. He wants to take a look around, let him rent a car and take his own chances. We do," I added.

"You know, I always thought it was Johnson who did Kennedy, but now I'm not so sure," Anderson said, looking thoughtful and paranoid. "If he's coming here, now, I'd sure hate to think of what it means."

"That is one Machiavellian notion, John," Marshall said.

"If that shit gets the job of being boss of the world, he won't care how many of us get killed," John said. Then he put his rifle up to his shoulder and aimed down into the landing zone where Nixon's helicopter was going to land. "We oughta save the world a bunch of grief. Dipshit O'Dell oughta know better than to come sniffing around a bunch of crazy grunts. Could get his dick shot off."

"Yeah, I mean, how they gonna know? Charlie's got M-14s too. Ours," I said, co-conspiratorially. "You can do it, John. You're a marksman. The Green Machine says so. I couldn't hit shit with this .45, 'less I did a Jack Ruby. You could follow in the footsteps of that other famous Marine, Lee Harvey Oswald."

Jim laughed so hard he snorted canteen water through his nose. "These mutherfucker officers would hunt us down and kill us like dogs," he said. "There ain't a grunt here that wouldn't help us, but the officers, man, don't you know, they are counting on Nixon. Whitefang already has the vaseline out."

"John is right, though," I said, "It would do the world some good to get rid of that seething twit. We oughta shoot him, if just to save our own lives. I mean, we do exactly that all the time, and he's the same color."

As Jim was nodding his assent, we noticed that what we thought was a private conversation was being closely listened to by an ambitious staff-sergeant. The sergeant's face was ridged with rage. We turned away to ignore him, but the cat was out of the bag. The sergeant turned and ran up the hill to where Whitefang was supervising the guarding operation.

"We stepped in it this time," John said, "They can kill us for talking about blowing presidents away, can't they?"

"They can at least put us in Leavenworth until we're deemed psychologically sound enough to execute," Jim replied. "It sure don't seem fair. Those guys talk about getting us killed all the time."

"They can't do shit. He ain't no president," I said, trying to remain calm, knowing how easily the NCOs let their hysteria rule their thinking. "Nixon is no different than you or me. We all want to be president. Fact is, he's not even next in line. But maybe he knows something we don't."

Anderson was worried. He was the one the sergeant had seen pointing the rifle. He said, "What do they expect us to talk about? We wouldn't be armed to the teeth if we weren't out here to kill people."

"No, no, John," Marshall said, "You've got it twisted. We're only here to kill the enemy people. Those sneaky little yellow enemy people. See, The Trick is on our side."

"Now you've really got me confused. If the officers and the politicians can send us out to kill or die, and the dinks can kill us whenever they can catch us with our pants down, what is the difference?" I asked, trying to keep the joke rolling.

"With the dinks," Jim said, "at least we have a fighting chance."

We looked up and saw the whole headquarters contingent heading our way. Other sergeants and corporals were calling for the troops to fall in on them. Thinking we were about to be arrested, we were relieved when the entourage passed us by and headed out toward the landing zone. The staff-sergeant who'd overheard us and a buck sergeant broke off from the group and approached us.

"We know what you were talking about," the staff-sergeant said, emphasizing with a stubby finger. "You shitheads stay here. Get down in your hole and keep your mouths shut," he ordered, then ran to catch up with the headquarters group.

We were the only ones left inside the perimeter. The whole rest of the company left the wire and filed into the paddy that was to be Nixon's landing zone. They formed a square of men facing outboard, and an extra squad was assigned to watch the graveyard at the edge of the hamlet.

The helicopter that was carrying Nixon, a Cobra, landed in the center of the paddy, and the future president emerged, nervously smoothing back his hair.

The Captain greeted him, then introduced his fellow officers. Handshakes and talk all around. When the Captain pointed out our bunkered positions and we saw Nixon look up toward us, we waved, smirking, John waving his rifle. Then Nixon got back on the chopper and was whisked away. The possibility that he could have learned anything from his visit was beyond remote.

I reached into my pack and produced some lime Kool-aid to mix with my halizone water, and offered my canteen to my friends. "Confusion to the enemy," I toasted. And we each took a drink. We were selfish children who did not understand how complex the war we were fighting was, nor how complex we were. Neither did we want to be gunned down where we stood.

◆◆◆◆

Back to the BAS to resupply my kit, I stopped to pick up my beer ration and ran into Doc Monroe. I'd consciously avoided Monroe, he was violent and provocative. Not violent like the Marines, full of posture but so wired into each other that fighting among the ranks was discouraged by all, but violent in that he enjoyed inflicting bruising pain and humiliation on anyone foolish enough to fall to his challenges. He was short, five-five at best, and about as wide. He had a Saxon's head and no neck. His shoulders were massively muscled, his chest deep and he stood on legs designed for wading through the slaughter. His face was constantly furious, aching to be beaten. What he was doing as a corpsman and not a Green Beret or Marine was beyond me.

Once, in the hold of the USS Galveston, while we were docked in Olongopo, I stood watching Monroe and a Marine exchange bareknuckled blows until I was bored by their tedious crunching. The Marine traded him blow for blow, talking to him all the while, saying he was trained as a boxer, you could hit him all day and he wouldn't feel a thing, let's just give this up as a draw, then smashed Monroe a good solid crunching blow to his mouth, splitting his lip and tearing his thick nose from its moorings.

Monroe refused to verbalize a reply, Alabama mean and sullen. I left, then came back fifteen minutes later, my sense of duty to a fellow corpsman drawing me back. They were still at it. Finally, the Marine grew bored, turned his back on Monroe and walked away, an insult that threw Monroe into a rage. He was about to spring onto the Marine's back when I stepped in front of him, saying we better go get some stitches in his lip and nose. Exhausted, he came with me, and I led him down to the sick-bay where the duty corpsman iced him down and stitched him.

Monroe continued his fighting habit while he was out in the field with Foxtrot Company. Fighting among the troops was a seriously stupid thing to do. We needed each other like life itself, and with everyone armed to the teeth starting a fist fight could be fatal. He was sent back to battalion for the pogues to handle. In charge of the sick-bay tent, Monroe was lording over his territory when I came in holding my beer and looking for a place to sleep that night. I tripped on the step, spilled a dollop of beer and ignited Monroe's fuse.

An argument about seniority ensued, but he wasn't listening. He started backing me up, his fists clenched at his sides, tendons bunching in his face, me saying, now don't get your jaws tight, don't you remember, I helped you once. But he didn't care. All he wanted was a fight. Even though I was still wearing my pistol, the fight was going to be man to man, just him and me. One of the rules among fighting men is that if you have any self-respect, any personal pride, any foolish notion of self worth tied to your ability to fight and defend yourself, when you are challenged, you fight—fists, bodies, not weapons.

I was perplexed that so small an accident as spilling some beer could so deeply infuriate him, and I wasn't about to bend down with a towel to wipe it up while he kicked me in the head just to make the point that he was the king of the world. I blocked a few of his punches, figuring his hate of men born tall would win his fight for him. A left jab caught me on the cheekbone. Contact. His foot lashed out, trying to kick me in the balls, letting me know that he was absolutely intent on doing me damage. I had no choice but to fight back. I struck out, missing badly. Fighting back was a signal to him to pile into me with all his might.

He was still backing me up when I saw the BAS staff looking on in tired wonder, and I started backing toward them, hoping someone would stop the fight. Not once did it enter my mind that I could beat him. He got in a few more snapping jabs, stinging my face, which must have looked like that of a child being beaten by his father, frightened, bewildered, and which incensed him even further. My glasses went flying off somewhere. I saw a right coming at me, blocked it. I could hear my father saying, get in there and rip his eyes out. Schoolboy karate lessons don't mean shit in a street fight.

Then a crashing left smashed into my right eye. I'd never been hit so hard in all my life. My mind went black and studded with shock stars. I was sprawled on my back trying to figure out how I got there when Monroe dove on me, his knee landing on my chest, knocking the wind out of my lungs. The man knew how to fight.

What happened next is still muddled in memory. I saw his fist start to pound at my face with furious rhythm, and my arms rise up to block them. Even being nearly unconscious I lashed out and felt my fist connect solidly with his face, but it didn't stop him. I couldn't see out of my right eye, and the men who'd been watching my inevitable beating started blocking his blows, then pulled him off. They told me while they were coming between us, I bit one of them.

Monroe was panting, still furious, victorious, blood trickling from his nose, still ready to pummel me. The Chief was standing directly in front of him to block his view of me as I got up, stupefied that they had let the fight go on as long as it did, but nevertheless grateful that they had all come to my aid. I'd been beaten fair and square, so I didn't unholster my pistol. That the staff could allow so vicious a psychopath freedom diminished them in my opinion, but he had them cowed, too.

Back at the company position the next day several friends greeted me with, "What happened, Doc?" My eye was badly bruised, and I was embarrassed over coming back to the company beaten up. Orrick saw me, and ridiculed, "Ha, ha, Doc got his ass kicked." Orrick and Monroe were birds-of-a-feather, headed for the same end. My friends and I went down to a bunker to smoke and tell the story. And upon hearing it Marshall picked up his rifle and said, "Let's go man. We'll do the mutherfucker." And I said, no, it was a fair fight. But his were the sweetest words I'd heard in that horrible place.

To The Shrink

But I was crazy, no doubt about it. So eager to please, so desirous of approval, so needful to be heroic, so urgently wanting manliness, so aware of my surrounds that I became sullen, morose and withdrawn, while asking officers impertinent questions of great complexity, exhibiting an unpredictable state of mind that challenged authority. The doctor who pulled a .45 on me when I was back at the Battalion Aid Station picking up supplies, rounding a tent corner, coming up short at the barrel of his gun, the doctor's body contorted in a twist of paranoid defense like he was being crushed from within, a who goes there seething from his rubbery lips while he stalked his own perimeter back and forth behind the medical tents, had said so. The other Battalion doctor, a fine competent man without enough to do, agreed.

Calling me into a hardback tent for a private consultation, he asked me what I thought about the war, a fair question. And though I don't remember exactly what my response was, I do remember that I stacked up enough references to institutional malice and enough concepts to confuse even me. I wanted out. I wanted to go home, even if the future looked as vague and empty as when I'd left. I was in deep anguish and pain, suicidal, my body working through the motions of being a soldier, my brain working in some cerebral zone only peripherally connected to Vietnam and the Marine Corps. My lies had become so numerous I could hardly remember what was actual truth. The entropy of the ground and war was churning through me so fast I was mind strobe, calm and energetic on the outside, willingly taking chances, but so wracked within I could feel my soul becoming a florid vapor like burned film. I wanted out, but I wasn't going to take the coward's way by shooting myself in the foot. I wanted to escape from being subject unto death or maiming by men who were clearly stupid and intent on getting me and mine killed. How to be well adjusted amongst a collective of maniacal loonies was a trick I hadn't learned, yet. Mental health was conditional, you were supposed to simply accept the monstrosities you were subject to, don't bitch, these are the same conditions your fathers lived through, and all the men who sought union with the combat soldiers all through the past, and they did OK, well, most of them. Except for the ones who ended up in the VA hospitals from drinking and smoking themselves to death, or remain in their stasis of depression simply maintaining life functions, frightened that the truth they've seen at the impact of bullets or exploding shells or body parts flying through the air at them and the knowledge that it is other men just like them that have delivered the shells and bullets and gas chambers and atom bombs, even so prettily wrapped in technological wings and lethal circuitry that the pilots and generals never have to see the exploded bodies of their results, but they are out of this examination.

"None of that matters," the doctor said, "really, there is only you."

"That is what I'm saying!"

"I want you to go over to Regiment and see the Regimental psychiatrist," the doctor said, ending the talk. He wrote out a reference chit, diagnosing me with one word: Intellectualizes.

My brain was condemned. My childhood injuries, paranoias, tantrums, defensive silences, verbal attacks, registries of every bomb dropped on the North, every man I knew who got killed or blown up, every constant urge to be either among the heroic or among the dead, surfaced after the many months without sleep and the continual privations inherent to being combat infantry. I was having a reality attack among serious fantasists. Why I wasn't like everyone else was the question at hand. All the other field corpsmen, all the other combat field Marines had suffered what I'd suffered, and they weren't intellectualizing in front of doctors. Some of them were merely indiscriminately blowing people up, or shooting women in the back, or gunning men down from helicopters, or testing their weapons against insubstantial villages, or applying electrodes to the testicles of suspected Viet Cong sympathizers, or dragging VC behind amphtracks like cowboys in the movies, or throwing themselves in front of machinegun fire because the camera was rolling, or killing our own men by complicity or mistake, or sleeping sixteen hours a day then going out looking for the dreaded Cong, blood glacial cold, or strenuously maintaining the enormous fiction that it was OK to kill these little brown people because they were peasants or niggers or dinks or gooks—not really human—Ho or Westmoreland, wherein lay the essential difference? They were going along with the program, butch bullies at every turn like the only way to survive in the world was to manifest asshole, or turn it to them.

In school the teachers told we new minds that war was an inevitable process of nature, as natural as the earth orbiting the sun, as natural as Mother Earth resurrecting your bones. They neglected to inflict us with the details. Man, part God, was part of nature, so what man did was nature, ergo cum dumb-dumb. The unselfish sacrificial dead are on the menu. Cannibals ken Corpus Christi. The beautiful Vietnamese woman shot in the back is buried to be eaten later, her flesh-stuff filtered into the best rice paddies, next to the graveyard, her ghost astride the soul of her killer or lost to worry folks into fitful peace.

So, sitting in the back of a six-by on my way to Regiment, like going to see the principal, turning over my choices between suicide, medical discharge, imprisonment, self-inflicted wounds, hanging out with the pogues at Battalion, or going back to the field, I could muster no argument against nature. Achieving personal merit offered the only form of salvation. So, even before I'd seen the shrink I'd decided to go back to the field and take my chances, counting my seconds like every man around me, but when my tour was done, it would be finished. No proving my balls by extending, re-upping, shipping over, getting sucked further and further into the fetid chasm of gore, good going boy, now you're one of us men. No thanks.

A childhood music of comfort for the lonely boy, the sound of the turn of the universe, was insisting there must be another way as I jumped off the truck at the rise that overlooked Regiment.

Down in a shallow valley lay the tent city that formed the nexus of military operations for three battalions of Marines. It was hopelessly vulnerable to attack. The concertina was appallingly close to the core of regimental leadership, as if by neglect they wanted to be overrun. The perimeter was defended by too few tired men occupying too shallow fighting holes spaced too far apart for adequate defense. Ten good sappers with mortars and machineguns could devastate the complex in five minutes of concentrated mayhem, with little fear of retribution. At the end of the sprawl of hardback tents stood a mountainous warren of military supplies, including enough explosive death to blow a meteor sized crater in the valley. A dozen mortar rounds in the ammo dump and that would be the end of Regiment. I was stunned by the lack of organization, at the thoughtless choice of placing such a significant military post on indefensible low ground when the Marine Corps' avowed policy was to take the high ground. At the moment the only reason I could figure that the Viet Cong hadn't blown the place to smithereens was that they either hoped to capture the supplies or that they wanted to humiliate us deeply, the whole panoply of death and maiming machines taken on and sneered at by the corpses of their brethren. The treasuries of half the world were being looted to finance the military buildup in North Vietnam to counteract our incursion into Asia, including the life-force of a billion people conscripted to foster or squelch our nasty war disease, each side permitting each other's side's existence in a tacit compact that spent the lives of the wretched.

A jeep carrying something long and lumpy, covered with a poncho, passed next to where I was standing. At first I couldn't figure it out, until the wind blew the poncho back and I saw the body of a healthy robust Marine who'd been shot through the head. A large scabbed gape where the bullet had smashed his skull open fixed him in my memory forever. The jeep drivers seemed so casually disinterested over their gory cargo that I shuddered at their numbness. The jeep continued down the red road to Graves to add the dead Marine to a row of a dozen others. They were wrapped in ponchos or in bodybags, olive drab packages destined back to their mothers, the flies rising in laconic clouds at the disturbance. The men detailed to Graves were angry at having to lug the offal leaking sacks in the pressing heat, and even though I wasn't privy to their nightmares I felt my heart harden for them, cloaking itself in passive fatalism.

Sitting in the metal folding chair beside the psychiatrist's desk I was fumbling at my bootlace, nervous and tired, trying to appear sane and able, but doing badly. I was expecting to find a kind sympathetic man with a notepad and a pipe, but I was looking into the seamed face of a career Marine dedicated to the maintenance of the beloved Corps. He didn't waste any time.

"What do you want?" he said, threatening. He'd heard it all before, they all wanted the same thing, they were all homesick and tired of the bullshit, they were all scared down to their socks of getting gutted or having their balls blown away or having their feet and legs and arms blown off or getting killed outright, sane responses to relentless conditions, they all wanted out, that's why they found their way to sit in front of a safe man who had the power to release them from their fear and bondage.

The hard wisdom in his eyes demanded the truth. If this corpsman wanted out he was sane. Not that he'd get what he wanted, the Corps got what it wanted first, mother green machine, inexorable history.

"Doctor Williams at the Battalion Aid Station sent me over to you," I said, avoiding an answer, and handing him my one word diagnosis. Then a portion of the blurt and tumult in me came out.

"I'm pissed. I don't know what I'm doing here. I gotta follow the orders of a stupid sergeant and be around people who say they *like* to inflict pain and kill people and I can't stand another minute of it!"

He listening patiently, his exasperation quickly becoming boredom.

"You're not getting out."

And I looked at him with sad supplicating puppydog eyes that couldn't hide the frightened lonely boy or the accumulated fury of the past months. He wasn't buying.

"You are here, and this is where you are going to stay. It's time to grow up, right now," he said, his voice as gruff and authoritative as a gunnery sergeant's. I was almost relieved just because he was doing the talking. I was ashamed that I was seeing a psychiatrist, that I was perceived as crazy, no matter how crazy the people around me were. I already knew I wasn't getting out, the military didn't let you go unless you were really nuts, completely unresponsive and uncontrollable, hitting officers, beating-off thirty times a day, shooting your friends for fun, killing your officers and NCOs with grenades, not taking the Corps seriously. And you better take it seriously. You may be on temporary assignment, but the Marine Corps goes on forever.

Being withdrawn or noisy didn't constitute a destructive threat, merely an inconvenience. By the time I reached the psychiatrist's hardback I'd already decided that I was going back to the field and was in fact hoping to impress him enough with my sanity that he would allow that. Travelling through the augury of war was a socially acceptable journey, while travelling through therapy invited lifelong stigma.

"It says here that you intellectualize. What do you think that means?" he demanded.

"If I knew, I could fix it," I said. It wasn't a good answer, but the question had only been rhetorical. He pointed at my head and said, "What it means is that you think you shouldn't have to put up with the same suffering that everyone else has to put up with. You think you are somehow above all the petty bullshit that comes along with serving your country. You think you are better than everyone else. And that is why you are going back to your outfit. Right now. And you are going to do your job. You are going to learn. Now, get out of here."

"That's it?" I asked, hoping for, expecting, wishing for some magic healing touch to end my misery.

"That's it. Go!" he said, and made a note on my chit, ignoring the begging forming on my lips. Of course, he was wrong. I didn't think I was better than the men around me. I was so disconnected from my real self and so dissassociated from my body that with the accumulation of suffering and the maintenance of a fictitious self, ignorant of empathy, hardcharger field Doc, that I felt inferior to all of them. They were men. I was something else, I didn't even have a name for it. Did already deciding to go back to the field mean I really was crazy? Would I spend the rest of my life, if I happened by luck or stamina to survive the war, defining myself in terms of neurosis and self destruction instead of health and joy? Should I have pushed harder and gotten shipped home to the Oak Knoll Naval Hospital Psychiatric Ward to join Don Bumgarten, the pretend Hell's Angel who'd persuaded me to ship for FMF, a kind of pinball irony? At bottom I was really just a man, capable of and hence responsible for every action ever committed upon the world, and my conscience was screaming for nurture. Om mani padme hum.

I went to see a friend.

I found Duke out behind the Regimental mess tent scrubbing some large aluminum pots. One of the benefits of being a corpsman was never having to stand KP as long as there were Marines to be of service, so finding him so engaged surprised my sense of military order.

"So what are you doing, Duke?" I asked, at once sorry to see him demoted to such mundane circumstance, and stifling a laugh, knowing there'd be a funny story of explanation. "Practicing for your future as a civilian?"

"Hey, man. I thought you were humping the hills, scoping out gookdom, getting shot and stuff," he said, flashing his big Irish grin. "I'm being punished. I got thirty days KP Plus my regular job," and he kept scrubbing, dexedrine sweat pouring off him.

"You must have stole the Captain's jeep," I said.

"Naw, I couldn't find the keys. It was my boss, the big bad dentist from Detroit. We were setting up the clinic, I mean he was supervising, I was working, and I couldn't find enough tent pegs to keep the fucking flaps open so I used my rifle for a tent peg. I mean, there ain't been any VC around here for months, but he gets a hair up his ass and tells me I'm a tar spot on the history of the Marine Corps, abuse of man's best friend is what he called it. So he writes me up and the Colonel tells me I'm not showing proper respect, I'm suppose to keep that gun clean all the time so I can protect the big bad dentist from Detroit from Communist attack when they come charging through the wire. Like I would." Then, turning to me, he asked, "What are you doing down here in pogue valley? Checking on one of your buddies?"

"The BAS doctors sent me over to see the shrink. They think I'm crazy."

"We're all crazy, man. We wouldn't be here if we weren't. You think we got here by accident? Only a full-fledged loco would sign up for this. What were you really doing?"

"I thought I was trying to get out, to go home."

"Oh, bad juju. That's the big prize, man. You don't get it if you can still walk and talk. I never would of thunk it of you. Hard charger, an' all," Duke said, and laughed, adding, "You always did have more sense than me, though. How'd you do? What did his nibs say?"

"He just levelled my trash. Told me to get back to my unit and do my job."

"And you don't want to go?"

"I don't want to. I want to be in pussy heaven, but I don't seem to be able to find the right ticket."

He laughed again, but continued scrubbing. "Stick around here. I can get you transferred if you want. We have a pretty good time. Hang around until tonight. We'll go down to the club. We'll get some toads."

"Toads?"

"Yeah, toads. Frisky little fuckers. They live around here. Pure blooded Annamese toads. We have a contest. Each guy gets a toad, puts him in the ring, sprays him with lighter fluid and torches him off. The one who gets outside fastest wins. We make bets on how far they get before they, as we say in our vernacular, succumb to the trauma."

"So this is corpsmen doing this?"

"Everybody, man. Marines, officers, doctors."

"No Duke. I can't make it. I mean we dropped napalm on a bunch of VC having lunch, but that costs too much. I'm gonna split."

"OK. Take it any way you can get it. Where you going now?" Duke said in perfect lucid American.

"I'm going AWOL. I'm going to Da Nang. I'm going to get laid."

"OK. Good seeing you. Good luck," and went back to his scrubbing. The cook was even more demanding than the dentist.

◆◆◆◆

Such heaven was but a bubble in the magnificent steam. Da Nang was much closer. I caught a ride with a happy Marine driving a gun-jeep, heading back to town to pick up his officer. "Seen much action?" he asked, the constant comparisons between men, the details of personal dramas, a way to establish status and rank in our enlisted adolescence. "Compared to what?" I asked back, just as sure that his actual question concerned my cock size. The retort was enough to give me a quiet memory of the last liberty in Da Nang, while he grinned and bounced to his own music.

Back then, so many long nights back, the Captain had offered us his benediction, congratulating us and himself upon our baptism by fire, apologizing for the lack of gratitude expressed by the Vietnamese for our sacrifice, and warning us about the virulent strains of venereal disease that might prove embarrassing to our loved ones if we ever got home, then granting us a liberty. Visions of soldier-of-fortune dinners at the Continental Hotel followed by drunken orgies danced in our heads.

We loaded onto six-bys, bragging, one man saying he went blind every time he got a hard-on, another claiming the ability to grow another member from sheer desire, and another claiming he could pole vault to the city faster than these fucking trucks could get us there; not to mention the oceans of beer about to be consumed, the fights to be won, and the revolution in the country's economy resulting from all the money about to be spent, big talk on ninety a month plus combat pay. We passed the corrugated tin roofed resettlement camp and marketplace down the road from Le Mai, and rolled past the ARVN shade shelter at the crossroads. It seemed curious that the VC hadn't mortared so many government troops in such a state of relaxed vigilance as we usually found them, as if their evolution of the war gave merit only to the hunt and the fire fight, as if mutual murder was the local sport.

We passed old women and young children working in the paddies, women carrying heavy loads on bamboo poles, dismembered men on cyclos selling Coca Cola and fruit ices reputed to contain fragmented glass. As we approached the outskirts of the city the devastation of thirty years of warring appeared as a ramshackle slum consisting of huts made from ammo-crates and flattened beer cans, cardboard and corrugated tin, teeming with wailing women and children. Rats competed with pigs for the garbage strewn in the narrow alleys. Pimps and blackmarketeers hawked the residue of violence. Children with running sores clung to their mothers with withered limbs. To pass through strung you to every slum in the world, the images of their destitution freezing in the soul. To attempt to cure that little pocket of hell with weapons and munitions was the height of arrogant insanity; just seeing Dogpatch released a longing that peace and well-being should reign throughout the world forever, that compassion should waken in every heart.

The trucks stopped in front of MACV headquarters. Starched uniformed men passed in and out of the doors urgently pursuing their purpose, steely glints in their eyes, as if they were consecrated with absolute right. If the energy of their collective resolution to win the war quickly, ignoring the clearly stated tactic of the North to exercise an eroding patience, could be divested of the bemedalled warrior fantasy that sent jets to vanish villages and the lives they contained in flames, if they could have been disabused of the notion that even in Asia American cash carried the morality of a contract, perhaps the mounting mayhem could have been averted. They were men who looked at the maps, sifted the intelligence, allocated the resources, organized the efforts of men, declared villages pacified or free-fire zones, called the airstrikes, channeled the mountain of destruction into the hidden battalions of NVA and the jungle enclaves of the VC by sheer force of decisive mind. We shied away from them as if their thought-waves were toxic.

Then we were on the street, at liberty in Hinoko or Tiger Town or China Town Yokohama or Ologopo, all the same town. After the months of humping the paddies, jungles, villages of devastating poverty and misery, after sustaining the injuries of battles and snipers and booby traps until it was hard to imagine that life was any other way, there we are standing on Asia whoretown street, watching round-eye fever spread like chain lightening. The street was crowded with the thousands of people forced into the city to escape the constant brutality in the towns and hamlets, their husbands and sons taken off by the current of killing. Kids sold cigarettes, condoms, porn, lighters, Paper-Mates from boxes hanging around their necks. Other children offered shoeshines and the services of their sisters, TJ, Da Nang, same-same GI. Their parents rode bicycles and pedicabs, or pulled carts and rickshaws, proffering weapons, drugs, assassination, slaves, any way to stay alive at all.

We broke into buddy groups, the black men drifting away from the chucks quickly, and a friend and I found ourselves threading our way down the crowded tree shaded streets of what was once a beautiful seaside town toward a club called Paradise.

Down at the end of the street where trucks were rolling up from the Navy transports docked at the wharves, in the stark bleaching sunlight, I saw a strikingly beautiful French woman watching the phenomena of bringing the wrath of God to quaint fierce Vietnam. There was something in her posture as she leaned against the dock rail in the distance, her gauzy dress showing a lithe luscious body, that bespoke a cultural deja vu, as if she possessed the secret of history and was deeply injured to see it come to ruin the fragile nation she'd come to love, a Versailles that refused to stay in its crystal globe. Preposterously presumptuous, I wanted to pick her up, but my friend reminded me that I was just another soldier grunt, therefore she was unattainable. "But she's the first round-eye we've seen in, god it feels like forever," I protested, but he led me through the doors of the Paradise Club.

A few tables with a few chairs at each table. A curtain over the doorway that led to the alley that led to the rooms upstairs. Wire grills on the windows to prevent some patriot from blowing up the customers with a grenade, mildew musty, geckoes skiddling over the stucco walls. A half dozen peasant girls dressed in Chinese silk or European cotton sun dresses were waiting for us. As much paradise as a soldier could hope to find.

Were the girls our own sisters we would have dragged them away and forbidden any young buck access to them, but they were the daughters of the war conducted just for us, and were flesh three dreams removed, driven into the city and sexual servitude by the fury occurring in the selves of their fathers and husbands, and in us, a furious dance in which we slashed each other unto death, leaving them to balm our spirits, and that balming reduced to a few minutes of beer and negotiations wherein we played at getting to know each other, ships in the night, heroes passing through, and a few more minutes of fast flat pleasure upstairs.

Upstairs was a high ceilinged long cool room painted pale sunny blue, the color you'd expect to find at a seaside resort. A passageway led to eight or nine cubicles, and in each cubicle was a raised platform that held a soggy mattress and a chair. Calico curtains were provided for modesty. They smelled of sex odors and mildew. The graffiti of feverish boys scratched the walls. Through the narrow windows I could see red tile rooftops and palms, then down to the docks where the great grey ships were unloading mechanical destruction.

I didn't know her name, it didn't matter to either of us. She was lovely and innocent, her eyes luminous and wideset, beautiful, yielding and accepting, and her thick long black hair fell down her supple back. She was from the country, perhaps working off a family debt, pretty and playful. Taking off her cotton dress she exposed small dark-nippled breasts, and the hairless vulva of a girl. Coaxing me to hurry by opening her thighs I saw the rose of her labia surrounded by brown venereal warts. She giggled coyly and while lying back on the ticked mattress seized me by the genitals, slipping on a condom before I had my trousers off. This wasn't going to take that long. That so small a young woman could bear my weight, and the weight of hundreds of other young men like me attested to her country strength. That she could so gladly assume the pent aching lonely joylessness of so many loveless war living young men attested to the strength of women.

In the clank of tank tracks and truck rumbles the easy glide into her, all I could think of was how delicate she was, how fragile beneath my thrusts, how the long sought welcome warmth was just a seizure of muscle, the yielding organ a slick hollow tube empty and dark like the long nights in Vietnam, how her nostrils flared from heaving through the breaths that expelled my desire to reach her, to be known by her as a living man, that somewhere in her future she'd remember my gentle gesture, hoisted on my elbows, my fingers caressing behind her ears. That, and the spasm releasing the knot of realizing who I was with, and who I was, another facet on a ball of mirrors worried that my money was going to buy the guns that would kill my future brothers or my future sons, that in my soldier loneliness I'd compromised my own resolution against supplying the enemy, not knowing whether the girl was a VC or South Vietnamese or MACV sex slave pimped for by brother or cadre or government official, theirs or ours, compounding by one to another thousand upon thousand the injuries done against the Vietnamese people. Fertile seed on barren ground, washed away into the Tourane, food for the long yellow streams of brit in the South China Sea, no babies who'd grow to know the course of stars flowing through them. Business completed, she wiped the condom off with a towel and dismissed me with a flip of her hand. Next.

Making it back to the street, emptier than when I'd gone into the Paradise Club, the urgency of my body to make contact with another human soul for our comfort or commiseration led me to meet up with some friends for another round of beers and another momentary woman, she nearly unrememberable, an aging dark face reflecting on dark water, my same action being repeated several hundred times by several hundred men roiling through the Da Nang afternoon, sending an energy through the nationsphere to manifest a long season of lust unquenchable by mere purchased pussy. By the time curfew came around the streets were rolling with drunken men who'd had their money stolen, gotten their rocks off, told their war stories so many times they'd all won Silver Stars and battlefield promotions, of course refused, and were piling puking into the backs of the six-bys in tangles of legs and arms and singing, headed back to our bunkers and concertina, weapons and fear. And while we were able to forget for a moment, the Vietnamese cyclo drivers began vanishing into their work of the night, slipping back onto the speed trails that led them to where they could ambush us or watch us, or ready their plans for when the big push came.

A week later a third of the company bared their fleshy butts to a line of corpsmen who injected them with their standard issue of two million units of penicillin.

That was the good time. By the time the happy jeep driver dropped me off in Da Nang round-eye fever had become such an epidemic that all that remained of the original city were its core of stucco buildings, Vietnamese scale, and leafless trees that had once shaded the sidewalks. The long slow riot of destruction was at hand. Dogpatch had grown to an alarming abysm of filth and despair, the diseases of the dispossessed carrying through the benjos into every niche and cranny of the city, curling up against the mud splattered walls, scratching its back on the hordes of people who were dealing black-market goods, consuming the minds of children changing money, being a hot copper scent in the nostrils of the thousands and thousands of new troops who were so thickly confusing the streets they were bouncing off each other like fry in a trout pond; a monstrous organism made of impacted rage, dysenteried bowels, teeth gnashing greed, marketplace frenzy, roiling drunkenness, Americans seeking pleasure and release as if Asia was the sexual supermarket built to accommodate our furious desire unanswerable at home. Trucks bullied their way down the streets, followed by jeeps carrying mounted .50 caliber machine-guns, followed by half-tracks. Streams of officers poured in and out of MACV headquarters, and rivers of enlisted men poured in and out of the hundred new bars, backslapping and shouting, hunting a new dark corner that hadn't been visited too recently so the girls would be fresher, hunting that last moment of knowing a woman before maybe getting blown apart or killed or going crazy.

I was easy pickings. Alone, stricken by the foresight that the war was growing in intensity and violence, that every child I'd grown up with was going to be touched deep in his soul by its steel teeth, that the stench of the city in the clasp of starving refugees turned to dishonor by our money and our childlike demand for women's bodies would sour all our days to come, if we had some, seeing that the war was growing grotesquely and fearing that even once my tour was over that I would be called upon again to serve, to do my duty, to lend my experience to the saving of lives and bodies, but I wanted no part of it, I'd refuse, I'd go to jail, and for that I was ashamed. I remembered telling a Hong Kong tailor—he asked, hating the Vietnamese—that I'd killed two VC, but he knew I was lying. Now I wanted nothing more than to resume a kind of magic innocence, a wish to abdicate my passage through Vietnam, to cleanse myself of what I'd seen and done and collectively wished into existence looming around me and a tremendous tumult of machines and men, but that would be like trying to throw away your skin.

Alone, the rain and men crisping my mind like ten days of acid, not even drunk but nevertheless incapable of doing anything other than what was going on around me.

"Number one good pussy," the cyclo driver said, pulling up beside me as I wavered on a street corner, half my money gone into the pocket of a sharp ten year old moneychanger kid. I knew he'd shorted me but it was his country and his future and he deserved it. Enough piasters left for a short-time and a couple of beers. They were going to get everything we had anyway, it was just a question of when.

Before the cyclo could be commandeered by a clutch of new guys I climbed in, feeling sorry for the pack animal life of the driver, seeing also in his face that same implacable fierce resolution I'd seen in the VC my friend Dale had shot. How versatile to be able to scalp us first, then kill us, bringing more and more dangerous fools to scalp and kill, but for their confounding machines. The sorry war economy stuffing the future into the now as fast as you could truck. The Chinese and the Russians weren't giving their munitions away. And if by off chance the cyclo driver wasn't VC, when they came, he'd need a way out. Scurry and run, pick one and deliver him, take your cut and go get another one, two more, maybe three, fish in a barrel.

The cyclo driver weaved through the crowds, taking sidestreets for a few blocks until we were in the off-limits part of the city, me worrying about being picked up by the roving squads of MPs without a liberty card. Market stalls selling fatigues, clips of ammo, M-1, M-14, AK-47, grease for whoever could afford it, pistols, cases of C-rations, whiskey, cigarettes, war fuel, spreading down the side streets like the ties to the future were being snapped like spider webs in a gale.

"You pay, you come," the cyclo driver said, demanding his five dollars. Ride and throw, one price. I stepped out of the cyclo, paid my driver who in turn paid another man waiting at the entrance of an alley. Several more Vietnamese men stood at the alley entrance, as menacing as pimps in the Tenderloin. No hats, pistols visible under their short sleeved shirts. The deal was made, the choice was to go through with the transaction as dictated by them or walk away, lose the money and your claim of being a soldier.

From inside the alley I heard the muffled grunting of dozens of men and the labored breathing of dozens of women. Several Marines passed by me, looking ashamed and shy, zipping their trousers. A woman, her expression that of a mother exasperated with her children, grabbed me by the arm and led me into a vast warren of curtained stalls that seemed to stretch in every direction endlessly. Several more Marines passed me on their way out. Several more women followed after them, taking the next group of men by their arms and leading them into the curtained warren. Their eyes were twisted and furious, having absorbed thousands of war-boy climaxes, the energy of the thrusts mounting in them no matter how often they muttered the mantra that it was just a job, just a dream of quick nameless cocks.

The woman whose lot I'd drawn looked to be about thirty, or forty, it was hard to tell in a face fated to suffering. She led me into her stall, and on both sides of me I could hear other soldiers grunting toward their spurting, pretending that pussy, access to the feminine void, was all that mattered, humping away wheezing and sorrowful. Inside the curtained stall she untied her kimono and lay back on an army issue cot, a kapok pillow at its head, a towel draped over its middle, stained and spotted cum yellow. She hitched the kimono up under her back, spread her legs and motioned for me to enter her. There was no point in undressing. She let out a sigh like a channel of Hell was open in her and she no longer cared enough to try to close it. If its consumptive energy spilled back into the men who were fucking her, number one fucky-fuck, it was only what they were bringing to her. The flesh of her once muscular thighs and hips sagged from supporting the weight of the men come there to deliver their message of salvation. Her breasts had been fondled and sucked by so many hands and mouths that stretch marks showed through dirty fingerprints. Her vagina was bruise purple, flaccid, oiled smooth with condom lubricant. With each thrust she let out small grunts of animal suffering. From pity I finished as quickly as I could. And around me, from behind their own curtains, duplicating like one bed in a room full of dusty mirrors the self-same men and women as she and I, were going through the same sexual assembly line, the same wretched fleshpain charade. And as she absorbed me, I absorbed her and all the men before me to carry as human memory, wishing her thereafter a freedom from us, a wise liberation, wishing her nurture and dignity, protection and peace, children and well-fed futures for them all, forever and ever, amen.

But there was nothing I could do for her but leave. I was just another member of the vortex swirling through the country and through her small soul forced to accept so many, so many men that we no doubt all became the same solid flesh meaning only a dull aching pain that would, pray to hope, go away before she was fucked to death or uselessness and thrown away by her pimps, Hollywood and Ford something she'd never heard of, but felt.

I may have been crazy, but I knew that I had to get back out into the field, get the tour over with, make no mistakes, make no waves, follow and be compliant, float like a leaf upon a stream, and get out of that place as intact as I could remain. I wasn't any tourist or reporter, I was a maker of war, a willing participant, the center of it just as the people selling weapons on the black market and the pimps and the whores and the colonels and the grunts and the VC dedicated down to the last cell of our bones to the execution of war.

The Useful Boy

I would be compliant. I would be useful and happy. I'd go along with the program and keep my mouth shut and not make any waves. When the officers commanded, I would respond. I'd go out on the ambushes, and go out on the operations and hang back inside the wire when I could, when we all could, when it was safe and there was no enemy activity afoot, passing out the white pills every day and the red pills once a week, and the crab ointment, and the vitamins, and the gook-sore ointment, and I'd take off the leeches, and debride the sloughed off skin of my men's immersion foot, and I'd attend to the colds and depressions, and comfort the men who got Dear John letters, and agree with the sergeants. I'd pass out the Lomotil even if someone had stolen its active ingredient of opium and the men suffered from dehydration and fever. I would shut-up and do my damndest to not be different, and retract my obdurate challenges. And if there was the faintest hint of a silly grin on my face, if someone felt a current in the air that one of us was secretly praying not for war but for release from its maniacal grip, I wouldn't mention that it was me. Death before dishonor would be my motto, Semper Fi mutherfucker, do or die. But by the time I got back to the hill everything had changed.

There were new faces everywhere, new squads composed of new men from other companies, men I'd never seen before occupying the bunkers we'd dug and sandbagged. Half my friends were gone. The ones who'd stepped on land mines, and the ones who'd been shot, and the ones who'd gotten malaria or vanished in some other way were vapor beings still familiar in the air. But they were replaced with tougher looking men, men with the lines of combat furrowing their faces, the tired hunting staring eyes, the hunched shoulders, the pared down to nothing but the essential ergs motions of body movement, the absolutely sure invincibility of Marines, how could you survive without it. They were new, but within a few days well integrated, we were finding ourselves interchangeable, just like we were always told, Marine, trooper, grunt, all the same word, all the same man.

A couple of nights later, after yet another long patrol, there was something knocking on my bunker. It was night. I could tell by the flare light in the gunslit. I don't remember going to sleep, I must have faded out after we'd come in through the wire. But there were these repeated impacts banging into the sandbags. Then there was someone standing in my doorway shooting his rifle with quick sure shots. A machine-gun started firing short bursts from the bunker across the road.

The smart thing to do, I remember thinking, would be to just lie here in my own good hole and wait for someone to call me, no point in going out there if the gooks are shooting at us, and if it was a full scale ground attack there would be more than two guns firing, the sandbags were adequate to protect me and I was even lower into the ground than any bullets could penetrate, it would have to be a rocket or grenade or mortar to take me out of my bunker and I was out of range of grenades, if there were rockets or mortars being fired I would have heard them by then, the smart thing to do would be just lay chilly, wait, let what was happening either grow in intensity or dissipate, hopefully the latter, hopefully it would go away and I wouldn't have to doubt my courage any longer. Stick to your role, don't be putting on those warrior airs, a dufus jerk like you could get shot.

The M-60 fired a few more bursts, probing, not sure, the tracers impacting out in the paddies beyond the road. I heard the man in my doorway shift his weight, getting a better footing, then cracking off a few more rounds. Another illumination round popped in the air above us, and before I knew what I was doing some other part of me made the decision to put on my boots and glasses, grab my medical kit and jump into the personage of hard charger field doc, not even afraid of dying.

"Coming through," I said, and pushed my way past the man firing from my doorway, staying low, taking cover behind him and the end of the bunker. I couldn't recognize him. He was one of the new men. He was shirtless in his flack jacket and had a olive drab sweat towel around his neck. No helmet. A thick purple scar ran down his neck and disappeared under the flack jacket. The firing stopped, and I asked, "What's happening?" Not really sure I wanted to know, more interested in letting a Marine know that I was there, subjecting myself to the same rigors as he was, except the killing. My eyes were scanning out in front of us in an adrenal strobe, the ground was grey silver, black and yellow, from the illumination round and the machine gun was spitting a tight red arc of tracers, but I couldn't see the targets.

A few bright muzzle flashes came from down by the gate and the bullets hit my bunker again. The Marine fired again, and the M-60 opened up again. In between firing the Marine explained, "Probe, steal our Claymores, who knows? Who are you?"

"Corpsman," I said. A pang of disappointment crossed his face. "Better keep your ass down, Doc," he said, firing a few more rounds. I'd never seen a face so fiercely earnest, so beautifully concentrated, so confident. A few more bullets hit the bunker and I took his advice, ducking with him, waiting for someone to call for me. The M-60 opened up with a long stream of firing. No more muzzle flashes came at us from out of the night after that.

"Catch some Zs, Doc. No more fun tonight," the rifleman said, relaxing, a smile of self congratulation coming over him.

"What about the gooks?" I asked, wondering if they had accomplished their task and ran away, or been killed while I watched, not even wearing my pistol, not even ready for repelling a ground attack if they were staged out there ready to wipe us out to the last man.

"Fuck 'em," the rifleman said, "Let 'em fetch their own dead." Then he turned and left, and I never saw him again.

The next morning we went down to check the Claymores and found them untampered with, intact, and there was no blood scabbing the road dust, just some scattered brass.

A few more days passed, they wouldn't even have to call me, the squads would start to assemble on the road above my bunker and I would go out and join them, and we'd walk out through the wire, into Le Mai, or down the road past the paddies and the tree lines, or down the mined trail behind the French fort.

And at night the squads would argue over who would get to take me, and I'd join them on a sand-bagged ambush, and Martinez would say, "Go to sleep, Doc," and I'd lay down on the soggy ground, not really sleeping, my mind working constantly to extend itself, to stretch itself into the very fiber of the land, hearing the leaves on the shrubbery grow, hearing the footfalls of insects landing on weeds, hearing the rain seep through the granules of laterite, registering the rate and rhythm of the men around me breathing, delicate tendrils of sense webbing out over the rough ground, and I'd wake at the slightest movement within a hundred yards. I had the ears. And Ramirez knew that, seeing me more that once bolt upright completely alert, startling the watching ambush squad, and seeing a small group of blacker shadows cross between some trees too far away for quick aim and firing. Can't radio in the sighting because we bagged it, stay awake now, they might be heading our way, but it didn't look like it. No sweat, we're the only ones supposed to be out here. Doc knows. Like the night we were out in the dark bush and I woke about to fly out of my skin with terror but there was nothing around to generate such fear. We'd sand-bagged the ambush again and there could have been other Marines hunting through the dark and about to come upon us, no one in authority had our coordinates, but no, it wasn't ground pounders, "What is it, Doc, What Is It?" Ramirez fiercely whispers. "We better move, get behind a dike," I say. And just as he decides I might be right and we crawl on our elbows over to a dike, slither over, and hunker down deep in its shadow in the dark of the wretched mosquito heat of night, the glare of a scanning search light catches the spot where we were hiding, then we hear the jet popping whops of a Cobra rushing down on us, the M-60 in the door spits bright yellow, a stream of tracers kicks up the dirt where we were lying, and we're huddled down deep in the deepest shadow afforded by the life-saving mud paddy dike, not even breathing, not even allowing the sweat to run down a hair and sound on the ground, the night was filled with whirling ghosts armed with knives, unfindable and unkillable, and on top of them the Cobra night patrols were trying to find us and kill us, and maybe it wasn't us they thought they were firing on, maybe there were VC who had found us out and were just waiting for the Cobra to fly past before they slit our throats, and you can't even scream at the Marines in the helicopter, you fucking idiots don't you know you're trying to kill your own men, so the scream gets stuck back in there and some years later primal therapy releases it, but you still duck every time you hear or see a chopper, and the Cobra circles around, the search light scanning all around, but it doesn't find us, and we can't see any VC also hiding, and finally the chopper goes on about its deadly business, and dawn is too far away and we wait sweating in the terrible dark, but dawn comes and we go back in, not even being able to tell each other what happened, but your sympathy for the Vietnamese is compounded, making them that much less the enemy.

And such confusion cost, like when a few weeks later Cpl. Ramirez stepped through the thorny hedges of Le Mai like he had twenty or thirty times before, and the wire he tripped loosed the C-ration can that released the unpinned grenade that blew off his right foot. Down to the left was the village well, and that was where the kids hung out and the old women came to fetch the kitchen water. The explosion blew his foot off at the ankle and he was thrown back through the hedge opening, laying on the ground, looking at the women and children lingering around the well. The other men in the squad hit the deck, looking for cover. For a moment he looked stunned and disoriented, like he couldn't believe that something horrible could happen to him. Then he saw that his right leg was shredded below the knee, and shake his leg as hard as he could the foot refused to appear. His foot was in his boot, and his boot was somewhere out behind him in the tall grass beside the graveyard, and there wasn't any way, not even an act of God, that could rejoin it to the integrity of his body. It was smoldering and no one wanted to touch it. The shard of bone and blackened muscle was showing the veins and arteries fused bloodless by the searing heat of the explosion. Two old women were watching from inside the ville, and Rameriz focused on them as the ones who had set the booby trap, or at least knew and watched it being done and had failed to warn him. He reached for his rifle, his only form of revenge, and started screaming, "You fucking cunt bitches!" repeatedly, all the while trying to stand, to get up on his good foot, to stand, to be a man again.

Then his sergeant was kneeling beside him, pushing the rifle away from him, calming him, talking to him, saying, "Hey, man, you're gonna be all right, really man, take it easy, going home for sure," he said, saying what were the most comforting phrases he could think of without mentioning the wound. "I'm gonna kill them fucking bitches!" Ramirez screamed, again reaching for the rifle, but the sergeant held it away from him. "Let's just worry about getting you out of here," the sergeant said, "We'll take care of the Gooks later." Then he yelled, "Corpsman up!" And while the rest of the men were hiding behind tiny knolls of dirt and grass facing outward in the event that the booby trap wasn't just a random maiming and foreshadowed an attack, the women who were watching were standing just out of range of the grenade, like they knew. The corpsman ran toward the gate in a crouch, his kit banging against his hip. A man was down, his whole purpose in being was to get to his man, life and death held no distinction, the moment of proof of courage, of human usefulness, was at hand. He reached Ramirez quickly, and saw the corporal slipping into shock and incoherence.

The corpsman saw the wound, a wave of revulsion rocking him backward. It wasn't there. The foot just wasn't there. All of life demanded congruity, wholeness, but some diabolical terrorseed had smashed into Ramirez with controlled fury and ripped off his foot, leaving a blackened congealed stump. To be wounded in combat, to be killed in combat where a man had a chance, was an honorable mortality. But a booby trap was insidious, the product of a dishonorable hateful people denoting a loathing contempt for all life. Retaliation for random mortar attacks, but up close, legs, balls, bowels, the message of humiliation so powerfully felt that they were willing to sacrifice their babies and children to deliver it to us, to leave their dead bodies in our wounds and souls when we went away.

Oh shit, what do I do now? So horrible, fucker could die, he's got labored breathing, he could stop breathing and croak, gotta stop the bleeding, elevate the wound, wound! traumatic amputation, these devious little shits sure put out the fear, Morphine, respiratory depressant, what the fuck, the dude is hurting. "They fucked you up good, Corporal. No lie. But you ain't gonna die, no more Vietnam for you," the corpsman promised, but he had no idea how long it would persist—on and on, lives mixed until crisped and gone, wrapping a battle dressing over the stump, then slipping a Morphine styrette needle into the corporal's shoulder. "It'll stop hurting in a second, Ramirez. Stay awake, now. The chopper'll be here any minute," and turning to the sergeant, saying, "Put your flack jacket under his head so he can breathe. Have two men put their packs under his leg, we gotta elevate the wound. Call an emergency medevac, do it now." And there was such conviction in his voice that the orders were followed immediately. Ramirez's eyes were taking on dreamy Morphine relief, his rage quieting, burrowing back into his deeper self to wait and gnaw and spring cynical and relentless upon a callow hometown. To Regiment to be stabilized, to Japan for surgical reduction, to some sleazy VA hospital for wingtip retro-fit. Gone and gone again, clerking, computers, boozed to death, who knows?

Some men made a stretcher, and four of them carefully carried the corporal to the H-34 as it landed out in the paddies. Passing through the rotor wash and reaching the door, the men transferred him to a regulation stretcher the door gunner had tossed out, thus retrieving their gear. The gunner had seen all this many times before, though he couldn't get the look of shock and worry to leave his young face. And just as the chopper was about to take off, in some bizarre gesture to affirm the wholeness of the world, the corpsman approached the gunner with Ramirez's helmet in his hand, and handed it to the gunner. The gunner took it, then dropped it. In the helmet was Ramirez's oozing congealing foot. The gunner stuffed it under one of the web seats and told the pilot to take off. After that we never saw the corporal again. I missed him.

Oh the World. We'd talk about it in our bunker, Jim Marshall, the company radioman, John Anderson, and Stevenson, the closet homosexual writer from New Orleans, an outcast, so welcome, and me. We'd proffer visions of how it was going to be, adrift in manna-pleasure. We'd have elegant rooms where we'd be safe and warm, and pillow-breasted women would sing us vulvic lullabies. Infinite tunnels of delight would be plugged directly into our veins. We'd eat sumptuous delicacies from jewelled services, opium canapes would be delivered by wish. In eternal youth and vigor we'd generate majestic works; a bridge across the Bosphorus, solar desalinators for the Palestinians, a great golden lotus for Alcatraz. Stevenson wanted black-tie parties, yachts and cities, and to own all the ships at sea. There was never any mention of victory parades or the President pinning CMHs on our chests. Those notions had vanished after the first fire fight. Larry Burrows from *Life Magazine* told us he'd been to 54 wars in the last six years, delivering to us a telling blow that blew out our superman candle and told us our exact worth in the larger scheme. Neither was there any mention of how we would pay for these ambitions, nor who we would have to enslave to get the work of them accomplished. It was just boy dreams in a brotherhood that knew no real future.

◆◆◆◆

But Sergeant O'Neill, weapons platoon sergeant, doesn't concern himself with the petty worries of the low-life ground pounders. He's got his Ontos and his mortar pits to run from the flat just before the climb up to the CP He patrols the installation, ceaselessly checking the cleanliness of the tubes, making sure the increments and rounds are stacked for easy assembly, even going so far as to hold inspections of his crew, lining them up in platoon formation to be sure they've shaved and kept themselves as clean as they could considering there was no shower, only the gook laundry down at the marketplace. Sergeant O'Neill is from Birmingham, a farm boy who grew up in the Marine Corps. He is lean and taut, fiercely patriotic, though he flies a Stars and Bars from the Ontos radio antenna, a snap-to, on-the-stick noncom thrilling in the power of his weapons. His tubes were always ready to send up illuminations rounds, to fire harassment missions, to do the bidding of the captain immediately, if not sooner. That asshole college jerk lieutenant on the four-deuce had nothing on him.

And today he is expectant. We are lazing around after morning chow, waiting for mail call, watching him lead his crew in side-straddle hops. He is getting them prepared to execute a harassment and interdiction mission on the village across the river. It's been a long time since he's been allowed to drop explosive death on people. And the mission was to mortar shrapnel on the known VC village that had fired on every Marine patrol that had ever swept through it, the same village he'd dropped mortar rounds on when the captain ordered the diversionary action over there in Indian Country, but he didn't know if any of the rounds had struck home. It was the same village that was rich with good wells, plenty of firewood in the jungles around it, river access for sampans, a road that led to the bridge that led to Hue and Da Nang, and good well-tended paddies. Even though most of its men had already been taken off by the war, and it was full of widows and sick children, it was still V.C.

And it was going to be a righteous mission, decency was going to prevail. The day before helicopters had dropped bright pink leaflets into the village, announcing that it was going to be mortared for the crime of harboring Viet Cong. We all knew the village was used for rest and staging by the Viet Cong. The trail leading east from it led to a narrows in the river where they could cross and gain access to the plains around DaNang, and the shelling was ordained by Regiment as a dissuasion. The sentiment among the troops was that the people over there knew the rules by now, you got a Commie mind, you're dead, tough shit, they'd do us if they got a chance.

After the calisthenics, O'Neill was so energized that he came down the hill to gather an audience. He called the group of men I was with over to him, announcing that he was going to drop some mortars on the ville, but would'ya take a look at this? Gathering around him, he held out a black and white photograph of a beautiful blond woman, German plump. Looking at it, being compliant and encouraging, friendly and innocent, I said, "Your wife, Sarge, she's sure good looking?"

"Yeah. My wife. But look at this one!" he says, excited as a boy with a box of firecrackers, and he shows us the next snapshot. And there is the beautiful pulchritudinous blond sucking on a cock she can barely fit into her mouth. "That you, Sarge?" some other trooper asks, and O'Neill says it is, flashing several more of the same. O'Neill's red face can hardly contain his exuberance, his eyelids are twitching, his mouth is a spasm of expectation. I didn't say so, but I'd already seen the same set of flicks brought in by a man who'd spent his R&R in Australia. O'Neill got some envy and adulation from a few of the men, deserved or no, and it was enough to send him back up the hill to his fire mission, a dozen of us following behind, induced and invited. The mission was to fire twenty-five rounds of H & I into the village, a warning, a sign of our growing omnipotence, an indication of our murderous resolve, no matter if thousands upon thousands of NVA were working their way down the Ho Chi Minh Trail to harass and interdict us or any villager fool enough to resist their swarming tyranny.

So there we were standing in a giddy group behind the mortar pit, Sergeant O'Neill orchestrating the team. And as tough as I was pretending to be, as tough as the men standing next to me were certain they were, the act of dropping mortar rounds on people who weren't attacking us still felt like a circlejerk, a clusterfuck, a group grope gone insane. Looking into the village my vision was crisp around the edges, like the focus of the sun had become a ring of acetylene, and the currents and rivers that ran through the lives of the villagers were seeking an avenue of escape.

The bandy sergeant stepped up to the tube, received the .81 round he demanded, and said, "Let's get this show on the road!" and dropped the round down the tube, and it was immediately whistling through the air and impacted in the direct center of the village, throwing up red dirt and grey-white smoke, sending lightening quick shrapnel into the flimsy thatch hootches. The report reached us just after we saw the explosion. "Put out two more for effect," O'Neill said, exuberant, working hard to hold on to himself. He put two more rounds down the tube in rapid succession. They exploded in the village near the site of the first round's explosion. "Right on, Sarge," a trooper said, and agreeing, O'Neill said, "Adjust left a hair," then handed the next round to one of his team. "Your turn, Private," he said, conspiratorially, catching the trooper's eyes with his own like now was the moment of proof, action talks, shit walks, spread the load and it won't hurt as much. The pitman twisted a knob and the other man dropped in two more rounds. In the village a banana tree exploded, and a thatch house exploded, then collapsed. For a moment I thought I could hear the screams of women and children carried up to us on the stale air.

Then O'Neill turned to those of us in the awed chorus, his eyes making the same demand on each one of us, either drop in a round or don't call yourselves men, chickenshit girls. It would have been easier to excuse yourself from a gangbang than to get out of committing the violence being exercised in the name of repressing the Viet Cong. Each one of us took a round, and while O'Neill adjusted the tube's aim, we paraded by and on his signal dropped in our round. The explosions walked up and down the length of the village, impacting and exploding in or beside the thatch houses, hot orange bursts, hissing shrapmetal, brief smoke, a house catches on fire, the banana trees are cut down, another house is afire, a water buffalo has broken out of its pen and is limping through a paddy, my eyes can see the red slash of flesh hanging from its haunch, it keeps twisting its horns around in bellowing incomprehension, gored by an invisible enemy, but we don't see any people, and sit around the edge of the mortar pit avoiding O'Neill's antic posturing and also avoiding looking at each other, as if what we'd just done would go away if none of us saw it in each other. After looking down into the far village for a half an hour or so, the show was over, no sign of significant damage, and we began drifting back to our bunkers.

Then there are small groups of people moving around the edge of the village, none of them are men, and none of them are armed, and I'm not making the connection, the time elapsed between our attack and the people getting their circular boats down from the rafters of their thatch houses isn't like a movie or like work. The people have waited until they were absolutely sure that we have stopped our attack and that we had no reason to continue to drop mortar rounds on them anymore, if we ever really did. And I can't figure out what they're doing, they're holding the round woven baskets, boats, that's what they are, boats made like baskets woven out of bamboo strips, and they're loading some people in the boats, there must be four, five, maybe six boats, maybe they're coming over here to attack us in broad daylight, what balls that would take to come charging up this hill right into the blast of an Ontos and a hundred-fifty Marines just itching for a fight, but those aren't rifles they're rowing with, just paddles, and there are some people huddled down in the centers of the boats, and they wouldn't be bringing children over if they were going to attack us. They look so fragile and injured. Their weeping is carried on the river. It sounds like birds spun in a drum.

Then we see them hobbling their way across the paddies, past the spot where Wilks shot the beautiful young woman, and they are all women and children. Some of the women are holding the others up, and some of the women have their babies clutched to their hips, they are moving slow and labored, but resolute.

And I am so deadened that I can't understand that they are the victims of our mortar attack, that they don't have a doctor they can go to, that there isn't a medevac helicopter that will swoop out of the sky and pick them up and take them to an air-conditioned operating theater where expert surgeons will remove the shrapnel they received as punishment for believing the power of the gun was superior to the fickle power of brotherly love that just rained mortar rounds down on them.

We see them gather at the wire, there are fifteen women and six children, their faces are contorted in anguish and their high-pitched voices are demanding admittance. They may have no doctors, but they know we do. The sentries at the gate can't admit them, though, the Captain has issued a standing order that there will be no gooks inside the wire without his express permission. But the women keep clamoring and the children are whimpering, and when I get down to the bottom of the hill, the Captain right behind me, I can see the dark wet splotches of blood soaking into their black pajamas. One woman is holding a flap of skin that was her cheek in place with one hand, the other hand comforting the baby clinging to her hip. The baby has a wound in her shoulder. They are pointing out their wounds to the Captain, but the Captain is in a rage, demanding, "What are those people doing here?"

"Caught in that shit we just laid down in that village across the river, Skipper." I said, the consequences starting to register. It was all right to explain what we were all seeing, but it wasn't all right to volunteer to do anything other than act against the enemy.

"I don't give a shit if they got blown up here from Da Nang. Didn't you get the word?" the Captain snarled, his own incomprehension no doubt forcing him to retreat into formula, rules. Sgt. O'Neill was having no part of it. He preferred his imagination, and stayed up on the hill with his tubes so he wouldn't have to look.

"But they're bleeding, sir," one of the sentries said, incredulous that he would have to state so clear an observation.

"The whole fucking country is bleeding, Private," the Captain said. "Let their own people take care of 'em. Fucking VC probably sent them over here to do their psywar stuff on us. We oughta send them back. They know the rules!" His face was still fuming red, but he was relenting, the sight of the women's and children's injury inviting instinctive mercy. After a few minutes he asked me, "What can you do for them, Doc? It's up to you. You don't have to treat them if you don't want to."

The ball was in my court. The assembled troopers were looking at me. The women and children were moaning and sobbing in the relentless heat, and a decision had to come about soon. If I administered care to them I would be aiding and abetting the enemy, a criminal act among soldiers. If I used up my limited supply of Morphine and battle dressings just to stabilize their wounds I would be possibly depriving my own men of needed life saving materials. If I demonstrated the least shred of compassion for them my status as a willing soldier would be jeopardized and I would be diminished in their eyes.

"You don't feel like working on 'em, Doc, we'll tell 'em to di-di," the Captain insisted. But his arms were folded across his chest and he was waiting. He was remembering my defiance, letting me learn my command lessons with the fates of the women and children in the balance. Better my conscience than his.

I didn't know how many dead lay over in the village, how many other women and children we had killed outright with the smashing down of bursting mortar rounds, or how many people lay too wounded to travel. But I did know that I was part of their suffering, I had dropped that round down that tube and sent it flying over into their midst to explode shrapnel through their bodies. And though I was the one supposed to be compassionate, allowing all the other men to exercise their cruelty and sadism, their killer instincts, when I came to the decision that suffering was suffering, enemy or no, women and children were standing in front of me bleeding with the metal that I and we had sent tearing through them and that deeper self that doesn't know anything about enemies or skin colors or even danger had already decided, so when I led the women and children up to the shade inside the amphtracks, the Marines and officers who'd been waiting for me to decide, to see which way their own sympathies should wend, even if it was contrary to the professed sick evil notion of kill them all and let God sort them out, they were visibly relieved. Life was being affirmed whether they liked it or not. An old Buddhist priest in Bangkok who gave me his blessing, maybe even foresaw my path, suddenly appeared in mind.

"These bitches booby trap us, it'll be your fault, Doc," a trooper warned. Whitefang relaxed, and seemed satisfied that the decision had been made. He wasn't the one who had had to do so, hence the onus of aiding and abetting the enemy didn't fall directly on him. His honor was protected, mine besmirched. The only things the women and children were carrying were each other and their loads of pain.

The amphtrack crews had been watching from the shade of the open vehicles, resting on their cots, reading *Sgt. Rock*. They seemed resentful that they'd be disturbed to provide comfort for the wounded people, but gave up their cots. The Vietnamese women quieted once they reached the amphtracks, and gratefully took the canteens of water offered by several of the troopers.

I took care of the baby first, injecting him with a quarter dose of Morphine, and when he was quiet, slumbering in his mother's arms, probed the wound in his shoulder with a forceps I'd cleaned in a canteen cup. The shrapnel had only ripped the skin and muscle open, and wasn't embedded. There was nothing more I could do but clean it as best I could, and bandage it.

The wounds in the women were surprisingly free from bleeding, just open tears in their labor hardened flesh where the shrapnel had knifed through. There was no way I could do a complete surgical procedure to sew the baby's mother's cheek shut, all I could do was clean it and bandage it, giving her the other portion of the Morphine. The women watched me closely as I pulled her pajama bottoms off to administer the styrette. As soon as the narcotic hit her, another of the women took the baby from her and she lay down on the cot, sleeping. The rest of the women lined up for me to probe their wounds. Most of them were superficial, and I extracted pieces of fragmented steel when I could feel them. I cleaned and dressed a large flap of skin that had been torn away from a woman's scapula, baring the bone. I took several pieces of shrapnel from the withered breast of another woman, giving both of them Morphine. There were arm wounds, hip wounds, scalp wounds, leg wounds, and I took out the metal when I could find it, dressing them, conserving the remaining Morphine when the victims weren't whimpering too much. The CO had called for a chopper to take them into Regiment for better medical care, and being there was no adequate antiseptic, a good chance that if I probed too deeply I could accidently enter a body cavity or puncture a lung, I'd leave the suturing to the surgeons.

By the time I'd finished my emergency comforts the chopper was landing. The officers organized the troopers who were watching and the women and the two children I'd bandaged and who needed further attention were carried to the chopper on the cots. They were woozy from the Morphine and couldn't walk. The rotor wash blew red dust into the bandages. Then they were gone, left by their sisters and aunts to our trust, maybe to never be seen again. The remaining women then just turned away, not looking back, not gesturing thank you or acknowledging our help in any way, just walking away and back to their boats to row back across the river and continue their terrorized living.

Back to helping the Viet Cong and the invading NVA. Back to providing rice and shelter, and sons, and babies who would pick up the gun as soon as they demonstrated that they would do what they were told to do. And it wasn't those particular women who rigged the booby trap that blew Ramirez's foot off, but women who were just like them, subject to the same pressures and intimidations, the same starvations and injuries, and I had helped them. The next time we went into that village they would lay out a boobytrap or send their men out to ambush us, or not warn us when the Viet Cong were near by waiting to kill or maim us. That I had taken the shrapnel out of their bodies did not obviate the act of putting it into their bodies. And if the good Samaritan, the mouse and the lion, the

230

Hippocratic Oath, had not been wasted on me, I could also see the pain and suffering tolerated by those women as being involute, turning back upon itself to further temper their resolution, strengthening their affirmation to be free of us and our sick evil tenet of killing them all and letting God sort them out, how deeply sad for us. It was humiliating to have our naive big brotherly generosity rejected in favor of tyranny. We'd won no hearts with our violence. And there it was in small, my dilemma, everyone's dilemma, how to free us each and all from the gun; our mechanically superior fury against their soul's capacity for suffering, long practiced, adept, ready to be regenerated as new life. There would be no winning. There would be nothing final. It would be like Uncle Ho said, a continual armed struggle until all the guns of Southeast Asia pointed at the Pacific and monster China, the narrow concentration of their thinking murdering anyone who opposed it; until angry with their enemies the cadres in Nanking dragged them outside and shot them in their heads, throwing them onto a pile of bodies, ending the tedious arguments. And while my simple act of helping our potential killers may have been a foolhardy sacrifice, it was still defensive and held mere hope; there was no deal. If I couldn't hear what the troopers were saying, if I couldn't win the war by myself, if I couldn't say what I was thinking to whoever could change their minds and release his violent charges back to farm the land and make the goods, then what was there left to do but fight when you needed to, and live until you could leave?

I don't know how many people we killed with our mortar attack, maybe ten, maybe one, maybe none, maybe they all listened as the only reader in the village read the leaflet to them and they spent the day in their family bunkers, the six women and two children who'd been wounded maybe staked out by the Viet Cong to absorb the shrapnel and deliver their torn bodies to our guilt. Like they say, in a war conducted at distances, you never really know. You push the button and the bomb-bay doors open and the people on the ground die, but you never have to see them screaming or evaporating into clumps of living flesh, your torment lying not in what you saw but what your spirit made you think.

Only a month to go, maybe it would be quiet, maybe the blowing off of Ramirez's foot and the helicopter night attack and the mortar attack and the loss of another squad from Foxtrot Company to ambush were unrelated. Random incidents in a horrible landscape. Maybe a magic mantra denying the existence of war, a mental capsule to keep me safe from what I was seeing and doing and would serve, would keep me safe. If I was only mind without a body maybe the bullets and the fragments of flying steel and the poisons and the knives could not find me. If I could send a part of myself out to each man in the platoon or in the squad that would make him that much more alive, that much more alert, maybe we'd each stand a better chance. But, of course, that was already happening, we were there together.

The next day I heard that Hurlock was in the ambushed squad from Foxtrot. He was dead. "It's just a short distance," he would say. And the only way to stay safe from war was to make real peace, every day, all the time. And even then, it's chancy. When it comes it is of no consequence that you were a warrior of the mystic nation, sworn to protect the liberty of the human spirit, or that your dearest roar was the restoration of belief, the resurrection of national faith, your country JesusBuddha liberator.

THE RESCUE

I'd lay in my bunker at night, staring up through the torn poncho roof into air dense with the sulphur scent of illumination rounds, and listen to the men settling into their night defensive positions, having one last cigarette hiding in the bowl of a helmet, getting quieter, turning the squelch knob down on the Prick-10, putting a round in the chamber. And out beyond the wire the lamps in the villages would grow dim until there was only shadow black in black, the stucco ruin ghostly grey in starlight residue. The insects and centipedes would start moving around then, the mosquitoes and fire ants, and I'd hear their crisp metallic chirps among the slithers of habu and kraits, cobras and bamboo snakes. Night was when the mongeese and the VC hunted. Night was the province of the lethal creatures.

Despite my magic denial, the war was getting worse, whether I was able to realize it or not. The radio crackles and the urgent grasping voices from on top of the hill would sound well into the night. More and more frequently the sudden jolting snaps of rifle fire would unleash the fears, were they coming this way? how far? ours? ARVNs? how many? another trooper trips over his dick? can they handle it, will we have to go? do the tighten-up, boys, he's out there for sure, you bet your life. Just because the hill had never been assaulted in force didn't mean that the NVA. didn't have such plans for it. We'd been seeing them more and more, too, reports that some other outfit had killed two or three in full uniform; pith helmets, gold star buckles, AK-47s. And we'd even see some of our own troopers carrying the spoils of fire fights, scowls of envy, not even the officers could dare to claim weapons won in battle from men so dangerously serious.

And as many patrols as Lt. Wurtz had personally gone out on, and as many times as he had sent his platoon out on ambush, not once had he killed a Viet Cong, or been shot or been blown up. The enemy were all around us, but he was charmed, fated it seemed, to never enter into the supreme conflict, to test himself against the death that the enemy was ready to bestow upon him. He would volunteer for every mission the CO would assign. His was the hardest working platoon in the company, he was out to get his reputation, to get some blood on his soul, and his men were his tools toward that end.

Wurtz was determined, well schooled and well-trained, blond, fit, with blue eyes that were constantly searching for the advantages of terrain. He was always ready, like his blood ran pure adrenalin. Even in the hottest parts of the days of patrol, he'd never even take off his pack, his stamina a constant intimidation to his men. I was up on the hill visiting my friend Jim, the company radio man, when I heard Lt. Wurtz talking to the Skipper.

"We gotta get over across the river if we're gonna get some kills, Captain," Wurtz said, like he was convincing a priest to do a bank job. "And I don't mean any daylight patrols when they can see us coming and sky out. I mean, a night assault. Catch those dink mutherfuckers with their pants down."

The Captain was cautious. The men didn't like moving around at night. They sandbagged the ambushes, he knew, but they were out there to serve as warnings if the enemy ever decided to mass an attack. Indian Country was a different story, though. Across the river was indisputably theirs, they told us so every time we went over there, and this last fiasco with the wounded women was a further reminder that Charlie had the high ground. The red dots on his maps said so, Christ, the red dots on the maps said they were everywhere!

"Of course, you're right, lieutenant, but I don't think so. Be patient, they'll come to us, you watch," the captain said, showing receding gums with a reassuring smile. But Lt. Wurtz wasn't satisfied. The point of being a Marine officer was to charge the hill, to go where angels fear, to tread on the wily little yellow fuckers, to go out looking for it as long as there was one atom of strength left in one fiber of muscle. In the crackle and hiss of the radios, in the light of the dial monitors and the radium watches, he persisted.

"We ain't been getting shit, Skipper. These chickenshit assholes sandbag the night ops. We haven't even seen a VC on this side of the river for weeks. Regiment wants bodies, Skipper. I mean to get them some."

Sensing his lieutenant's irresistible drive, his commitment to duty, to the good of the Corps, his willingness to relinquish any credit for kills to the reputation of the company, the CO humored him.

"And just how are you going to do what we've been unable to do?" he asked.

Wurtz was ready for his challenge. "A night op. We'll get some rubber boats, sneak across the river, set up an ambush right out side the village, and cream their asses."

"We don't have any rubber boats, Wurtz. Rubber fucking boats."

Ridicule was OK, it wasn't no. Valiant action dreams, Sneaky Pete in the dangerous dark, kill the evil fuckers and steal their women, the Captain was a man, after all. "Another diversionary maneuver, then. Choppers over, we'll lay chilly for a day, and work up on them at night."

"Can't do that. We're spread thin, lieutenant. We're down to almost half strength, as you oughta know. Besides, we send you over there in a helicopter it'll be like you wearing a neon sign that says 'shoot me.' I'm glad you're gungy, but there's no reason to be stupid."

It still wasn't no. Yes was closer, and good men got what they wanted. "You know, and I know, they are over there. Only way we are going to get them to engage is to go over there and force them."

The Captain wasn't listening anymore. His mind had slipped into commando fantasy, and he was stroking across the Song De in a rubber boat, knife in his teeth, eyes that could cut down trees.

"So, what is your plan?" he said, exasperated, like he was granting his brash lieutenant a huge huss and he would be expecting repayment.

It still wasn't yes, but Wurtz could feel the approval of his daring warming in the Captain, knowing the keen weight placed on aggression. Nothing was more highly prized than the willing courage to engage and kill the enemy. Even if it went bad and got people killed. The Captain couldn't say no. All he needed was a workable plan.

"Well, we sure as hell can't wade the fucker. We go down to where Charlie crosses, he'll be waiting for us, for sure. We'll take some tracks over. We'll jump off just as they come up on the bank and slow down, lights off, then the Tracks will go on further downstream, and we'll already be in place. Slick." His voice was a zealous whisper, the moments of setting up the ambush and readying the men, and squeezing off the death forming in his mind as certain and solid as a stone, the thrill like a crystal seizing in his blood. The muscles at the sinuses tighten, the kidneys switch from urine to adrenalin, you couldn't bleed if your own daughter needed a quart. And, just at the moment of decision, Battalion called for a situation report, distracting the Captain. Taking the handset from Jim, he looked sternly at the brave young lieutenant and said, "Just a squad, Wurtz. No point in squandering men."

And that was all the permission Lt. Wurtz needed. He had difficulty not running down the hill to his platoon's portion of the perimeter, instead, striding purposefully and smiling.

Seeing him coming one of his men said to another, "Better watch it, Wurtz has a hair up his ass."

"I wonder what we volunteered for this time? Anderson's platoon has the ambush tonight."

"That fucker looks dangerous. I'll bet we're going someplace special."

"I don't want to go no place special. We're short, man. That lifer mutherfucker can't do no shit to us."

"I wanna go home. I wanna go home. Oh Lord I wanna go home," another man sang.

Most of the platoon had been sitting on top of their bunkers, silently looking out into the gathering dark, but gravitated toward Wurtz by habit and attraction to his zeal. When he had their attention, he looked at each of them, saying, "We're going across the river."

"Tonight?" a man asked, stricken by the idea of wandering around in Indian Country at night.

"Right now," Wurtz said, tolerating no further questions. "This is a strictly volunteer mission. First squad, you just volunteered."

"Oh, thank you, Lieutenant," a lance corporal mocked.

"Knock off the shit," Wurtz replied. This was not a discussion. Lives depended on the men getting his word.

"We will get into one of the tracks, cross the river, and get out just as we come up on the bank. The track will proceed further down the bank on the other side, then come back. The gooks will be watching it, not us. We'll move on in toward the village, set up an ambush, and nail whoever goes out to take on the track. Now get your gear together, no noise, no smoking, be ready to saddle up in five minutes. We are going to kick some ass tonight. No doubt about it. Doc Wilson, you stick with the sergeant. I'll take the lead." End of message.

Wurtz didn't wait for assent, but moved further down the road to make the arrangements with the Track driver. First squad was complaining, "That dipshit is gonna get us greased, man, I can feel it."

"He's got his commando bullshit going again. Swear to God he shoulda gone recon."

"What are you people bitching about. Isn't this why you came? We're just gonna go for a little moonlight walk and grease some gooks, no big thing, no sweat. Be home for a midnight snack," the sergeant chides. But for his bravado everyone knew he was just a talker; he'd never killed a bunch of gooks on an ambush. None of them had.

"I got a bad feeling about this one," the machinegunner admitted. He was a big, powerful Cherokee who seldom spoke. His admitting to a premonition was an omen, a good reason not to go. But he had his machinegun and his orders and there was no possibility of refusal.

In the few minutes the nine men met the lieutenant in front of the Amphtrack. There was the gunner, Bear, and his 'A' gunner, the M-79 man, the young black corpsman, Wilson, and five riflemen, counting S/Sgt. Monk.

"They are going to step in it tonight. You watch," someone watching them assemble prophesied. Someone else said, "This is the dumbest dumbshit thing I ever heard of. Don't that fool know who is over there?"

"He's mad because they won't come out and play."

"Anderson did that shit to us, I'd leave him over there all alone," someone else said. But all the grumbling in creation couldn't change Wurtz's mind. He did know what was over there. He was possessed of the invincibility of immortal youth. He was Marine Corps officer, as good as any ten gooks. He was a leader of men, the scion of a rich family and it was his genetic destiny to perform the national duty of conducting his part of the war with deserved pride.

The patient men waiting in the dark for him and his squad suffered no such illusions.

The dozen Marines loaded into the track, and the huge green vehicle rumbled down the hill and through the wire. We heard the track's engine noise fade into the night, and we waited, smoking in the dark.

An hour passed before we heard the track returning.

"I guess they made it over, all right," a man said, his friend answering, "Don't mean shit. If I was mister dink, I'd pick 'em off on their way to town. I mean, it ain't like there is anywhere else for them to go over there. There's the hills, the paddies, the path and the ville. Now just where would you expect a bunch of Marines to go?"

The track roared up the road, spun on one tread and parked. We went over to ask the driver how it had gone, and he said it was no sweat. A few rifle shots sounded down by Iron Bridge, none of our concern. Another hour passed. I went inside my bunker so I could smoke and register the sense of Wurtz's patrol. I didn't know the men very well, but they were friends who would die for me, and I for them. Wurtz's stupidity didn't disrupt the fact that the squad was part of us, and some intuitive connective tissue was tracking them. Something horrible was going to happen. It was preordained by the structure of our lives, our being in that place at that time. We went looking for it. It was going to find us, and Wurtz was looking hardest of all.

We were safe inside the wire, and I was safer inside my bunker, and they were out there, across the river, in the breathing dark bristling with menace, walking through country that was pure trap.

First there was a short burst of AK-47 fire, the reports sounding to us through the dense air from across the river—maybe a click up from the village. For a second in the pause just after the firing I think, no, not ours, but the burst is too short to have done much damage, their guys get nervous too, hope nothing bad has happened. It can't be bad, the tracks haven't even been back ten minutes.

But the pause only lasts a couple of seconds. Four more rifles start firing simultaneously, the AK has signaled them to start the ambush and there are four, five, maybe six rifles firing, some on automatic, some single shot, the firing lasts for at least an excruciating minute, it is one-sided, different weapons, theirs. It's too far away to hear human voices screaming but I feel them in my heart. There is another longer pause, then several M-14s open up on automatic, but it's only three or four men firing, the sound feels desperate, unaimed, terrified. But it is enough to keep the VC quiet for a several minutes. I am waiting to hear more firing, more firing would mean that some of them were still alive, that they hadn't all been killed or wounded to stillness, though silence could mean that the VC broke off the ambush and left Wurtz's squad to bleed and die.

Part of me is insisting that nothing bad has happened, that it was all just a big mistake, that even men as angry and dedicated as the Viet Cong would not be so murderously bold as to kill Marines outright in an ambush, especially an ambush of men I knew, I'm taking it personally, ego and self tied by love and paranoia to every man around me, including the VC, to ambush Marines invited massive retaliation, napalm, miniguns, helicopter gunships swooping out of the night sky, freezing your eyes in a halogen spotlight while the 20 mm cannons blew your body apart, how the little yellow fuckers with their small arms could hope to withstand such onslaught bewildered me, such guts to get in close and kill us straight on from fifty feet away, the willingness to take on overwhelming odds, two to one, three to one, ten to one, to almost certainly die behind their courage, was so stunning in itself that to go against them was both enormously courageous and like killing your own noble reflection.

But it was night, there were no gunships in the air, the firing was close in, there would be no rescue from the air. In the pause between firing the men on the hilltop were screaming orders. The mortar pit launched several illumination rounds, and as they lit over the ambush site, more firing came from both sides. The fire is sporadic, aimed, they've got each other in their sights, there is more firing from the M-14s, desperate, urgent, each trigger squeeze feeling like a little boy calling help me. The AKs and the SKSs felt like enraged punches to the mouth that drove your brain into the ground, splintered teeth and skull, the last knowing moments, sky and vengeance.

As soon as I heard the fire I was out of the bunker, bolting into the dark like the rest of the men in my platoon perimeter, hearing the gunshots, lighting up pensively, automatically putting on web gear and flack jackets, getting ready, the motions more dictated by unity with our brethren than expecting orders. A runner came down the hill, moving fast, followed by the XO, Gunny Mead and the company corpsman, HM-3 Broad. By the time the XO and the Gunny reached us, Lt. Anderson had already passed the word for the platoon to saddle-up.

Seeing the three of them I was expecting the senior corpsman to go along with us. It was clear that we were going to load onto the tracks and cross the river and get the men who'd stepped into the ambush, it was our duty, our singular and unit obligation. If we would leave no dead for the enemy to mutilate, we would more certainly risk and spend our lives to save the wounded and the living. But Broad came up to me as I was heading over to the waiting gape of the tracks, stopping me, saying, "This is a volunteer job, Doc, you don't have to go."

And for a second I felt enormously relieved, I didn't have to go, I knew that we were about to enter into extreme danger, the firing had not stopped, and I didn't have to go if I could find even the flimsiest excuse not to. I could leave it to the other corpsmen, saying it's too late, I should stick around in case we were about to be overrun, it was another platoon, there was no loyalty bond, my back hurt, I had a sprained ankle. "I'm staying here to coordinate the medevac," Broad said, effectively cutting off any decision that gunfire might have inspired in me.

"I'm on my way, man, who else is coming?" I said. Scared down to your bones, so what, you are those men suffering out in the dark, you will go, there was never any real question about it.

"I knew you'd say that. That's what I already told the CO. You, Corry, and Bob Planter. They'll stay in the tracks. You go out and do triage. Good luck, man," and he gave my flack jacket a pat like I was going out to win one for the Gipper, but I didn't feel like I was going out to play some silly game. I'd won the honor of being just like the Marines, about to go out and throw myself in front of machinegun fire. One hero, hardly; dozens and dozens.

Approaching the waiting tracks, I asked some sergeant, "What's happening?" Verbal tic, getting a reply that summed up the Marine Corps approach to disseminating pertinent information. With as much cool as he could muster, the sergeant said, "Squad stepped in the shit, we're gonna go get 'em." Like we were about to go get some groceries. Obedience means action without understanding, like you don't have the right to expect to come out of it alive.

Everyone wanted to ride on top of the tracks, a way to hold the high ground, to shoot from a moving platform. But the sergeants knew better and insisted that we all ride in the belly of the beasts, mouths shut, weapons on safety, no smoking, no information. It was an urgent matter at hand, even if few of us understood completely what awaited us, so there was little of the usual grousing.

Clamor of gear and boots on steel floors, the ramps winding shut, engines thrumming, we're loaded in the tracks and the tracks are rattling down the road, sharp left turn, further down the road, then out across the dry paddies, heaving humps over the dikes, then into the green silt-laden ooze of the river. Inside, we are defenseless, incapable of action, disconnected from our sacred earth, sitting ducks to a rocket or a mine. Muscles and imaginations are tightening. Everyone has a different version of the story, no one in charge has deigned to tell us what has happened. Maybe Wurtz's squad was ambushed, maybe they sprung an ambush and had one backfire on them, maybe there were wounded, maybe there were wounded and dead, maybe they were all dead and the Viet Cong were just sitting over there in huge numbers waiting to slaughter us as we ran out the doors, just like the Japs. Every one has different expectations of what will happen once we get there, and what is expected of them. It will be up to each man to figure out what they are supposed to do once the tracks stop and the ramps open and we go rushing out, into what, no one is saying.

We're in the current of the river, water churning under the spinning tracks, the walls of the compartment cooling and condensing our rapid breathing, no longer faces of boys looking frightened, but the faces of reconciled men, just as frightened but absolutely resolute. When the ramp came down we would be out the door, no sergeant would have to kick our asses. The only way to defeat the enemy was to kill him first.

Another sudden lurch up the river bank and we're in Indian Country, mud and silt churning out from under the tracks, clumps and clods of riverbank kicking back into the river. We turn, heading east toward the sea, hoping that it would be all over when we finally got there, that we'd find our friends, some of them wounded, but basically OK, and we'd just have gone through the fears, better that than having to go through gunfire. The tracks are moving fast, the one I'm in taking the lead, the driver pushing the huge machine to its limits, engine straining its hulk over the rolling mounds of earth beside the river. The trip is taking so long, if it takes much longer the Viet Cong will have killed any survivors, I'm thinking, gone down and shot them all in the head to make sure, and to humiliate us. The trip is taking so long, long enough for the Viet Cong to gather their strength, regroup if Wurtz's squad was able to defend itself and kill a few of them, long enough that they could be waiting for us. Everyone in the tracks is too scared to talk, to venture a fear would be to invite disaster.

Bullets are hitting the side of the track. They are a harmless noise, strange and metallic, so distant in danger that no one even flinches, a curiosity. I remember thinking, oh good, they're only using twenty-twos, which wasn't true. Two Viet Cong were firing their AK-47s at our track as if mere bullets could halt the lumbering beast and pierce the armor plate and kill all of us men trapped inside. We heard the sudden crump of a grenade exploding behind us. I was only trying to make the threat smaller, manageable, mental magic to help get me out the door.

Soon now, soon. Soon we'd be out the door. There were Viet Cong waiting for us, in their loathing of the great metal beasts they had announced their presence, we knew they were there now, now we would be ready for them, it didn't matter how many they were, we were Marines. If there were more than a platoon they would have brought bigger weapons. They knew we came after our own, they planned, they were patient, they could afford to wait. "Fuck man, if they rocket us, we're fried, man, fucking fried!" a trooper yelled, making us all suddenly aware that the machine's gas tank was in the floor and we were sitting on it. A sergeant told him to keep his mouth shut, but the trooper's warning was just more reason to hit the door running when the track finally stopped.

The driver turned out the overhead light, ducking down under his hatch, steering the machine with his periscope. The driver's gunner started opening up with the twin .30s. There it was, all the information you needed, there were Viet Cong waiting for us out there, we were close, there was only one chance beside staying locked up in the track and running, leaving our men out there to fight for themselves until the Viet Cong killed them, and that was to get out there amongst them, fight, shoot, kill, make the horrible moments stop. Brass is clattering on the steel floor.

Lt. Anderson has the door seat, but he seems incapable of leading, so Gunny Mead stands in front of us, bracing himself against the roof of the track, waiting for it to stop. We hear the other track pull up beside us, more bullets hit the side of the machine. In the dark, the .30s are still firing, he can see in the flare light, but all we can do is hear. Gunny Mead's bulky form is outlined in the orange light. "When the ramp goes down," Mead's strong voice says, "hit the door running." And that is all the information we get. Just an order of what to do in the next five seconds, and we're all standing up in the tracks, except Doc Corry who is hanging back in the back of the hull, doing what he has been told to do. The ramp goes down, taking far too long, it's opening and we are vulnerable to fire during the time it takes to get low enough to let us escape.

Finally, we are out the door, worse than getting off helicopters, it is definitely a hot zone. At the split second the ramp hits the dirt the whole squad is yelling, releasing the voices, pouring out the door as fast as their legs can carry them, hunched low, the rifle fire is coming in at us now, the twin .30s are still firing but none of us has presence of mind to fire back, all we are looking for is a place to hide and find some cover so we can fire back, there are a half dozen rifles firing at us, tracers are flying past and above us, leaving retinal after images I can still see. In the sliver of sputtering flare light I could see our young faces hardened into fierce resolution. We are yelling the oldest yell in the world, reaching back millions of years, flushing the blood with the willingness to kill and die, making all life but the life here in this moment the only life.

In a strobe of rifle fire flashes I saw a ragged line of prone men strung out over thirty yards in front of me. The other men see them too, and rush toward them. Several of the men laying down are firing at the Viet Cong who are firing both at them and at us. A flare crackles over head, I can see two Viet Cong hiding behind a mound thirty feet away, two more are teamed fifty feet away from them, another Viet Cong is hiding behind mound about midway down the line of prone Marines, two more are further down, and those are the only ones I can see. But what I was seeing and hearing, what was happening, was not registering in the brain place that assigns names and meaning. There wasn't time to invent a story. What needed to be done was wired deep in the nerves, issued from the medulla, dictated by human character and immediate event. That I could die out there ceased even to be a comforting whisper. The officers and the trainers can claim influence, but it is the bones of being that do the work.

Another flare popped above us. To my right I could see a man laying prone, his hands were covering his ears, as if he could shut out the dangerous noise and the horrible world by not being able to hear it. The next thing I saw was Sgt. Monk up on one knee, calling for a corpsman. Beside the sergeant lay a man curled into a fetal position, clutching his abdomen, his pain and anguish rippling through the night. The sergeant patted him on the shoulder, then picked up his carbine, aiming and firing it in the general direction of one of the Viet Cong who was firing at the still on rushing burst of men coming out of the tracks. Twenty-five feet away from them was another man firing his rifle in short bursts, conserving his ammunition. His feet looked strangely detached from their legs. He seemed remarkably calm, like the world had slowed down by half, and if that slowing was to be fatal there was no impeding it.

Somehow I reached Sgt. Monk, and the man clutching his own abdomen. "Good to see you, Doc," Sgt. Monk says, his voice slow and measured, and I'm wondering how he can still be alive as tall as he is and as erect as he is holding himself while the fire is coming at us from fifty feet away. "Keep down, there are only five of us holding this line," he says, and two Marines flop down beside us, taking the aim of his rifle as the direction in which to fire. While they fire their rifles into the dark, keeping the ambushers' heads down, I tend to the wounded man at the sergeant's knees. He's got a battle dressing over his stomach, and looking under it in the flare light I see the grey protrusion of intestine indicating a through and through gutwound, maybe the kidney has been taken out, maybe he got lucky and the bullet just entered the gut just below the apron of his flack jacket, bouncing off the pelvis, tearing up the intestine, but that can be fairly easily fixed by a competent surgeon, biggest immediate worry is peritonitis, getting him out of danger and into one of the tracks where he can stop worrying about getting shot while he's defenseless, so I tell one of the just arrived riflemen to scuttle back to the track and get a stretcher and get the man into the track, superseding Sgt. Monk's order to fire on the enemy, and the man scuttles off quickly, and before the sergeant can say anything, I've got a styrette into the man's arm, my hand is soothing his brow and I'm telling him that he was going to be all right the others will be here soon with a stretcher, no I can't give you any water, you're gut shot, here let me put some water on this battle dressing to cool the fire and so the tissues don't dry out, I'll catch up with you later, there are other men here to get you, take it easy, we'll be out of this shit before you know it. But I didn't know, I didn't know how many Viet Cong were over there, or how many were waiting after we killed the ones that had ambushed Wurtz's squad, there was only one thing to do and that was keep going and I'm moving off down the line toward the man with the strange feet. Looking up for a split second I can see Gunny Mead standing over by the lead track, directing men to take positions along the ragged line of wounded Marines, and I can still see or feel the Viet Cong also in a rough line across the field from us, the chaos and the yelling and screaming, the rifles firing confusing beyond description, but the force lines of the fight bringing Marines into their right places, the Viet Cong holding their own with incredible perseverance. I'm not the first man out on the line anymore, there are Marines passing behind me, heading to reinforce the men in the ambushed squad who are still capable of self-defense. I don't know what I am supposed to do, I barely know what I'm doing, just moving through the fire zone trying to stay alive and keep the people who've been shot alive and mostly just moving toward the man with the strangely twisted feet.

When I get to him I find him being looked over by Bear, the machine-gunner, the man with the strangely twisted feet is his assistant gunner, and Bear is propped up on his elbows fitting the pieces of his machine-gun back together. He seems undisturbed, like there is nothing more important in the existence of creation than getting his gun back together, and there is no force in existence that can break his concentration. Blood scent and fear scent, cordite and gasoline, shit and urine, red soil and river muck, tawny Vietnamese flesh, scents in flare light. Ten men on the line are firing now, shooting indiscriminately into the dark at the Viet Cong, keeping their heads down, maybe they'll get lucky, and there doesn't seem to be any urgency about killing the Viet Cong, only in getting the ambushed squad out of there, if enough Marines are shooting at the Viet Cong there would be little chance that any of us rescuers would be hit, or so goes the unstated tactic.

The assistant gunner is a friend of Dale's, and he recognizes me, saying, "Glad you could make it, Doc."

"Where are you hit?" I ask, still watching Bear put his M-60 together, still feeling the Viet Cong looking for a position from which to fire not fifty feet away from us. I can feel him crawling, towing his weapon behind him.

"I'm shot through both ankles."

"Bleeding much?"

"I'm all right," he says, calm and clear, almost glad, "bullets went right through. Can't walk, but I ain't bleeding."

I see two men reach Sgt. Monk with a stretcher, and yell at one of them to get over to us as soon as they can, letting them know our position, stupidly letting the Viet Cong know exactly where we were too, as if they didn't already know. Bear has the gun together by then, and he's putting the belt into the feeding mechanism, pulling back the slide, sighing like it's about fucking time, and I'm saying to the 'A' gunner, "Let me get a dressing on those ankles."

"No point, Doc." he says, kind of dreamy.

"Doc Wilson already get to you?" I ask.

"Naw, Gunner Bear got his kit, gave me a jolt already. I'm OK. You better get to LeFever, he's all fucked up." I'm about to move off, and I lift my head for a second and not thirty feet away I see the tight muscular curl of a Vietnamese man untuck for a moment, lift his AK-47 to take aim at the three of us and I let out a scream as the tracers and bullets stream just over our heads. Bear ducks slightly, like he was impenetrable, like he could tell the trajectory of the bullets and knew even before the Viet Cong soldier fired that we would not be hit, and he pulls the M-60's slide back, the belt is started and without aiming triggers the gun, loosing a burst of bullets that hit the Viet Cong in the chest, blowing his upper body apart, killing him instantly, sending him flying back like he'd been hit by three huge fists, the force of the rounds entering his body rending him asunder. He doesn't even have time to scream.

Bear is still calm, and I don't have time to even see what has just happened, I must get on to LeFever, there are several Marines running up behind me, one of them catches up to me and asks me what to do next and I send him back for a stretcher to pick up Morton, and tell him to tell the other two to reinforce the machine-gun, I'm not even thinking, more just moving. Further down the line, near the tracks, a grenade explodes. Bursting crump. No screaming. A dozen men are running behind us now, and there are rounds being fired into their midst by the Viet Cong, but they are poorly aimed, as if they have come to sense that if they start shooting at us with deadly accuracy they will so infuriate us that we will neglect our wounded and hunt them down and kill them no matter how many of us it took, we'd blast their village, women and children, into nothingness, they were outnumbered and outgunned, the two tracks had four machine-guns between them, lights and mobility. If they dared back off the very air itself could suddenly fill with violent fire and steel. Sensible men would have given up the fight when they first saw the amphtracks coming across the river, but not these Viet Cong. No. It was their women and children we'd dropped the mortars on, and we would pay. They were sticking, fighting to the death, but staying cautious and low, prescribing what death and maiming they intended us to absorb.

I can see LeFever's long lanky body laying still and pain wracked a few yards away, and feeling the bullets going over my head and at the Marines running behind me, I scuttle over to him. The Marines behind me hit the deck, catch the flashes with their eyes and start firing, barely missing me. "Hold your fire!" I yell, my voice automatic, unthinking, the blood doing all the talking. But it works, and I hear a voice slightly hoarse and shamed say, "Sorry, Doc."

LeFever was unconscious. The gunner said he'd taken a round in the leg, so he couldn't be dead, I thought, but checked for a pulse at the jugular just to be sure. Slow and thready, he was in shock, he stirred when I checked his body for wounds, flinching when my hand located the battle dressing the gunner had applied to his leg. The bullet had torn through the large muscle of his left thigh, but there was little blood, no arteries had been severed. No tourniquet needed. He was out, I only had one and one-half styrettes left, the corpsmen on the tracks could dose him if he came around, there was nothing more I could do for him but get the Marines behind us to come to his aid, to protect him, the Viet Cong were readying themselves to fire on us again, I could feel them moving behind their grassy mounds in front of us, taking position. There were still two more clumps of men I had to get to.

Another flare washed the field in stark white light. In my peripheral vision I can still see Gunny Mead directing the operation from his position beside the amphtrack, the twin .30s are putting out sporadic fire to keep the Viet Cong's heads down, Marines are still running to take up protective positions beside the wounded men, and I can see men with stretchers heading toward LeFever and Morton is being carried back to the tracks. Sgt. Monk is still kneeling beside the man with his intestines hanging out, Monk is firing into the grassy mounds. Several Marines on the line are firing, single shots, unsure, firing to make the horrible thing stop.

I could also see several Viet Cong crawling into positions behind the mounds, towing their rifles by the slings, sliding over the grass like serpents, like vicious black mouths about to eat us. But I was so intent on getting to the next men who might need me that the thought of getting out my pistol to shoot them simply did not occur. Some prescient personnel officer had me pegged, oldest son of a broken home looking for God, and while I was aware that men around me were being killed and wounded, that I was in profound danger, that we all were in profound danger of losing our lives or being maimed, my killer instinct was not awake, the others would make the Viet Cong stop, they had to, we had to get these men to medical help, they had rifles and grenades, it was their job. I had my own work to do. I could trust them. I moved on to the next two men, both were lying prone, scoping the mounds, waiting for movement before they fired.

"Either of you hit?" I asked, seeing the tension in their bodies as a sign that they were still intact, still whole and worried, defending themselves, tied into each of us, knowing the Viet Cong only as the enemy to be stopped and killed, as the enemy who had done this outrageously horrible thing of ambushing them in the heaving dark, shooting them without warning, killing them without the courtesy of honor, vile and loathsome, deserving death. But that cut both ways. Only one thing to do in a firefight and that is to stay alive.

"We're OK. You better check Washington. He took a hit, he's over there somewhere," was all the information they had for me, enough to get me moving toward the moaning sounds coming from thirty feet away, the supine form of his body trying to lay as still as he could so the pain would cease. It was my friend Washington who thought I was crazy but followed me with his rifle after the Viet Cong kid who later sniped us, ready to defend me. It didn't really matter that I knew him. He was a man down, the complete and utter purpose of my being. I felt a few rounds fly overhead, heard the pops of an SKS, heard the two men I just left open up with their M-14s. I ran my hands over his body, he was still conscious, checking for broken bones, bullet holes, cold where the blood no longer flowed, hot and sticky where it did. His respiration was labored, his pulse strong and regular, his eyes in the flare light beseeching, those of a child both terrified and angry, something horrible had inflicted this terrible pain in him that stopped him from moving, from even defending himself, making him lie still on top of the hole in his hip that he didn't want to explore with his fingers, that he didn't want to know how much damage was done, that if he moved the pain would explode through his nerves like yellow lightening.

I could see where the blood had crusted in a jagged blotch on his hip, showing blackish green in the flarelight. I touched his hip, and he winced, moaning low and saying, "Not there, man, don't touch me."

"Gotta get in there, man, gotta see it, gotta know," I said, deciding to use my precious morphine, his breathing was OK, the pain rippling through him in waves. I jabbed the needle through the sleeve of his fatigue jacket, squeezing the tube empty, talking to him, telling him it was going to be OK, that the men with the stretchers would be here any second to take him away, don't worry, nothing more bad will happen to you, making promises I couldn't keep, the grunts didn't call us witchdoctors for nothing. I don't knew if he was even aware that we had come to rescue him in the tracks. When the morphine took hold, I rolled him over on his back.

Then I found the hole where the bullet had entered, and with two fingers, tore open the fabric of his trousers. In the start shadows I could see a neat hole filled with torn tissue and bruise blue blood. Simply touching around the wound sent the man into a spasm of excruciating pain. Under my fingers I could feel the fragments of bone move. The bullet has smashed into his iliac arch and was lodged there, hard and stubby.

"You're gonna be all right, man. That ain't shit. Hurts like a mutherfucker, but it ain't gonna kill you. Home, baby, home to the World for you."

I stuck a battle dressing over the hole, telling Washington to hold it in place, there was nowhere to tie it to, and yelled to the men next to us to get the word to the men in the tracks that we had a wounded man here, need a stretcher, get moving. I get to my knees to start moving off, remembering that someone along the line of the wounded had told me that the lieutenant was somewhere in back of us, badly wounded, maybe dead, and I had to get to him next.

Something sharp whipped past my ear, then two more. I know they are bullets but there is nothing I can do about them, I'm moving toward the lieutenant, there is nothing that can stop me and therefore I can ignore the bullets. I hear the rifle fire coming at me, and turning toward the rifle flashes, eyes drawn to danger, drawn to light, I see a Vietnamese man less than twenty feet away. His face was contorted into a mask of profound anguish. The muscles of his arms stood out bunched and taunt, and his aiming eye was focused on me, I could feel it see me. He was ignoring Washington, I was moving, Washington was already down and gone. I can see the Viet Cong's finger tightening on the trigger of the old M-1, the muscles of his arms and shoulders contracting to pull the trigger and I know he is going to kill me but there isn't anything I can do about it, there isn't even enough time to duck or dive away. I am going to be dead in the next split second, I can already feel the great black emptiness getting ready to swallow me, I can feel the hint of unutterable peace. It doesn't matter if I am a good man or a bad man, a good Doc or a vile enemy. I will simply end. I see the Viet Cong's face explode. Two more bullets smash into him while I'm seeing him come apart in pieces. Then I see the bright yellow-white rifle flashes register in the air just past my left field of vision, and feel the Marine who is rushing toward my left side. He is going down on one knee and firing again. I am not dead.

It was Wilks.

"You better learn to keep your head down, Doc." he said. He was smiling. "These people ain't fucking around." And he is happy, looking at the product of his work in the fading flare light, seeing the black blood smashed clump of man flesh totally inert. "Fuck man," I said, not fully understanding what I'd just seen, the readiness to die still coursing through my brain. Wilks's posture is solid, carved out of absolute flesh, he is the supreme ruler of his piece of ground. "You better check the lieutenant, Doc, he's back behind us," Wilks commands. Other voices were still shouting orders, some directing the fire, but none were calling for help. I was almost done.

"That's where I was headed."

"Get going, your ass is covered," Wilks said, and I move off again, more bullets snapping past my head, several Marines returning fire. But I feel protected, like nothing horrible can happen to me. A grenade detonated behind me in a burst of white light. A piece of shrapnel seared into my left arm. I kept moving, ignoring the pain, maybe not even knowing that I was hit, not caring, just keep moving, if you are moving and working you are alive, forgetting that I'm hit until the metal works out eleven years later burnished smooth as a streamstone by my blood. Moving toward the dark shape that is laying still as death behind the ragged line of men I'd just left, moving toward the man so motionless, so devoid of divine presence, a kind of blackness seeming to hover over him.

Even as still as he was the thought that he might be dead refused to enter my mind. He was apart from the fight, his face relaxed, his eyes rolled up into their sockets and showing the whites. His web belt was on backwards, the gunner had already been to him and dressed one of his wounds with his battle dressing. I felt under the flack jacket for the thick wet of blood on the body cavity, but found none. He was so still though, his body temperature was dropping, he was closing in on death, the wounds had to be in the legs like the wounds of the others, the flack jackets were worth their weight in diamonds.

A Marine flopped down beside me while I was palpating the lieutenant's legs, feeling the give in his left femur where a bullet had cracked it.

"Sorry to bother you, Doc," the Marine said. He was so polite. A bone fragment jagged out of Wurtz's right calf. The gunner had used his own battle dressing to cover the wound, remarkable sacrifice, the lieutenant must have been the first man he'd reached, but the dressing was slipping off. Another battle dressing had been applied to Wurtz's upper right hip, that bandage taken from Doc Wilson's kit.

"They're out of morphine back at the tracks. Sent me to get some from you," the Marine said, his voice is soft and consoling, like being gentle would alter the mood of the violent air. I felt for the lieutenant's pulse, slow, thready, I had to dig deep under his jaw to feel it.

"Lieutenant here sure don't need it," I said, reaching in my kit and handing him my last styrette, saying send some people back with a stretcher. And the Marine took it back to the tracks, even though there were bullets aimed at him, he was running as fast as he could to help ease the pain of the other men; guts, love, a brave act by a loving man.

The firing was slowing though, not hearing the rifles shooting, not hearing any more grenades, I felt like I had a few moments to work on the lieutenant, he was hurt bad. But I didn't have the slightest clue as to what to do next, except try to make him comfortable even though he was near death and unconscious. Talk about refusing to accept present reality, about not having the mental capacity to understand what I was seeing. I was reverting to hospital care procedures. I tried to cut his web gear away with my bandage scissors, make his breathing easier, but they were too dull.

Two more Marines showed up dragging a stretcher. They'd crawled over to us on their knees. "Glad you're here," I said. "Lieutenant here's got five wounds in his legs, he's got compound fractures. I'm amazed he's still alive. We gotta get him to the tracks and get him back to Regiment, or he's gonna die." We settle the stretcher beside his prone limp body. There is a large spreading scab of blood seeping below his right leg. I take off his belt and put it around his leg up near the hip and cinch it tight, even though the seep is slowed, his heart not pumping much.

"Easy now," I say to the Marines, but we all know what to do, and how to do it, it's in our brain and flesh. And we carefully lift the lieutenant onto the stretcher in the dark, me cradling his legs against further trauma, trying to keep the compound fractures, the bone sharps, from cutting further into his skin and muscle and blood vessels. Then the two men take off, hauling the lieutenant toward the tracks with me holding his fractured legs between the splints of my arms until we get to the Tracks and they take him inside.

Gunny Mead is shouting, "Let's go, people, let's go, get in the tracks, get it moving!" But the men holding the line have already broken off the fight and have started peeling back toward the tracks, the Viet Cong have stopped firing, the men are crouched low and facing into the mounds, a few of them shooting at the mounds just in case.

Inside the tracks I can hear the moaning soft sobbing of men wounded and laying on stretchers, and the murmurings of men bending over them in the dark, soothing them until the rest of the men can be loaded aboard and the hatches closed and the lights turned on so they can see to help them further. To get them back into the comfort of the light.

And the Marines are coming in now, crouching low, backing into the tracks, some of them still firing into the dark, but the floors of both vehicles are full of men on stretchers so they have to climb up on top, and finally the engines start.

But the count is wrong. Two men are missing. Morton and S/Sgt. Monk are still out there, and two troopers are immediately dispatched to go out and get them but there are no more stretchers and someone asks me what to do. No time to devise something, there was no telling how soon the Viet Cong were going to re-group or even if they were, or if any of them were still left, I know I saw two of them killed, I don't know how many others were killed by the other men in the ambushed squad or by the rescue platoon, maybe three, maybe ten, maybe a whole platoon, we'd never know. And I remember the cot that the amphtrack driver slept on tucked behind his seat, and I say take that. So they do, and I can see their dark forms take the cot out to Morton and Sgt.Monk, and Monk never relaxes his vigil over his man even to help load him on the cot, he is absolutely dedicated to protecting his trooper, he is in love with life and with his man, and they all four come back, taking Morton into the track. The ramps close, the lights coming on before they are completely closed, but there is no more firing. And the rest of us climb up on the tops of the lumbering machines, and it is done. All but the leaving.

THE AFTERMATH

In the headlight glare we silently looked into the field of grassy mounds to be sure we'd left no one behind, then turned and quickly left. There never seemed to have been a question of trying to defeat the Viet Cong, only to get our men out of the deep serious, and if the Viet Cong chose to stick around and get blown up, good. Either hiding behind the mounds or sinking into the darkness dead, even from the vantage of being on top of the tracks we could see no evidence of the fight, no enemy bodies to count. I wanted a smoke in the worst way. Even though the wounded men were safe inside the hulls and being cared for by the other corpsmen, even though I had done everything I could to help save their lives, even though Gunner Bear had already done first aid on them before I got to them and by our mutual work kept them alive, even though the tracks were too full to admit even one more person, I still felt guilty about so desperately wanting a cigarette that I chose to ride on top of the tracks, to be able to treat someone if they were wounded on our way out, I rationalized to the sergeant. I lighted up in unison with every other man on top of the heaving vehicle, a method of touching my own mortality, a way of selfishly letting my brain know I was still alive.

We were facing outboard in case some fool VC decided to shoot at us from the dark, but every foot we travelled away from the site of the fight let our faces relax into those of elated, spent, completely confident warriors. We had made it out alive. We had thrown our lives into live fire to help our friends stay alive and come away alive, none of us even seriously wounded, we had won.

"That was somethin'," a trooper next to me said, a gaunt face showing an ecstatic grin. "Yeah," I agreed, not considering whether we'd won or even what we'd done, only greatly glad that we were on our way out of there, on our way to where the choppers would be waiting to take the wounded men to where they could be properly taken care of, on our way back to the safety of home behind the wire, in our bunkers, back to sleep in the ground. There wasn't much talking on top of the track, the thoughts and memories turning inward, becoming real in the time to reflect. There was still danger out there, too. Keep your mouth shut and your eyes open.

We rushed along, bouncing, sliding down the riverbank, churning back through the river water, then up the other side, heading for the red beacon of the helicopters which had already landed in the paddies outside of Le Mai.

The rest of the company had come out to make sure we got back in safely, setting up a perimeter around the helicopter, opening as we passed through the ranks on the tracks. They looked jealous, envious that we had engaged the enemy and they had to stay back in the company area. The CO was there, along with the whole headquarters contingent, including the company corpsman, Broad. Broad and the Captain were standing together as we jumped down from the tracks. They looked pleased, like their lives up until that time had just been justified.

Feeling each other, everyone already knew what to do, and started taking the wounded men to the chopper, hurrying, expediting the work to shorten the pain and reduce the chance of any one of them going into deep shock that would kill him. Doc Corry and Doc Planter both supervised the loading of Lt. Wurtz, getting six men to carry him, admonishing the chopper pilot and the doorgunner to take it easy with him, he was hurt bad. And Broad calls me over to the track where some men are taking Morton out of the hatch, and asks me what Morton's problem is, and I reach down and pull back the battle dressing to show the twisted grey bulges of intestine, then put back the dressing and wet it with water from my canteen. Morton's eyes are looking into mine, thankful, full of blessings, and Broad wants to know if we should transfer Morton to a stretcher, but I say, no, he's comfortable, it would generate too much pain, and Morton smiles back up at me through his morphine pleasure, he's going home, alive.

Then they are gone. The chopper lifts into the night sky, turning off its lights, and we hear the rotor pops fading out over toward Da Nang, our friends will be safe and cared for.

There's not much backslapping or self- congratulation, it has been a job of work and we are tired, walking the slow triumphant walk back inside the wire to our bunkers, self-absorbed, gathered in groups of friends, not giving much to the others who weren't with us. Unless you were there, you didn't know. Tomorrow we could pretend we liked it.

Getting to my bunker I slept the deep dreamless sleep of a man wrapped in the womb of love.

Nor did there ever seem a question of us losing the war. It was an American enterprise, righteous and bold, blessed by God. The power available to be brought to bear was immense, the materiel copious—but not strong enough to crush the posture of intensity I saw in the spine of the Viet Cong who was going to kill me.

The morning was tropical day shine, the sky so blue a lungfull lights your blood with pearl-fire; horsecock and beer for breakfast. I wanted to be with the men up on the hill, to talk about what we'd gone through, to hear them say you did good Doc. I wanted to see Gunner Bear and Gunny Mead, and even Wilks. I wanted to know what had happened to Doc Wilson. So I saunter up the hill, grinning and smiling, and the troops are buoyant around me, we're filthy, our faces smeared with cordite and sweat and mud, and there is blood and scorch marks on our fatigues, but there is also a kind of luminous sheen around us, like we might disappear any minute, we know it, but it's all right.

I had expected to find Gunner Bear on top of the hill being wreathed in laurel, men fawning at his feet. But I found him instead standing behind the serving counter in the mess tent, re-erected over the offal of our own killed dead, slinging sliced fried baloney and white bread, kid food. He was being punished, doing KP, being humiliated. How a man calm and self-possessed enough to field strip his machine-gun in the middle of a fire fight, to tend to and bandage five wounded men while still under fire, and to get the gun back together and kill a Viet Cong could be being punished was beyond any sense of honor I'd ever heard of. I couldn't even hold my tin tray out to him, if someone were to be served it should have been him.

"What the fuck are you doing here?" I asked, his own anger fueling mine. His eyes were furious, but his shoulders were hunched with chastisement.

"Beats me," he said, shrugging like he wanted me to leave him alone.

"I don't understand why they'd put a good man like you on KP, you must'a popped the CO a good one."

"Captain says I fucked up," he said, heaving like he'd been whipped. "Got the squad shot up because my gun jammed."

"Bullshit!" I said. Guns jam. People hide in the dark and try to kill you. Fools lead you into death.

"Everybody knows what happened. It was that dufus Wurtz..." but I couldn't finish. The XO was coming through the tent flap and I could see he was listening hard to my loud protest. There was nothing to be done to raise Bear from his punishment. The Corps had spoken. I reached in and took the serving tongs from Bear and served myself, saying to him quietly, "We know what you did and what happened. And no one can take it away. Those shits don't know nothing. They weren't there. They won't ever know." He didn't say thanks, but I didn't expect one.

Up on the hill the mood was high among those of us who'd gone out on the rescue mission, and desultory among those who'd been left behind. Those who'd been left behind were watching the hamlet and the village across the river, staring out into the empty green paddies, sagging with the weight that the other men had been in a big firefight and were hence elevated, more fully Marines. S/Sgt. Monk was still asleep on his rubber-bitch, next to the CP The men of my platoon were milling around, recounting the events of the night, high and sharp featured, eyes glinting, posturing dramatically. Wilks was sitting apart from them, resting on his haunches, pointing at them and laughing.

Also sitting apart from Anderson's men was one of the two men in Wurtz's squad, besides Wilson, who hadn't been wounded. Uncontrollable tremors shook through him, the consternation of being a victim and a survivor who'd failed at being better than any ten VC, who hadn't defeated the enemy single-handedly, who was selfishly satisfied to have just lived through it but couldn't say so because of the code, said, "Howdy, Doc. Glad you made it."

"Glad you made it too. Hey, man, I saw you. You and whatshisface, you were laying down some fire, man. You stuck man, you kept your people alive."

He smiled like he'd been forgiven, then asked, "How's Wurtz? He looked pretty fucked up."

"I don't know if he's going to make it. He was shot up pretty bad. Five wounds in his legs, compound fractures, but I don't think they hit the femoral artery. If he makes it, it'll be an act of God."

"Or Congress, eh?"

"But you made it all right. You came out in one piece." I said, but he was still shaking like some part of him wished that he had not been spared, that there was something unworthy about surviving an ambush.

Gunny Mead approached, putting an overtly friendly hand on my shoulder. "Lieutenant is going to be all right," he told us, "He's on his way to Japan right now. We just got the word."

"Hey, I saw you last night too, Gunny. Standing up in a fire fight. Got to say you got some balls!" I said to Mead. The Gunny just smiles, letting us come to our own conclusions about him, then says, "I don't recommend it. Besides, I had that twin thirty firing right over my head. Not even them Viet Cong are that brave." Then he nodded in the direction of Doc Wilson who was sitting on the edge of the old brick wall, kicking his feet. "You better go over and take care of your man," the Gunny says to me, and gives me a smile like I was his son and he was proud, he could trust me with his life. If you want to get a man to follow you anywhere, give him that one, and mean it.

"What happened to Wilson?" I asked the Marine as the gunny moved off.

"Hate to tell you, Doc. He froze."

It was the ultimate condemnation. Being each other's lives, taking care of each other, collectively eliminating any threat as if possessed of a singular will, made us tribal members. To abandon one's duty to each other was to resign from the race of men. To freeze under fire was utterly selfish and useless, and seen as a more reprehensible act than leading your men into an ambush. Scream, shit your pants, piss all over yourself, buckle and dig with your fingernails into the dust coating a rock, hide behind your best friend's dead body; all forgivable if you rose up and got off a few rounds, if you looked around and helped your friend. It was your and their only chance. But to freeze was a declaration of total isolation, making you untrustworthy, and that he was a corpsman put his onus on me. But he was still a man. I snagged up a couple of beers and went to talk to him.

I didn't know him, he'd been transferred in after the debacle of Operation Starlight. He was a slight, scholarly looking man, maybe his ambitions to be a doctor getting braided with war-fate, that disease possessing life currents of its own.

"Mind if I pull up a rock?" I said, sitting next to him. I handed him a beer, but he refused it, clearly indicating that he didn't think he deserved the reward.

"Pretty tough last night?" I said. But he wouldn't respond. "You never know what you're gonna do when the shit hits the fan," implying forgiveness and acceptance, but he'd have none of it. He still refused to respond, to tell me anything about the night before. I could see him withdrawing further and further, mulling the incident into every angle of explanation and self justification, blame and apology, but always coming back to the true fact of the matter, he froze. He didn't even acknowledge my, "Get 'em next time, man. You'll be all right," as I was leaving him to himself. When he was sure I wasn't looking, I saw him sob. With his dishonored self to haul he would be no good to the men around him on patrol. He was transferred back to Regiment.

I fetched a few more beers and went to sit next to Wilks, who'd been watching the men spraying each other with foam and grab-assing. Handing him a beer I said, "Looks like I owe you one."

"You sorry ass mutherfucker, Doc," Wilks says with psychotic glee. "You don't owe me shit. You think I killed that Slope for you? Ha Ha. I thought he was shooting at me! Goes to show you. Gotta keep your head in a firefight." And for a second I couldn't tell who was more alone, Wilks or Wilson.

Leaving him to his personal reverie, I could see it inside him, he was welding the lives of the Viet Cong he'd killed to his own making himself huge as Kali. I stepped off to join up with Gunny Mead and the CO. They were coming back down the hill, followed by Doc Broad, the XO, S/Sgt. Monk, two riflemen and my friend Jim.

It was a day off. No patrols, just the headquarters group wanting to go across the river to visit the scene of the crime. "Come on, Doc," Gunny Mead invited, "I'm sure you want to see where we were." So we loaded into an Amphtrack, rode across the river, and stopped a just about the same spot as the track had stopped the night before.

Emerging from the track we seemed to step into a vacuum of dead air. The ambush site felt like it was encased in a silent bell, and inside the bell the released angers and souls were furiously seeking escape. We walked over to a small knoll overlooking the ambush site, and what had seemed large and furious and violent in the dark seemed remarkably small and contained in the daylight. The only remaining evidence that such fury had occurred were the wrappings from the battle dressings, several large scabs of dried blood and several circular scorches left by exploding grenades.

In the night the Vietnamese had come to police up the brass, scavenge the scissors I'd dropped, retrieve their dead and wounded, cleansing it of all sign. They knew we'd be coming back, and they were going to leave us no satisfaction. All that remained was the spirit of our sacrifice humming in the empty air.

A click down the trail the village was also still. No smoke from the cookfires rose from the hootches. There was the feeling that we were for the moment safe, that nothing could happen to us in the sterile daylight, as if the psychic charge between us and the Vietnamese had exploded and been expended, leaving the ground sacred. The village was in mourning, as were we.

And once in love with the men of war, then so in love with life I came to realize the day by day, second by second urgency to live, to be alive and to know that you're alive, and that all life around me was my own life, and I held that thought like a glowing pearl, making the faint wish that no harm should come to anyone again, and more, that the pearl be known to everyone.

Later in the day Jim was pointing at my arm, asking what caused the scabbed and spreading bruise that was turning benzoate brown, and making it stiff enough for me to use my kit strap for a sling. We were heading down to a hootch in the hamlet to buy some sodas and write letters home.

"Centipede bit me, I guess," I said, too numb to remember that shrapnel from a grenade had torn into me, too insistent that some magical protection kept me from injury and made me different from the flesh bodies of the other men. Magic to deny death its dominion or war its reality.

We took seats at a government issue picnic table that served as a counter in the hootch. Two beautiful young women were grooming each other, picking lice from each other's scalps and pretending to eat them, giggling at our aplomb. Jim kept asking me what had happened during the ambush and rescue, but there was little I could tell him that he hadn't overheard while acting as radio relay during the fight. Neither could I tell him how terrified I'd been, and how stupidly I was denying the danger we'd all undergone, or my shame for not having taken up the gun and defended myself and the lives of the men, even if I was well occupied doing my job.

"You know, man," I said, "lots of yelling and screaming. Lots of bullets, a couple of grenades, nobody knowing what the fuck was going on. But it all got done OK. I mean, we didn't stick around and go after the slopes, but I know we killed a bunch of them.

"You know, that amphtrack driver told me he wants me to pay for that cot we used for Morton's stretcher."

"What'd you tell him?"

"I told him Semper Fi, and take a flying fuck at the moon. Some guys got no heart at all."

"But you tell me something, you're hanging out up there with the big boys, how did Whitefang handle it? I mean I found Gunner Bear doing KP. That fucker deserves a Navy Cross," I said, thinking of how many seconds it would be before we got to leave.

"Gunner was that good, huh?"

"Kept those people alive, took out a gook for sure, probably more!"

"Don't mean shit to the officers," Jim says, "And you know the CO," he added, looking around to be sure we are not being overheard by an officer or their toadies, "Whitefang has to look good for the boys upstairs. He's the dumbshit who authorized the mission, and now he ain't even got a verifiable body count, plus he's got half a squad shot to shit. It's that Annapolis training, figures punishing us will get the Colonel's dick hard and maybe make him forget."

"What about us. I mean, I guess I was expecting him to say something to the platoon, something like 'Well Done,' or good going hardchargers, something like thanks."

"Hey, he writes the company history the way he wants it to read. We're just guts and noise."

I bent to concentrate on writing my letter home, pretending in it to be the brave man performing his expected duty selflessly, belittling the power of the enemy and the power of bullets to maim and kill, claiming that because we had survived the little battle that everything was OK now. But the handwriting looked like the wracked scrawls made by men after six months of fighting in the jungles of Guadalcanal.

Heading Home

It was true, it was true! The Army was coming. After all the lies, rumors, scuttlebutt, word, all the jive and bullshit coming from Battalion and Regiment, all the misinformation and false intelligence that would send us out to dark and lonely ambush sites and call life by names that had lost their connection to life, the Army was coming to take over our positions and relieve us from our dreams full of guns and maimed dying. Soon, soon there would be sleep that didn't crackle with electrical fear and burn with every labored breath. Soon we'd be in a protective hull of steel, headed for Okinawa.

We were standing around in squads, or what was left of squads, watching the six-bys convoy a whole reinforced company of Army boys rolling toward us on the dirt road. We'd been packed for hours; haversack, rubber bitch, fartsack, poncho, weapons, ready to go, no arguments. When the trucks stopped and the officers started forming up their units we started shying away from the bunkers we'd lived in for nearly a year.

The Army officers were very brusque and military, ordering their men to march up the hill and through the wire, taking charge like an occupying force. They started assigning our bunkers to their men as if we weren't even there, as if we had already disappeared, as if the war was theirs now and we had been no part of it. Six men were assigned to the grave where I had slept, and I hoped it was not prophesy.

The Army boys stood in front of their new homes, staring at us as we lounged in salty postures. No one spoke. No one said hello to our counterparts. They were green kids, their uniforms fresh and starched, their weapons clean and new. Their expectations were no doubt as full of anticipation of the yellow peril as our own were. It was going to get worse for them, though we didn't really know how bad, even as we didn't really know how bad it had been for us or how bad it was going to be once we got back to the States and the alienation still waiting in the grinding heartbreak of America, balmed by greed and bright toys, weapons and misery. We were a ragged bunch, the plaques of our flack jackets showing white through the worn fabric, our uniforms pale and sun bleached, our faces gaunt with fatigue and sleeplessness. We carried our weapons with the nonchalance of simple body extensions.

I remember recognizing a few of the faces in that group, those of men I'd spent the entire war with, but not those of others who had joined us sometime during our stay there. It didn't really matter if I knew them or not, they were the men of my platoon, my company, my life was theirs and their life was mine. Not even the promise of the glories of the World could ease the sadness of having to part.

I spotted the caduceus on one of the Army men standing in front of what had once been my own sweet home, and it seemed two great armies should not meet without some sort of ceremony, some exchange of knowledge. The Army was shy of us, maybe we looked crazy, or had the look of men who'd killed or had come so close to knowing their own nature that to touch or speak to us would pox them, or they believed the Marine Corps myth of men who knew no fear and would use their weapons at the slightest provocation. Certainly the Army officers were aghast at the depth of our poverty, our wretched living conditions, our worn clothes and rusty weapons. Already they were ordering their men to lay more concertina, expand the bunkers, dig new bunkers, dig fighting holes, perhaps ignoring us like they would derelicts on downtown streetcorners. I approached the Army medic, my grin no doubt ironic.

We'd made it, we had the stuff, we'd survived, some of us had actually been heroic, none of us had raped or severed body parts from the dead or burned down villages, we'd lived and fought, suffered and done our defined duty. He and his men were about to do their year in war, each of them nursed on movies, myths and the news. I introduced myself to the medic, all he wanted to know was how it was going to be. I stammered something about malaria, dysentery, keep your head down, immersion foot, good luck, then in imperial gesture spread my arms and said, "Now, this is all yours."

"Yeah, thanks," was all he could say.

◆◆◆◆

I could wait to get back to Okinawa. I could bask in the warm Pacific sun and the clamor of men's voices, and I could watch the billion-starred night glow deep blue with the breath of God. I was in no hurry. The APA that held what remained of our battalion was moving toward Okinawa at about ten knots, plenty fast, the trip could take as long as two weeks, two weeks to watch the streams of yellow brit and the wakes of swimming sea snakes and the magnificent sunsets over the South China Sea. No more war for me, but for the war going on in the heads of the men around me. I didn't have to want it anymore, didn't have to pretend that the rigor and the violence was warming and stimulating, that the friendships and bravado were tight and close, though some of them were.

Like most of us on the ship I was giddy with not being in the Zone anymore, the weight was gone. Out on the ocean the boys back in their four-foot thick concrete bunkers couldn't call us up and send us into death and danger—like they did the night before we were going to get on the ship, sending us into the middle of the Regimental ammo dump to expel some sappers. I was content to laze quiet and play backalley on the grey steel decks. To re-speak what had happened would be a long time coming, and even then it would be only partially true.

Sending us into the ammo dump was a profound reminder to impose on us as we waited for dawn, hunkered safe behind aircraft revetments. They would get one last thrust of force from our unit. The war was going on, was getting larger, and did not have

269

provision for units that thought their tour was over, the war's timing didn't correspond to our expectations. If they didn't pull us out after a year, we could be there forever, every one of us, a soldier for every three South Vietnamese. But there were reports of sappers in the ammo dump, we were close, the trucks that had brought us there were still standing-by, so we were the natural choice. So close to being gone, ripped out of our reprieve, to swarm through the ammo dump terrified that one mortar round would come in from the surrounding hills and blow us all to hell, working that warren of death in boxes all day, finding nothing. Then going back to the Da Nang pier and loading onto the ship, our nerves set with the sure and certain knowledge that if you are alive you can act, no matter how dire the conditions, no matter how long between the demands for action.

The war was spreading. When we docked in Subic Bay, looking forward to Philippine women and San Miguel beer, looking forward to a three day bacchanal, heaven help any fool who got in the way of our good time, we were not allowed off the ship. There were three other troop transports in town, and the women were so well occupied that the sick-bays were overflowing with contused eyebrows and broken jaws, noses, hands and arms, stabbings, skull fractures and lacerations. The boys going in were out for a good time before they died. Adding us proud veterans would just fuel the burgeoning conflagration.

Even after we'd left the balmy waters of the South China Sea and entered the greening grey of the East China Seas, on toward the Ryukyus, becalmed and drifting for five days while the crew repaired the boilers, the mood of the men was mostly quiet resting, releasing the tensions of laying curled in a fighting hole, in the rain, in the mud, in the perpetual fear, sleeping finally safe in a steel hull afloat on the Pacific. The official word was that our battalion had lost nearly half of the men we had started with, six hundred men who had been killed or wounded or contracted a disease or been wiped out in some horrible way—but the losses had occurred so slowly, their singular disappearances happening so suddenly, that to recount them or even remember them while we rested was like trying to remember how your legs moved during a firefight, or what you dreamed the night you heard your buddy screaming he'd been hit. The number seemed phenomenally large, like the brass was trying to make us feel good by telling us we had suffered great losses. And as I milled around on the ship I'd run into men I hadn't seen since before we went into Vietnam, and men I'd run into in-country, and men from my company and from my platoon, each and every one of us happy to see each other, we were there, we were alive, we'd made it, we'd been utterly changed and transformed, some of us even becoming what we expected we'd become, most of us becoming something altogether different, possessors of a magnificent mystery of significant enough value to devote the rest of your life to its unraveling, not just who you were when the fire got thick, but who you were while you were waiting for it, wishing for it, hoping first for the test to start then praying for it to end, not only for you, but for those other men around you—the prayer spreading to encompass even those who were trying to kill you.

And the magic was still upon us, we could roam the ship without fear of restriction, we were known killers. And not much had changed among my friends, I was still a connection, and they'd send me to raid the sick-bay for drugs to experiment with: librium, darvon, relaxants, depressants, stimulants, mood elevators, anything to change the mind to approximate that stunning awareness brought on by deprivation and danger, the firefight, the long nights peering into the murderous dark on ambush, the sting of the steel, rather than the tedium of work or rest, the want of that heroic sensation so compelling that it sent men back into the war, or into crime or into work where your life was risked daily, dope dealer, steeplejack, salesman, teacher, finding ways to keep even a psychosis in check with marijuana or speed or cocaine until it has gathered so much power the cumulative memory manifests itself in taking potshots at a piece of road maintenance machinery for waking you up twenty one days straight, or goes the other way, a vow to never handle a gun again because to pick one up is to heft the weight of the whole year of war and the subsequent years suffered by the same men as you were, to heft it is to again pick up the suicide you were able to leave maundering in the grave that became a bunker, equal with a vow to never again be subject to those who would threaten your being alive.

Between typhoons, in the December chill, we reached Okinawa, no dancing girls to welcome us this time, just the dock, the trucks that took us to Camp Schwab, where we were kept confined for three days until our exuberance at arriving home safely dissipated. But many of us felt the haunt of ancient memory coming from the town next door, and ignored the threat that we wouldn't be sent back to the World on schedule if we went AWOL, climbed the fence and had at the women until our money ran out.

It was a moment of joyful abandon for me to turn in my rusty .45 and my depleted medical kit. Giving them up I was relinquishing any further claim to warring against the Vietnamese, though I had to keep my decision private. The first news I learned upon getting to Okinawa was that I was being transferred back to the Navy, service fleet. Hearing that I wasn't there amongst the Marines anymore, I made a show of being glad to be leaving, glad to be out of the big green machine, out of all the Mickey Mouse. But I was profoundly saddened when I heard the men I'd lived with cheer when it was announced that they were going back to Camp Pendelton for further training, then back to Vietnam, further inland, to patrol the hills around Khe Sanh. No matter how much I loved them, there wasn't enough of me left to volunteer to go with them, so I let the impersonal benevolence of my orders dictate my direction.

But we were still salty dudes, no doubt about it, and when the gate opened for our first liberty in Hinnoko, Jim and Gordon, the reporter from *Stars and Stripes*, and Anderson and I rushed to the taxis for the quick ride down the hill and into town to find what we'd left behind. And it wasn't long before we had set up a Mojo party, sukiyaki and a typhoon fifth with a mamasan to cook it and four women to attend to our needs. The procedure was to eat, drink, go into one of the rooms with one of the women, fuck, come back and drink some more, repeated until each man had fucked each woman and got plastered enough not to remember how much fun they had. Yab yum by the numbers, numbly humping and puffing. Even after one of the women smeared her loving tissues with alum to tighten the friction and pretended to climax, I still couldn't cum. No cum, no deal. The transaction is invalidated. It was clear that an evening of ersatz human connection, the flesh separated by a condom a thousand miles thick, was not what I needed. I excused myself and headed out into the Okinawan village not sure what I was looking for, but sure that whatever it was, it did not lie in the pretence of bought fuckery. I was going home, I could afford to feel, even if I didn't like the turmoil tearing through me, the whole of the war seemed predicated on the enslaved rape of women.

There was something nagging in the back of my mind, some hint or whisper of hopeful innocence barely remembered. The town was filled with drinking rollicking Marines, arms around each others' shoulders, crashing through bar doors, spilling into the dirt streets holding women and beer bottles, shouting and laughing, free at last, for a little while, until payday anyway. In the far distance the lights of the bombers and the military transports could be seen leaving Kadena, the swirl and mix of energies spinning out a maelstrom that would touch down in North Vietnam and Travis Air Force Base, the bombs and men made of the same mind.

Wandering, drifting, hooking up here and there with old friends, I ended up at the Texas Club, remembering Hurlock's contribution to my education, squeezing in through the crowded door. The mamasan recognized me, surprising me that she could distinguish me from the thousands of other young men passing through her women and her doors. I asked her if Michiko was around, oh yes, she remembered, no, she wasn't around. Babysan was here, yes, down in Naha with his grandmother. Michiko and two of her other girls had gone to Saigon to make big money. War was good for business. She had some new girls now, very fine, number one pussy, Doc go stateside now, butterfly boy, no sweat, bye-bye.

A few days later there is the equivalent of a weapons-reinforced company of Marines sifted together from all over the war, sitting very quietly in the tubular fuselage of a Trans World 707, crossing the Pacific, heading for home, Japan, Alaska, California, heading for the land of the big PX, heading back to the World. But everyone is subdued, there doesn't seem much to say. We can't even talk to each other because there is no framework on which we can hang our experience, our experience not being the one we'd come to get. I'm sitting next to a beefy gunnery sergeant who reluctantly tells me that he has spent the last three years in the jungles of northern Thailand, shooting VC, Pathet Lao, bandits, any kind of dink. At first I think he is sneering at me in contempt for my youth and my relatively insignificant war experience, but later I realize that it doesn't even matter that he's been sworn to secrecy by the CIA, he can't talk because no other human hearts but his exist for him. We are soaring through the stunning air, and I am remembering the woman I lay with the night before we left, and how I could no longer restrain myself in the name of health, and bending her to my mouth I slipped my tongue into her leathery cleft and drank deeply from the seminal traces of thousands of men before and the thousands of men who would come after me, each joining the milling throngs on their way to Vietnam to exercise their own tragedy on the Vietnamese people. In the stunning air I am trying to figure why we each and all went to Vietnam, and figure that it was to get back what we'd lost, the Kennedy spirit, the WW II spirit, our own mystic toil evidenced in the lives of the Vietnamese. The Vietnamese were now part of my blood, teaching from within their strength, their capacity for absorbing pain, absorbing one of our blows and rising to demand another, and another until their very soil of existence was poisoned by our maniacal rage and we recoiled in horror at our own capacity to injure, and still they came up mocking, grinning, aching for more, sending us off to try to extinguish our conscience by splitting into a thousand freedoms that no glorious thought has yet mended, leaving each man to his own effort toward merit, his obligation to the singular soul of us to reach in under the bloody battledressing and seize the fractured self and breathe life and light into it, burnish it with love, commit to virtue, seek its central benevolence, polish it until it brightens with its own essential wholeness, yours, theirs, ours, the same soul, and then hold forth the shining heart. The deepest human contract is mutual protection.

And if we are all one life, then extend compassion to yourself: make heaven everywhere apparent, plant the garden, weave the artistry, heal the sick, build the harmony, add to the soul. Add, add, add to the soul.

Dan A. Barker is a Vietnam veteran. He is the initiatior and director of the Home Gardening Project, a nonprofit corporation that builds complete raised-bed vegetable gardens for the aged, disabled, or single-parent mothers of Portland. The Home Gardening Project has built over 800 gardens to date.